UNLEARNING
WHITE
SUPREMACY

A Spirituality for Racial Liberation

Alex Mikulich

ORBIS BOOKS
Maryknoll, New York 10545

Founded in 1970, Orbis Books endeavors to publish works that enlighten the mind, nourish the spirit, and challenge the conscience. The publishing arm of the Maryknoll Fathers and Brothers, Orbis seeks to explore the global dimensions of the Christian faith and mission, to invite dialogue with diverse cultures and religious traditions, and to serve the cause of reconciliation and peace. The books published reflect the views of their authors and do not represent the official position of the Maryknoll Society. To learn more about Orbis Books, please visit our website at www.orbisbooks.com.

Copyright © 2022 by Alex Mikulich.

Published by Orbis Books, Box 302, Maryknoll, NY 10545-0302.

All rights reserved.

No part of this publication may be reproduced or transmitted in any form or by any means, electronic or mechanical, including photocopying, recording, or any information storage or retrieval system, without prior permission in writing from the publisher. Queries regarding rights and permissions should be addressed to: Orbis Books, P.O. Box 302, Maryknoll, NY 10545-0302.

Manufactured in the United States of America

Library of Congress Cataloging-in-Publication Data

Names: Mikulich, Alexander, author.
Title: Unlearning white supremacy : a spirituality for racial liberation / Alex Mikulich.
Description: Maryknoll, NY : Orbis Books, [2022] | Includes bibliographical references and index. | Summary: "Weaves together historical, theological, ethical, and sociological analyses to understand the origins and evolution of anti-black white supremacy and how to overcome it"—Provided by publisher.
Identifiers: LCCN 2021049827 (print) | LCCN 2021049828 (ebook) | ISBN 9781626984660 (trade paperback) | ISBN 9781608339280 (epub)
Subjects: LCSH: Racism—Religious aspects—Catholic Church. | White supremacy movements.
Classification: LCC BX1795.R33 M55 2022 (print) | LCC BX1795.R33 (ebook) | DDC 282/.73089—dc23/eng/20220128
LC record available at https://lccn.loc.gov/2021049827
LC ebook record available at https://lccn.loc.gov/2021049828

For Katherine and Tyler,
that you may experience a fullness of mutual respect,
justice, and equality rooted in divine intimacy.

Contents

Part I
The Colonial Context
of Anti-Black White Supremacy

v

Part II
Living Decolonially

Acknowledgments

Most works of nonfiction, even if they were written by an individual author, are products of collaborative and communal endeavors. I believe that anti-racist scholarship and activism demand an even more expansive and enduring collaborative labor because they must be oriented to the collective transformation of individuals, institutions, structures, and culture.

I am indebted to many wise, compassionate, and encouraging friends, colleagues, and activists who inspire and ground my own commitment and reflection on white privilege going back decades. I am especially thankful to Jim Forest, who was the first to listen attentively to my argument and encouraged my interpretation of Thomas Merton. Jim's affirmation set me on the path of writing this book. Matthew Cressler, assistant professor of religious studies at the College of Charleston, contributed critical feedback that helped me to clarify and illuminate my focus on God's grace drawing all of us into ever deeper relationships in participatory love, mutuality, and belonging in which White people put their lives at stake for Black and oppressed peoples.

I thank Paul Pearson, director and archivist of the Thomas Merton Center at Bellarmine University, who invited me to be the first white scholar to give the Ninth Annual Black History Month Lecture in 2015. Paul served as an invaluable dialogue partner as I began to turn that lecture into this book. I am indebted to him and Mark C. Meade, assistant director of the Thomas Merton Center, for their wise and skillful guidance as I conducted research titled "Merton's Analysis of White Innocence and Racial Superiority" as a Shannon Fellow in 2015–2016. That research, as well as the retreat I enjoyed at the Abbey of Gethsemani, were made possible by the generous funding of the International Thomas Merton Society (ITMS). The sacred spaces of the Merton Archives at Bellarmine, as well as the church and grounds of the Trappists' Abbey of Gethsemani, continue to nourish my mind, body, and soul for this prayerful work.

I extend gratitude to editors and publishers who granted permission to publish excerpts from my previous work that appears here in rewritten, expanded form. I thank Maura Thompson Hagarty, editorial director at Anselm Academic, for permission to reprint part of my chapter "Where Y'at Race, Whiteness, and Economic Justice? A Map of White Complicity in the Economic Oppression of People of Color," in Mark Allman, ed., *The Almighty and the Dollar: Reflections on* Economic Justice for All (Winona, MN: Anselm Academic, 2012). In the present volume, I have included revised and expanded essays originally published in the *National Catholic Reporter* (*NCR*), specifically "Merton's Letters Call for White Atonement" (January 13, 2013), and "Indigenous Scholars Invite Decolonization of the Anthropocene" (October 8, 2019). *NCR*'s Stephanie Yeagle, who has skillfully edited my essays for nearly ten years, graciously adds light and life to every essay.

I thank Andrew Grant Thomas, editor in chief of the *Journal of Othering and Belonging,* for his kind invitation to write a response to the inaugural edition of that journal and the opening essay by john a. powell and Stephen Menendian. I was honored to enter into conversation with powell and Menendian, whose scholarship and leadership guide me and many others to envision and practice belonging and inclusion every day. My essay "Embracing Ecological Intimacy" for the *Journal of Othering and Belonging,* which I revised and expanded into chapter 6 for this volume, is reprinted with permission from editor Rachelle Galloway-Popotas and the publishers at the Haas Institute for a Fair and Inclusive Society at the University of California–Berkeley.

I thank Professor Barbara Wall, former vice president for mission and ministry at Villanova University, for her invitation to me to present "Embracing Racial Intimacy" in October 2017 as a part of the Catholic Social Teaching and Racism 2017–2018 Lecture Series, which was sponsored by Villanova's Office for Mission and Ministry. I am also grateful to Suzanne Wentzel, publications manager for mission and ministry, for publishing and granting permission for me to utilize my essay "Catholic Social Teaching and Race: Embracing Racial Intimacy," in the *Journal of Catholic Social Thought* 16, no. 1 (Winter 2019): 65–81, which I have revised and expanded into this book.

I thank Hans Christoffersen, publisher at Liturgical Press, for granting permission to revise my chapter "Contemplative Transformation in Sophia-Wisdom: A Way of Decolonizing Faith and Society," in Laurie Cassidy and M. Shawn Copeland, eds., *Darkness, Desire, and Hope* (Collegeville, MN: Liturgical Press, 2021). I have revised and expanded "Contemplative Transformation in Sophia-Wisdom" into "Engaging Impasse: The First Will Be Last," which is chapter 4 in this text.

I thank Mark Pawlak, permissions manager at Hanging Loose Press, for permission to quote two lines of Jayne Cortez's poem "I've got the blues ooze," published in *Jazz Fan Looks Back* (New York: Hanging Loose Press, 2002).

I am thankful to Sheila Sturgis-Craig, former associate commissioner, Texas Health and Human Services Center for the Elimination of Disproportionality and Disparities, for inviting me to serve as a keynote speaker for the 2015 Texas Cross-Systems Summit. I deeply appreciate her critical affirmation that a contemplative spirituality is integral to the struggle for the elimination of racial disparities, both in movement organizing and public policy advocacy.

I am deeply indebted to many colleagues and friends who inspire me on this journey every day. Laurie Cassidy, who is a most trusted friend and colleague and who is always available to provide critical feedback, daily witnesses to the presence of Sophia-Wisdom. M. Shawn Copeland's public encouragement for nearly twenty years keeps me keeping on in this shared struggle. Other friends whose listening, encouragement, and support make this project possible include Gerald Beyer, Wanda Correa, Al Alcazar, Rosa Gómez-Herrin, John Sebastian, and Stephen and Dina Karam.

My deepest gratitude goes to members of the editorial team at Orbis Books. I thank James T. Keane, formerly of Orbis, and Robert Ellsberg for their endorsement of my initial book proposal. I am most grateful for Jill Brennan O'Brien's wisdom, patience, and compassionate support through some personally harrowing and unstable times over the past years, including six physical moves of our home, caring for loved ones in the hospital, and job transitions. Jill's sharp editorial skill and sensitive eye helped me eliminate unnecessary repetition, clarify awkward sentences, and ultimately illuminate a fuller depth and breadth of my argument.

I pray with Saint John of the Cross, who prefaced his *Sayings of Light and Love* as follows: "May there be nothing of worldly rhetoric in them or the long-winded and dry eloquence of weak and artificial human wisdom, which never pleases you."[1] Wherever there may be worldly rhetoric or long-winded and dry eloquence of weak and artificial human wisdom in this text, I alone am responsible. Finally, I am eternally indebted to my beloved life-partner, Kara, who energizes all of life with joy.

[1] Saint John of the Cross, *Sayings of Light and Love*, in *The Collected Works of Saint John of the Cross*, trans. Kieran Kavanaugh, OCD, and Otilio Rodriguez, OCD (Washington, DC: Institute of Carmelite Studies, 1991), 85.

Preface

The genesis of this book finds its primary inspiration in Thomas Merton's *Seeds of Destruction*. It is perhaps Merton's most underappreciated work both because of the moral and spiritual challenge it directs to "white liberals" and because of the way it witnesses to an anti-racist life that integrates contemplation with prophetic action with and for Black Americans. As soon as I opened *Seeds*, the kernel of wisdom that inspires this book initially puzzled and later struck me with clarity. Its epilogue draws from Saint Paul's Letter to the Romans:

> What if God, desiring to show His wrath and make known his power, has endured with much patience the vessels of wrath made for destruction? (Rom 9:22)

Saint Paul's phrasing sounds deliberately provocative. Indeed, Paul asks rhetorically in 9:14, "Is there injustice on God's part?" It sounds as if Paul assumes that the God of Israel and Jesus Christ is wrathful. Paul immediately answers in 9:14, "By no means!" He emphasizes throughout Romans, "Neither death, nor life, nor things present, nor things to come, nor powers, nor height, nor depth, nor anything else in all creation will be able to separate us from the love of God in Christ Jesus our Lord" (Rom 8:38). So why does Paul, and more importantly Merton, seemingly taunt us with God "desiring to show his wrath" for "vessels of wrath made for destruction"?

Paul contextualizes Romans 9 within God's salvific history through Israel. God's mercy and compassion (9:15) reveal themselves consistently, even in and through Pharaoh's opposition and oppression. Ultimately, Pharaoh's "hard-heartedness" (9:18) fails to derail God's desire to show mercy and liberate an oppressed people. While Paul celebrates God's goodness, compassion, and mercy, at the same time he warns his readers that we, too, may be just as obstinate as Pharaoh. Drawing upon the archetypal figure of the potter and the potter's wheel (see Is 29:16; 45:9; 64:8; Jer 18:6; and Wis 15:7), Paul imagines God as a potter who molds human beings at God's will. In other words, like a potter, God can crush the clay to bits or shape it into something beautiful. Although God may have been angered at Pharaoh's recalcitrance and "desired" to demonstrate divine power, God "endured with much patience the vessels of wrath," that is, vessels of obstinacy like Pharaoh. Paul essentially says to his readers that if God shows loving-kindness to Pharaoh and gives him time to repent, imagine how much time God offers the people of Israel and of Christ to repent. God's loving-kindness is immeasurable.

Interestingly, Merton never discusses his deployment of Romans 9:22 anywhere in *Seeds of Destruction*. He does, however, make three points abundantly clear throughout *Seeds* that may help us understand the epilogue. First, Merton warns White people of faith who profess to be racially innocent that we are the source of anti-black violence in the United States. We White folks need to begin by rooting out our own violence and stubborn insistence that we set the terms of change. Although Merton does not extend the metaphor explicitly, I suggest that we who cleave to the social position and privilege of whiteness in the United States see ourselves as a kind of Pharaoh—an oppressive, dominating power who obstinately opposes the liberating will of Jesus Christ and the freedom of God's people. Part I of this book invites readers who benefit from white privilege and power to learn how we have assumed roles akin to Pharaoh's foot soldiers over the past five hundred years.

Second, drawing upon the deep wells of biblical wisdom and Catholic contemplative traditions, Merton's *Seeds of Destruction* invites White people of faith to place our body, mind, and spirit on the side of Black people in order to practice the primary commandments to love both God and neighbor. I argue that loving Black people in the fullness of their humanity is a prerequisite of the gospel and of cocreating *basileia tou theou*, the new reality fulfilling God's loving desire for the whole of creation.

Merton's third and decisive point, wholly consistent with Romans 9:22 and Christian doctrine, is that God's grace alone makes love and liberation possible. The roots of authentic protest and liberation are rooted in divinely inspired contemplative prayer and action that reshapes us in and through God's grace. Merton's religious vows of obedience call him to be so deeply oriented to God's grace that he welcomes the disintegration of his false egotistical self in order to allow transformation to a true self oriented to truth and love. I extend his prayerful, contemplative orientation to God's grace in Part II of this book in two ways.

First, beyond Merton, I draw upon African American religious experience and Black Catholic womanist and liberation theology as sources of God's liberating love and transformation in the world. Womanist and liberation theologies are oriented to the experience and wisdom of enslaved Africans who "applied the Exodus story, whose end they knew, to their own experience of slavery, which had not ended. The sacred history of God's liberation of his people would be or was being repeated in the American south."[1] In this particular repetition of God's sacred history, predominantly White people of faith and churches have played roles much more akin to Pharaoh than of the prophetic gospel witness of Black Americans. People who believe they are white, a felicitous phrase I draw from James Baldwin, need to become humble and orient ourselves to the wisdom of the African American religious experience.

Second, although Merton does not say it, the insight of Romans 9:22 for Americans who maintain position at the summit of racial hierarchy and oppress Black and Brown folks is that we must work through our own idolatry of the lie of whiteness. How do we even begin to do that? Left to our own devices, we can't. So how might God, like a potter, be breaking up white preoccupations with a false self with its disordered attachments to power, privilege, innocence, position, and control? I contend that a condition of the possibility of transformation in contemplative wisdom is engaging societal "impasse and dark night."[2] The Carmelite tradition of "dark night" grounds and orients the path of transformation of the book's second part. Only through the affliction of dark night—that is, the loss of everything that gave us meaning and satisfaction, including disintegration all of the emotional, intellectual, moral, and spiritual attachments of whiteness—does Wisdom draw us into the transformative intimacy of participatory love, mutuality, and belonging. It is to this intellectual, emotional, moral, and spiritual work that I now turn.

---

[1] Albert Raboteau, *Slave Religion: The "Invisible Institution" in the Antebellum South* (Oxford University Press, 1978), 311.

[2] Constance FitzGerald, "Impasse and Dark Night," in *Living with Apocalypse: Spiritual Resources for Social Compassion*, ed. Tilden Edwards (San Francisco: Harper & Row, 1984), 93–116.

Introduction

I write as a partner, parent, scholar, and activist who longs to see my children and my children's children free to thrive as human beings, unfettered by the pain and suffering of death-dealing white supremacy and racism. I address these essays to and for White[1] people of faith who share a deep longing for racial liberation and who are willing to work through our shared complicity in the sin of white innocence and supremacy. My primary purpose is to offer a contemplative way of unlearning white complicity in anti-blackness and of living as followers of Christ who are authentically committed to act in love by "enfleshing freedom" with and for all our brothers and sisters.[2]

Although *Unlearning White Supremacy* is not an autobiography, my essays are inspired primarily by my personal, spiritual, and political experience of parenting biracial, African American children and being members of Black Catholic parishes in San Francisco, California; Hartford, Connecticut; and New Orleans, Louisiana. While this work is informed by my training in Catholic theology and ethics, the gut-level passion I share is shaped by interracial relationships of my family and our membership in these three parishes. I write in loving thankfulness for brother and sister Black Catholics whose uncommon faithful witness to the gospel endures in the face of death-dealing racism in church and society.

Having served as a lay pastoral associate at a dynamic Black parish in San Francisco in the early 1990s, Kara and I were deeply blessed by the uncommon hospitality, love, and joy of our Black brothers and sisters. Our experience at Sacred Heart drew us into the intimate embrace of Black Catholics and transformed our lives forever. Sacred Heart parishioners literally opened their arms to us—the entire congregation, all together, gathered around us

---

[1] I am following the National Association of Black Journalists (NABJ) style guide for use of upper or lower case when referencing Black and White people and Black, Brown, Indigenous, or White communities. Not all Black people are African Americans so I use a person's preference or specific identity where possible. Otherwise, I try to be as specific as possible in referencing, for example, Haitian American or Jamaican American. The NABJ does not capitalize "white" when referencing racist terms or actions, so I do not capitalize white supremacy, white settlers, or anti-black supremacy. I do not change upper or lower case where sources whom I quote use another style. See https://www.nabj.org/page/styleguideA.

[2] M. Shawn Copeland, *Enfleshing Freedom: Body, Race, and Being.* (Minneapolis: Fortress Press, 2010), 128.

and physically hugged us as members of their parish on the first three successive Sunday Masses we attended at Sacred Heart in 1992. We have never experienced that kind of communal physical hug anywhere else. Sacred Heart members made the gospel real in their passionate and intimate embrace of us throughout the years we lived and worshipped in San Francisco. Our own inherited bias and stereotypes were dissolved by people who cared for us as their own. Their intimate embrace brought us into unimagined depths of the Sacred Heart of Jesus. Their authentic witness to the gospel and the Sacred Heart of Jesus endures in my memory, heart, and soul.

I will never forget serving Sacred Heart as a lay pastoral associate. My primary mentors in ministry were eight to twelve Black women who met weekly for Bible study, prayer, and reflection. While I did my best to provide some insights from biblical scholarship into particular passages and books of Scripture, I was really a student to an exceptionally wise group of mothers, grandmothers, aunts, and sisters who ran the parish and who embodied Christ in the neighborhood community in how they cared for every single person from the youngest toddlers, to teen youth, young adults, and the infirm and elderly. Their joyful embodiment of the Beloved Community, especially in the midst of pain and suffering, provided living witness to their faith that "God makes a Way where there is no way."

On one occasion, when the Bible study group planned a parish retreat, they organized the retreat around one of the most powerful spiritual symbols I have ever experienced. The retreat was centered on remembering our ancestors through the African Tree of Life. While one can find many renditions of this image, the one at this gathering looms large in my memory. It was about two feet tall and equally wide. It depicts ebony human figures literally supporting one another and holding on to each other as they ascend the tree. The figures were carved out of African ebony wood in Tanzania. The image conveys a deep sense of intimacy both with nature and with ancestors who make life possible for the living today. The retreat facilitated reflection upon the African Tree of Life in relationship to each person's individual journey, to their shared journey as a faith community, and to Catholic teaching about the unity of all members in and through the Body of Christ.

That retreat remains one of the most powerful experiences of my life because the women shared without reservation their deepest sufferings and joys in the midst of personal and public struggles. One women's story is seared into my memory. Tears ran down her face as she gathered herself before she spoke. The African Tree of Life, she said, gave her inspiration to share memory of her own ancestors. She told us how her family was originally rooted in Arkansas but moved to San Francisco because they were terrorized by a lynching that made it impossible to stay. She and her family were still grieving long after they made the move to the Bay Area. I began to learn in that moment how lynching is not something in our past, limited to particular localities or regions. Lynching leaves trails of terror and trauma that tear families and communities apart all over the nation. Yet even in the wake of the bloodshed in Charlottesville and the protests in numerous other communities that are removing Confederate monuments, few White people are listening for ways to memorialize the victims of lynching and to find ways to heal these broken parts of the Body of Christ. Such forgetfulness and ignorance of the traumatic toll of history disregards our Eucharistic bond to each other and is a denial of our baptismal vows to repent for our participation in social sin.

Sacred Heart bestowed many deep blessings upon us, including the opportunity to learn from the great African American scholar and contemplative (I believe mystic) Rev. Cyprian Davis. I met Father Cyprian when he was visiting San Francisco to promote his recently published book titled *The History of Black Catholics in the United States*. In his book, Father Cyprian lifts up powerful stories about the courage of Black Catholics. One example is that of Catholic Hill Church in Ritter, South Carolina, where the Catholic community, led by former slave Vincent de Paul Davis, stayed together without priest, church, or sacraments for nearly forty years after the Civil War.[3] This is only one of countless stories in which Black Catholics nurtured their faith and community against seemingly insurmountable obstacles. When Father Cyprian visited Sacred Heart Parish, I asked him if the history of Black Catholics might be a "best-kept secret" even greater than that of Catholic social teaching, and if he thought that history might offer the broader church a source of spiritual and moral renewal. He responded positively that Black Catholic history provides great sources of hope and added, "Why don't you take up that work yourself?" I felt like Father Cyprian was Christ, personally inviting me into an entirely new way of looking at the world.

Sacred Heart Parish opened our hearts, minds, and spirits to a whole new way of viewing the world. It also opened us to the possibility of adopting Black children. We were humbled by the people at Sacred Heart whose joyful faithfulness to the gospel was forged in resilience to racism within the church and in society. Thus, when Kara and I were exploring and then preparing to adopt cross-racially in Chicago in the late 1990s, we consulted interracial families led by White and biracial parents. Parishioners from Sacred Heart and parents of interracial parents both underscored the profound need for us to take up anti-racism as a way of life so that we would care appropriately for our children.

Throughout our preparation we confronted our own white ignorance of how to raise Black children in a society that idolizes whiteness as it loathes

---

[3] Cyprian Davis, *The History of Black Catholics in the United States* (New York: Crossroad, 1990), 209–10.

Blackness. While I began to learn about the sting of racism through service to and participation in a Black parish, I felt that sting in a new way when I attended a Catholic Charities gathering designed to introduce parents to adoption. At one point in the session the leader presented a hierarchy of "preferred children" based upon statistics of whom white parents chose to adopt. Healthy White babies were at the top. Eastern European, Asian, Central American, and Hispanic American backgrounds filled out the middle. At the bottom of preferred children were disabled children of all races and Black babies. The leader presented this information without any historical or cultural context and without any reflection about how it related to, much less conflicted with, our Catholic faith and values. I left with a piercing sense of violence of how this unquestioned racial hierarchy feels for our Black brothers and sisters and a desire to be faithful to their love and care.

Truth-Telling in the Age
of White Nationalist Rage

Informed by this experience, I write primarily for White people of faith who share a deep longing for working through the racial contradictions of our way of life. If you believe you are innocent or see no need to work through the contradictions of the lie of white supremacy, this book may not be for you. Yet in the post-Charlottesville and post–George Floyd conversation, too many White people of faith took the easy road of condemning overt white supremacists without addressing the more pervasive and pernicious reality of how good White people of faith, including Catholics, maintain conditions of white Eurocentrism that elected an explicitly white-nationalist president in 2016—the first since the Jim Crow era. This book is for people of faith willing to work through our own complicity in the idolatry of whiteness.

While there is a growing academic literature addressing white supremacy and racism from multiple theological, pastoral, and moral perspectives, there are limited resources for White people of faith and justice who are not professional scholars. Nearly sixty years ago the Cistercian monk Thomas Merton wrote a series of "Letters to a White Liberal" that still ring true today. I am inspired by Merton's contemplative vision and practice as I attempt to understand and articulate how whiteness works. For Merton this meant unraveling the roots of assumptions of white innocence and superiority.

Drawing upon Merton, I invite White people of faith to take shared responsibility for the sin and idolatry of white privilege and racism. This is no easy task, for it involves the deepest core of our hearts, lives, and souls. Indeed, it will involve individual and collective transformation from arrogant racial ignorance to unlearning the roles we play in perpetuating the social sin of anti-black white supremacy. By "unlearning," I mean beginning the work of acknowledging, gaining consciousness of, and undoing the many ways we have been malformed and deformed by a society that idolizes whiteness. More than that, as I explain, unlearning white privilege and superiority means becoming accountable to ourselves and others and taking responsibility for the roles we play in perpetuating unearned privilege and conferred white dominance.

Embracing God's Intimate Love, Mutual Care, and Belonging

God's gift of creation draws all of us into an intimate embrace of love, mutuality, and belonging. In the contemplative tradition, Thomas Merton notices in the sound of a frog hopping into water, in the fluttering of a hummingbird, in a gentle breeze, and in all of the people he encounters at the corner of Fourth and Walnut in Louisville, Kentucky, the loving and intimate dance of God with and in the whole of creation. It is that intimate dance of God's loving embrace to which we are called as beings made in the image and likeness of One who offers intimate communion in absolute openness and vulnerability.

The divine call to sensitively embrace the whole of creation is universal. This is why the Roman Catholic Church opens Vatican II's "Pastoral Constitution on the Church in the Modern World" (*Gaudium et Spes*), with these enduring words:

> The joy and hope, the grief and anguish of men of our time, especially of those who are poor or afflicted in any way, are the joy and hope, the grief and anguish of the followers of Christ as well.[4]

The Catholic Church celebrates how "Christians cherish a feeling of deep solidarity with the human race and its history. This deep sense of solidarity with the whole humanity calls the church and the people of God to read "the signs of the times," "interpreting them in light of the gospel if it is to carry out its task."[5] Vatican II calls people of faith to deepen historical consciousness as a way of witnessing to Christ's intimate love for every creature throughout creation. Sadly, in terms of building racial solidarity, White Americans tend to be unaware of how the long history of white supremacy endures in the present. Part of the work of unlearning white superiority is becoming histori-

---

[4]"Pastoral Constitution on the Church in the Modern World: *Gaudium et Spes*," in *Vatican II: The Conciliar and Post Conciliar Documents*, ed. Austin Flannery, OP (Northport, NY: Costello, 1987), 903.

[5]Ibid., 904.

cally conscious of how our past shapes who we are in the present.

I elucidate in this book how the US Catholic Church and people of faith have failed to live up to the gift and task of God's love. As I explain, drawing upon the theological anthropology of Saint John of the Cross and contemporary womanist and feminist theologies, "intimacy" denotes a deeper level of solidarity. Intimacy expresses the deepest theological, spiritual, and moral issues at stake in the work for racial liberation in a way that solidarity language easily elides. Too often, solidarity language neglects how the responsibility of being with and for other human beings is rooted in God's gratuitous love. Precisely because "solidarity" is used so widely and frequently in abstract ways that miss its deeper theological, spiritual, and moral meaning of struggling for racial liberation, I use the term "intimacy" as a way to articulate how God draws all people into deeper levels of loving mutuality, care, and belonging.

White people and institutions often use the term "solidarity" without taking the real risks involved in the emotional, spiritual, political, and practical work of racial liberation. The most salient risks of racial solidarity that I address in this text include White people gaining self-knowledge of our participation in persistent racism and relinquishing the emotional, spiritual, political, and economic advantages and security we obtain to the detriment of Black, Brown, and Indigenous people, and other peoples of color. My point is not to jettison the use of the word "solidarity"; rather, it is to invite people of faith to think, reflect, act, and communicate in self-critical ways that notice how social justice language may become co-opted by euphemisms, abstractions, and interests that shield us from the real risks such work entails.

Solidarity raises difficult questions for White people and the Catholic Church in the US context. Where have we White folks been in the struggles of Black Catholics for full recognition as citizens and members of the Body of Christ? Our faith tradition is clear that people of faith are called to be in "vulnerable communion"[6] with and for people who are in any way oppressed, despised, or denigrated. The acid test of the practice of solidarity is whether and how it is practiced in the midst of social conflict. Bryan Massingale explains that cross-racial solidarity "is based upon the deep-seated conviction that the concerns of the despised other are intimately bound up with our own," in such a way that victims and beneficiaries of systemic injustice both realize that their full humanity and freedom are inextricably interwoven.[7]

In his articulation of a mystical political theology, German theologian Johann Baptist Metz (1928–2019) states,

---

[6]Thomas E. Reynolds, *Vulnerable Communion: A Theology of Disability and Hospitality* (Grand Rapids: Brazos Press, 2008).

[7]Bryan N. Massingale, *Racial Justice and the Catholic Church* (Maryknoll, NY: Orbis Books, 2010), 116–17.

A practical fundamental theology tries to hold on to solidarity in its indissoluble mystical-universal and political-particular dual structure, with the goal of protecting universalism from apathy and partial solidarity from forgetfulness and hatred. . . . In its mystical-political structure solidarity emerges as a category of the salvation of the subject at those points where it is being threatened: by being forgotten, by oppression, by death. It arises as a category of engagement so that men and women might become and continue to be subjects.[8]

Too often social justice and ecclesial leaders speak of solidarity in universal terms that miss Metz's concern with the Christian witness as the "partiality of discipleship"[9] and Massingale's call to practice conflictual solidarity in a specific, practical way in which "our sense of connection and commitment"[10] with despised others is unmistakably clear in the struggle to enact freedom and justice. In the spirit of Metz and Massingale, I suggest that mystical political intimacy means taking up sides in multiple forms of ritual, prayer, protest, and lament by being in vulnerable communion with Black and Brown brothers and sisters. I elucidate these ways of taking up sides in Part II as a way of embracing a deeper level of humanity that is not based upon White people purchasing an illusion of wholeness and autonomous self-sufficiency through wealth, education, and self-segregation. Rather, drawing upon the reality of mutual human dependence and divine giftedness of every person, the depth of our humanity is found in shared suffering, in what theologian Thomas E. Reynolds calls "vulnerable communion."[11] Being in vulnerable communion means becoming open to and being transformed by the fullness of other people, including their beauty and giftedness as well as their woundedness and suffering. Vulnerable communion means entering into enduring relationship with people such that brothers and sisters fully share the joys and hopes, grief and suffering, on the way of life and the gospel.

"For the Trumpet Shall Sound"

I do not share these reflections to gather praise or earn a pass for my privilege; rather, through this book I suggest a way of unlearning white superiority as a way of becoming fully human and creating the conditions for possibly healing the wound that is racism in church and society. Real healing requires

[8]Johann Baptist Metz, *Faith in History and Society: Toward a Practical Fundamental Theology*, A New Translation by J. Matthew Ashley (New York: Herder and Herder, 2007), 210–11.
[9]Ibid., 210.
[10]Massingale, *Racial Justice*, 117.
[11]Reynolds, *Vulnerable Communion*, 108.

the humility to let go of power and control and to become vulnerable and intimately connected with the entire Body of Christ. I offer these reflections about ways to unlearn unearned white privilege and power, including my own, in the hope that our church and White brothers and sisters in Christ will seek a more authentic way of life by working through our shared complicity in the evil of white innocence, supremacy, and terror.

In the context of US empire, colonialism, and white supremacy, I believe that it is a prerequisite for people like me, from dominant social locations, to be explicit about their commitment to antidomination. Too often White people take for granted our dominant status within the most powerful nation in the world. We tend to forget the history of how we gained this privileged position in society and we like to flatter ourselves with the myth that our own individual effort got us here. If we are honest, we know that we are born into a world that normalizes white privilege and confers a dominance that is undeserved and inhuman. As I elucidate in the chapters ahead, we tend to live under illusions of superiority and forgetfulness of our past that blind us to our own role in systemic racial injustice. We assume innocence and superiority even in the simple, necessary process of breathing. The chant "I can't breathe" evokes the memory of the police killings of Eric Garner and George Floyd, and ought to remind us how the taking of one life takes life from all of us.[12] This means that I must continually be unlearning how I am complicit in multiple forms of oppression in every sphere of life, a reality that Patricia Hill Collins names the "matrix of domination."[13]

Too often, the Catholic Church and people of faith have been focused on economic success and status whereby we foster ignorance of our responsibility with and for all members of the Body of Christ who are suffering within our cities, towns, and dioceses. I grew up in a relatively affluent family in a Midwestern university town where we had little concern about the interlocking violence of poverty and racism. While the founder of our Catholic parish faced Protestant resistance to the formation of a Catholic faith community in the 1950s, our parish enjoyed many benefits of affluence and connections to the local university that benefitted the parish elementary school, and we really had no self-reflective awareness of being a predominantly White community. As I look back, I also see how we assumed a certain racial innocence even as we failed to criticize the racial epithets used by various family members and in the community at large.

Our privilege was also evident in how my parents, extended family, and local community viewed the living Dr. Martin Luther King Jr. as a threat

---

[12]I wrote about the theological and spiritual implications of the "I can't breathe" chant in "Jesuit Institutions Must Do More to Undo Racism," *America*, October 13, 2015, www.americamagazine.org.

[13]Patricia Hill Collins, *Black Feminist Thought: Knowledge, Consciousness, and the Politics of Empowerment* (Boston: Unwin Hyman, 1990), 221–38.

rather than a prophet. More personally, while my parents celebrated my father's service in World War II and the graduate degree he attained with the aid of the GI Bill, there was no awareness or discussion of how that benefit was denied to African American men and women who served. When Black Americans expressed their anger in Detroit in 1967 and 1968, my family talked about the violence as if we had no connection with our brothers and sisters who were suffering racial and economic injustice. We and our Catholic parish unreflectively enjoyed our safe distance from Detroit's strife.

This work of unlearning white, male, heterosexual privilege is necessarily a lifelong task. Contrary to popular white practice and custom, I claim neither innocence nor achievement. This work does not inoculate me from privilege or from the responsibility to continue to unlearn and subvert white domination. Rather, I address myself as one who remains complicit and must take up the work anew every day, throughout my entire life. Conversion, like the sacraments, is a process into the always-transforming love of God and neighbor, not a passing event. My hope is that this book contributes to a larger conversation and shared struggle to become more deeply human and to find new ways of living whereby all people and creatures may fully thrive.

Mystical and Political Intimacy

God's gift of transformation in the intimate unity of love of God and neighbor is mystical and political because it expresses God's desire that we embody a "withness" for others in their trauma and woundedness.[14] By mystical I do not mean some kind of special knowledge, extraordinary vision, or Gnosticism. I look to the contemplative Trappist monk Thomas Merton as a helpful guide for understanding how and why the mystical and political are intimately interwoven. As noted in my preface, I am focusing particularly on Merton's *Seeds of Destruction*, his pathbreaking work addressing white complicity. My argument draws heavily from both Merton's *Seeds of Destruction* and his *New Seeds of Contemplation*, which I believe offer enduring insight into how White people of faith might integrate contemplation with the work of racial liberation. Toward the end of *New Seeds of Contemplation*, Merton invites people of faith into the "general dance"[15] of God's luring, gentle, loving presence in the entire cosmos and throughout the whole of existence. We are called to forget "ourselves on purpose, cast our awful solemnity to the winds and join the general dance."[16]

---

[14]See Flora A. Keshgegian, *Redeeming Memories: A Theology of Healing and Transformation* (Nashville: Abingdon Press, 2000), 190–98, here 194.

[15]Thomas Merton, *New Seeds of Contemplation* (New York: New Directions Books, 1972), 290 and 296.

[16]Ibid., 297.

This "general dance," along with everyday mysticism, encompasses the human longing for sacredness and union with God. That desire itself is God's presence within us, drawing us into a more intimate dance with the whole of creation. This is the giftedness of God's creative love always already present in every being and in the entirety of Being. This is what the great twentieth-century Jesuit theologian Karl Rahner called the "mysticism of everyday life." For Rahner, the gift of God's love involves the most fundamental invitation of the divine to the human: love of God and neighbor in the midst of everyday, ordinary life. The mystical is not something extraordinary reserved only for the rare visionary mystic; rather, in the most mundane moments of everyday life, the divine is present within us and all around us.

This call to intimate love with the whole of God's creation goes to the very core, purpose, and meaning of the Christian faith tradition. Too often, however, at least in North American culture, we have reduced mysticism to an otherworldly spirituality disconnected from human pain, suffering, and struggle. White people must confront the reality that we have been socially and historically constructed as the pinnacle of humanity for at least the past five hundred years. By the term "intimacy," I begin to articulate in Part I a deeper level of solidarity that includes White people becoming contemplatively aware and critical of the ways we have been humanly, morally, and spiritually deformed by anti-black white supremacy. Part I is an extensive reflection on the ways White people need to become critically aware of the ways that the worldly reality of white supremacy and anti-black oppression is *inside of us.* Thus Part I challenges White people to confront our historical amnesia (chapter 1), unlearn modernity's deceptive "white habitus"[17] (chapter 2), and trace the historical origins of anti-blackness in the Roman Catholic papacy's initiation of the Atlantic slave trade (chapter 3).

I use the term "mystical political intimacy" to highlight three intercon-nected Catholic theological and spiritual claims: that human beings are created in the image and likeness of God and endowed with the capacity for relationship with God, that human beings have a unique place within God's creation, and that human beings are made for communion with our human and nonhuman kin. Yet too often White people appeal to solidarity through these theological claims without any historical deconstruction of anti-black white supremacy. Thomas Merton's call to White people to develop critical

---

[17]Eduardo Bonilla-Silva develops the concept of "white habitus" as "a racialized, uninterrupted socialization process that conditions and creates whites' tastes, perceptions, feelings, and emotions and their views on racial matters." See Eduardo Bonilla-Silva, *Racism without Racists: Color-Blind Racism and the Persistence of Racial Inequality in the United States,* 2nd ed. (Lanham, MD: Rowman and Littlefield, 2006), 103. Chapter 2 in this book utilizes white habitus as a way of interrogating and understanding how White people are shaped within and contribute to a separate residential life that fosters a White culture of solidarity and negative views about Black, Brown, and Indigenous people.

self-awareness of our egotism and authentically embrace Black people as an expression of the unity of love of God and neighbor is, I argue, a call to enduring transformation and liberation.

I use the term "intimacy" in Part II as a gospel way of lived conversion of minds, bodies, hearts, and souls that is both transformation in God and transformation with and for racially oppressed peoples. Mystical-political conversion is rooted in God's grace and compassionate living and loving with and for racially oppressed neighbors. This is why I am proposing "intimacy" as a deeper way of nurturing solidarity as a gospel encounter of Jesus's way of healing and repair, connection in table fellowship, and transformation in walking the way of the cross with oppressed peoples and the earth. Ultimately, my argument is oriented to a mystical-political sensitivity, transformation, and liberation with and for Black people and the whole of God's creation.

However, the term "mystical political intimacy" may sound quaint, even oppressively naïve, to people who have suffered racial violence. This sensibility is not unfounded in the face of white supremacy, terror, and violence. People of color have endured slavery and every form of violence—including rape, torture, lynching, and imprisonment—and to this day have been continually denied fundamental humanity in every sphere of US social, political, and economic life. Yet throughout colonial and US history, many people of diverse racial and class backgrounds have crossed racial lines to create loving families and communities of resistance. These loving interracial relationships[18] witness to alternative ways of life that profoundly imitate God's intention for tender and caring relationships in the Lord's Prayer.

In North American culture, the word "intimacy" also tends to conjure up an exclusively erotic, sexual, reductively physical meaning. As Lisa Lowe demonstrates in her examination of imperialism across four continents, the "intimacies of desire, sexuality, marriage, and family are inseparable from the imperial projects of conquest, slavery, labor, and government."[19] Too often, US culture reduces and flattens the meaning and purpose of human desire to nothing more than self-pleasuring physical attraction, voyeurism, and possession. We miss how this demented desire corrodes racialized sexuality and identities, and drives white supremacy and imperialism. Even more deeply, moral theologian Bryan Massingale exposes the multiple ways sexual racism is a tool of racial domination and humiliation. The race-based sexual violence prevalent in law enforcement, pornography, and assaults upon women of color, he explains, finds its roots in the history of slavery, Jim Crow, and

---

[18]Sheryll Cashin, *Loving: Interracial Intimacy in America and the Threat to White Supremacy* (Boston: Beacon Press, 2017), 5–6.

[19]Lisa Lowe, *The Intimacies of Four Continents* (Durham, NC: Duke University Press, 2015), 17–18.

lynching.[20] I thus employ the term "mystical political intimacy" to articulate a deeper level of transformation to which we are called as coworkers in God's vineyard (Mt 20:1–16) for racial and ecological liberation.

My own encounter with Thomas Merton and the contemplative life began after I survived a bone marrow transplant for leukemia that nearly took my life in 1984. Looking the reality of death in the face prepared me to engage Merton's call to encounter reality as it is. Little did I know that his writing would draw me into the calling I attempt to live today. It was in the hospital facing death that I first began to notice that the condition of the possibility of my life rested so much on white racial privilege and power. I began to understand that being alive itself—including breathing—is an instance both of divine presence and conferred racial dominance. Our African American brothers and sisters do not enjoy the same health-care benefits that saved my life. According to the American Cancer Society, African Americans have "the highest death rate and shortest survival of any racial group for most cancers."[21]

Later, when I was in divinity school studying both Thomas Merton and Dr. Martin Luther King Jr., I attended a conference held in late 1988 at the Aquinas Center for Roman Catholic Studies at Emory University. That conference, titled "For the Trumpet Shall Sound: Protest, Prayer, and Prophecy," addressed the legacies of both Merton and King and featured, among many other famous scholars' presentations, Albert Raboteau's reflection on "The Hidden Wholeness" of Merton and King. A variation of that talk is published in Raboteau's book *A Fire in the Bones: Reflections on African-American Religious History*. His scholarship on slave religion inspired new generations of scholars who have emphasized two critical facts of the history of African slaves in America: that they were full of agency in the midst of slavery, and that they revolutionized our understanding of the meaning of Christianity and democracy itself. Like many others, I was also inspired by Raboteau's reflection on how King was planning to join Merton for a retreat at his Kentucky abbey (Our Lady of Gethsemani) that was in the planning stages before King's assassination.

The possibilities of joining the contemplative and prophetic, which Merton and King were not able to explore together, stand before us today. Most importantly, by taking up Raboteau's challenge to attempt to walk the path of contemplation and prophecy, I embarked upon an unexpected journey of confronting both my own complicity and the deep complicity of my faith,

---

[20]Bryan N. Massingale, "The Erotic Life of Anti-Blackness: Police Sexual Violation of Black Bodies," in *Anti-Blackness and Christian Ethics*, ed. Vincent W. Lloyd and Andrew Prevot (Maryknoll, NY: Orbis Books, 2017), 173–94.

[21]American Cancer Society, "Cancer Facts and Figures for African Americans 2019–2021," www.cancer.org.

Roman Catholicism, in US racism. Rev. James Forbes, who contributed a passionate sermon on the intersections of race and class at the 1988 Emory conference, also nurtured fire in my belly for racial justice. More importantly, it was Sister Antona Ebo, a Franciscan nun from St. Louis who had walked with King from Selma to Montgomery, who personally challenged me to risk my life for racial justice. "For the Trumpet Shall Sound" was more than just another conference; it was a rare, life-changing experience that shaped my deep sense of calling to address racial injustice in the United States.

Merton begins *Seeds of Destruction* by noting that the contemplative life is not an abstraction or a flight from the world. "The contemplative life is not, and cannot be," Merton begins, "a mere withdrawal, a pure negation, a turning of one's back on the world with its sufferings, its crises, its confusions and errors."[22] Monastic communities are fully implicated in the sinfulness of the world, Merton explains, and must witness to baptismal conversion into God's love in the midst of worldly egoism and injustice. To forget or ignore one's implication in the sin and injustice of the world, continues Merton, "does not absolve the monk (or any contemplative) from responsibility in events in which his very silence and 'not knowing' may constitute a form of complicity."[23]

Practicing silence does not disconnect one from time and place. On the contrary, silence connects us with the whole of reality, including the time and place in which we live. At the very outset of *Seeds*, Merton recalls that when monastic communities remained silent in Europe in the first half of the twentieth century, too often they were "publicly giv[ing] support to totalitarian movements."[24] Such otherworldly recollection and renunciation itself becomes complicit in the evil of the world.

On the other hand, Merton does not join any partisan political cause, and is clear that "monks should be free of the confusions and falsities of partisan dispute."[25] The last thing he would want, exclaims Merton, is a monastic movement in politics. However, the monk, the contemplative, and persons and communities of faith ought not concentrate only upon "ideal essences, upon absolutes, upon eternity alone."[26]

Even today, when spirituality becomes overly concerned with making individuals feel better with themselves and comfortable with the social status quo, Merton's warning endures. This is especially true when White people tend to be more concerned with personal "wholeness" while we remain ignorant

---

[22]Thomas Merton, *Seeds of Destruction* (New York: Farrar, Straus and Giroux, 1964), xiii.
[23]Ibid.
[24]Ibid.
[25]Ibid., xiv.
[26]Ibid.

or complacent about racial violence. Unfortunately, religion and spirituality have become deeply privatized in Western European and American culture, with disastrous consequences for the public good.[27]

These conditions result in much of spiritual life becoming overly individualistic. As religion focuses too much on individuals—providing them with a therapeutic spirituality that assuages guilt, pacifies anxiety, and accommodates disquiet with social injustice—we become blind to social suffering and begin to believe that social injustice is inevitable. As our economic system has become dominated by corporate capitalist practice, spirituality has become merely another commodity to be sold.[28] In America, this includes justification of the so-called prosperity gospel, a profit-driven and self-interested spirituality, at the expense of real concern for people who are suffering and excluded in society. Worse, the prosperity gospel rhetoric tends to blame people who are poor for their plight, and its adherents, many of whom are white and affluent, disavow responsibility for racism because they do not see color or claim to be "color-blind," a perspective that I discuss in depth in chapter 2.

Merton's contemplative practice and theological perspective offer a different approach. He does not acquiesce to a spirituality that justifies the status quo as the way things should be. Rather, he articulates how Christians must engage with the social injustices of our time. Christianity, he writes, cannot reject history. In fact, Christianity is centered upon a historical event that changes the entire meaning of time and history. The freedom of the Christian contemplative is not freedom *from* time; rather, the freedom of the Christian contemplative is freedom *in* time. Merton writes,

> It is the freedom to go out and meet God in the inscrutable mystery of His will here and now, in this precise moment in which He asks man's cooperation in shaping the course of history according to the demands of divine truth, mercy, and fidelity.[29]

Contemplatives, lay and monastic, are called to witness to God's mercy, truth, and justice in the midst of earthly conflict. The adversary is neither time nor history. The adversary is evil will and the accumulated inheritance of untruth and past sin. Merton recognizes how we are individually and collectively shaped by society as well as the history of sin that precedes us.

Although Merton does not advocate political partisanship, he states, "I

---

[27]Robert Bellah, Richard Madsen, William M. Sullivan, Ann Swidler, and Steven M. Tipton, *Habits of the Heart: Individualism and Commitment in American Life* (Berkeley: University of California Press, 1985).

[28]Jeremy Carrette and Richard King, *Selling Spirituality: The Silent Takeover of Religion* (New York: Routledge, 2005), 13–22.

[29]Merton, *Seeds of Destruction*, xiv.

speak not only as a monk but also as a responsible citizen of a very powerful nation." His point is not that the secular nation-state ought to be guided by an eschatological church. However, he continues, it is "a solemn obligation of conscience at this moment of history to take the positions"[30] that he affirms in *Seeds of Destruction*. That solemn obligation of conscience is now ours, in a nation that is retreating from its democratic and faith commitment to live up to the creed that all people are created equal.

If he is to live a vow of poverty, Merton reflected in 1964,

It seems illusory if I do not in some way identify myself with the cause of people who are denied their rights and forced, for the most part, to live in abject misery. To have a vow of obedience seems to me absurd if it does not imply a deep concern for the most fundamental of all expressions in God's will: the love of His truth and of our neighbor.[31]

Followers of the Way of Jesus

The premise and purpose of this book concern the heart of the gospel. It is easily communicated through the clarity of the Lord's Prayer. When Jesus offers his prayer that has become the primary prayer of Christianity, he prays that God's loving presence may be fully real, right now, right here. He invites followers to address God in the same intimate way he does. I take the Lord's Prayer as a way that Jesus draws us into his aching passion to transform our numb absence and lust to dominate others into God's desire to expand the caverns of our being into eternal love with and for every creature in the web of life. The Lord's Prayer is Jesus's invitation to us to orient our entire lives to intimacy with God and neighbor in the way we shape every dimension of our lives with and for one another. The Lord's Prayer calls people of faith to create God's Beloved Community among all of our human and nonhuman kin here and now.

Even when we acknowledge human finitude, too often we forget that God created the human person with an infinite capacity for God in the "caverns"—the "soul's most subtle rooms"—of the intellect, will, and memory, as the Carmelite Constance FitzGerald describes the theological anthropology of Saint John of the Cross.[32] She quotes John of the Cross's commentary on

---

[30]Ibid., xv–xvi.

[31]Ibid., xvi.

[32]Constance FitzGerald, "Transformation in Wisdom: The Subversive Character and Educative Power of Sophia in Contemplation," in *Carmel and Contemplation: Transforming Human Consciousness*, ed. Kevin Culligan, OCD, and Regis Jordan, OCD (Washington, D.C.: Institute of Carmelite Studies, 2000), 351, note 46.

The Living Flame of Love, where he explains that because the object of these caverns, namely God, "is profound and infinite," it follows that "in a certain fashion their thirst is infinite, their hunger is also deep and infinite, and their languishing and suffering are infinite death.[33] As long as we fill the caverns of the intellect, will, and memory with "human knowledge, loves, dreams, and memories that seem or promise to satisfy completely," FitzGerald explains, "the person is unable to feel or imagine the depths of capacity that is there."[34]

Paradoxically, FitzGerald writes, only when we become aware of our human emptiness, especially now in the midst of our fragility and breakdowns of all in which we have invested our lives, "the limitation of our life project and life love, and the shattering of our own dreams and meanings, can the depths of thirst and hunger that exist in the human person, the infinite capacity, really be felt."[35] Even as we seem to be falling into an abyss of sinfulness and idolatry of whiteness, God draws us into an infinite capacity for mystical sensitivity to the interdependence and bondedness of the whole of creation, to paraphrase Beverly Lanzetta's *Radical Wisdom.*[36] I explore this paradoxical insight in the beginning of Part II because it interrelates God's work and ours in the struggle for racial liberation.

Merton's concern for following God's will through God's truth and love of our neighbor is rooted in Jesus's intimate love for His Father (Abba) and his prophetic practice of compassion.[37] When Jesus calls his disciples to be compassionate as God is compassionate (Lk 6:36), he presents his listeners with a radically different vision of God than that offered by the religious elites of his time. During the historical life of Jesus, the religious and economic elites apply the Law of Moses legalistically to maintain the power and status of those same elites, while the great majority of people suffer grinding poverty. Due to their economic conditions, most people could not follow the purity rules of the Temple and could not pay taxes (i.e., the tithe) to the Temple.

In contrast, Jesus presents his followers and listeners with a much more compassionate vision of God and practice of the Law. The Hebrew and Aramaic roots of the word that Jesus uses for "compassion" are plural forms of a noun that means a woman's womb.[38] Rather than stressing external

---

[33]Ibid. FitzGerald quotes Saint John of the Cross, commentary on *The Living Flame of Love,* in *The Collected Works of Saint John of the Cross,* trans. Kieran Kavanaugh, OCD, and Otilio Rodriguez, OCD (Washington, DC: Institute for Carmelite Studies, 1991), 681, no. 22.

[34]FitzGerald, "Transformation in Wisdom," 303.

[35]Ibid.

[36]Beverly Lanzetta, *Radical Wisdom: A Feminist Mystical Theology* (Minneapolis: Fortress Press, 2005), 197.

[37]Maureen H. O'Connell, *Compassion: Loving Our Neighbor in an Age of Globalization* (Maryknoll, NY: Orbis Books, 2009).

[38]Marcus J. Borg, *Meeting Jesus Again for the First Time: The Historical Jesus and the Heart of Contemporary Faith* (New York: HarperCollins, 1994), 47–48.

laws or rules, Jesus's word thus evokes a vision of the wholeness of creation and of God as "womblike," an experience in which God feels for the whole of creation the way a mother feels intimate care with and for the new life in her womb. For men, this means feeling with and for others deep in our gut. While the text in Luke 6:36 is often translated as "Be merciful as God is Merciful," biblical scholar Marcus Borg contends that the English word "compassion" better expresses the vision and practice of love expressed by the historical Jesus. His womblike term for compassion invites people both to feel with others and to put that feeling into practice. By calling his followers to practice compassion, Jesus calls them both to feel passionate care for others and to act in a way consistent with that feeling God nurtures within us. Practicing God's compassion intimately interweaves our lives together in love, freedom, and justice.

Jesus's practice of compassion—as we find in the stories that he told—his practice of healing by gentle touching, and his critique of unjust wealth and power meant that Jesus chose to suffer with the despised, the forgotten, and the poor. Suffering with and for the oppressed, articulated as preferential solidarity in Catholic social teaching, defines Jesus's practice of compassion. A truly contemplative and human solidarity means that we are "pierced to the core" of our souls so intimately by the suffering of others that we feel the depth of another's wound within the very depth of our being.[39] This is where Christ's presence and ours are joined in the work of healing a wounded world. When we "feel and identify with the depth of another's wound," contemplative Beverly Lanzetta explains, this connection "generates an ethic of mutuality and compassion, a desire to share in and bring healing to the sorrows of others."[40]

In political and prophetic terms, Jesus's practice of preferential solidarity sets a radical example of resistance to the relationship between the privileged and the oppressed. Jesus clearly did not practice the elite norms of his day, such as piety and respectability; on the contrary, his practice of compassion threatened the economic, political, and religious elites. Indeed, his practice of preferential love and justice ultimately led to his crucifixion. The Catholic Church recognizes this reality today when it states that those who "stand up against [racial] repression by certain powers" will "face scorn and imprisonment."[41] Jesus's ministry and his suffering and death fundamentally witness to God's gratuitous, preferential love for the despised, and shape the transformative heart of Catholic social teaching. The way of preferential solidarity invites intellectual, moral, and religious

---

[39]Lanzetta, *Radical Wisdom*, 200.
[40]Ibid.
[41]The Vatican, Pontifical Commission on Peace and Justice, "The Church and Racism: Toward a More Fraternal Society," no. 26.

transformation to realize full human dignity and flourishing for all in human community. White liberation is intimately interwoven with Black liberation. The conditions of the possibility of shared liberation, I argue, are built through the narrow path of practicing the contemplative ethic of the intimate compassion of Jesus.

A Complicit Church

Work for racial liberation is both mystical and political precisely because of the unity of love of God and neighbor. It is political because US democratic and faith institutions and people have used all forms of power to oppress many diverse peoples of color. It is political because creating the conditions for the possibility of full human thriving for African Americans, Latinx, and First Peoples must involve complete transformation of the social, political, economic, and cultural levers of power that keep people oppressed. It is political precisely because Jesus Christ was executed for his witness to divine love and justice.

Violence against Black, Brown, and First Peoples continues unabated throughout the United States. For example, in the wake of the brutal murder of nine members of the Emanuel African Methodist Episcopal Church in Charleston, South Carolina, do we perceive the intimate connections between care for the whole of creation and care for Black lives?

Our African American brothers and sisters can't breathe (Eric Garner and George Floyd), can't eat Skittles or wear a hoodie (Trayvon Martin), can't play loud music (Jordan Davis), can't play as a child in a park (Tamir Rice), can't seek help after an accident (Renisha McBride), can't walk to a store with a friend (Rekia Boyd), can't move to a new city and job (Sandra Bland), and can't pray in their own church (Cynthia Hurd, the Reverend Clementa Pinckney, Sharonda Coleman Singleton, Tywanza Sanders, Ethel Lee Lance, Susie Jackson, the Reverend DePayne Middleton-Doctor, the Reverend Daniel Lee Simmons, and Myra Thompson).

In this context, poet Claudia Rankine shares how a Black mother told her, "The condition of Black life is one of mourning."[42] This is the reality in which a mother incessantly mourns the fact that she might lose her son at any moment. Rankine understands that while white liberals might feel temporarily bad about Black suffering, she explains,

There is really no mode of empathy that can replicate the daily strain of knowing as a Black person you can be killed for simply being Black:

---

[42]Claudia Rankine, "The Condition of Black Life Is One of Mourning," *New York Times,* June 22, 2015.

no hands in your pockets, no playing music, no sudden movements, no driving your car, no walking at night, no walking in the day, no turning on to this street, no entering this building, no standing your ground, no standing here, no standing there, no talking back, no playing with toy guns, no living while Black.[43]

She continues by noticing that eleven days after she was born on September 15, 1963, four Black girls were killed in the Sixteenth Street Baptist Church in Birmingham, Alabama. Now, fifty-two years later, upon the deadly shootings at the Charleston AME church, Rankine stresses that Black suffering means perpetual mourning. If predominantly White churches value Black lives, indeed all lives, then we would share in that mourning and work to end the conditions that cause such mourning.

Two things about the witness of the nine AME church members are especially troubling to theologian Willie James Jennings. First, Jennings is haunted by the fact that Dylann Roof was present

in the intimate space of that bible study, sitting there at a table with these saints of God who were seeking to hear a holy word just for them, just for this moment. I would feel less pain if he simply walked into the church and started shooting; then I could live with the fact that this young man did not give God's voice the chance to penetrate his contorted heart.[44]

The pain is that Roof "did hear the sound of grace and communion. God's voice was sounding in Emanuel. He simply resisted it."

Second, Jennings is haunted by the forgiveness that the families of victims offered Roof. He calls us to remember the words of Rev. Daniel Lee Simmons's granddaughter, who said, "We are here to combat hate-filled actions with love-filled actions."[45]

Jennings struggles to understand how Black folks are called upon throughout the centuries "in tortuous repetition to forgive those who kill us, and we do it. The only way I can fathom this grace of forgiveness is if the very life of God flows through people like these Black families."[46] Yet Jennings also struggles with how forgiveness is interpreted. Too often, it is used to avoid dealing with whiteness and the state of war it creates in America. Forgiveness can become a soothing high that does not address the lie that is white supremacy. I believe White people ought to be haunted too. We ought to be

---

[43]Ibid.
[44]Willie James Jennings, "Dylann Roof Was Wrong: The Race War Isn't Coming, It's Here," *Religion Dispatches*, June 26, 2015, www.religiondispatches.org.
[45]Ibid.
[46]Ibid.

haunted by the connection we have with White people who foment racial terror. We ought to be haunted by the fact that the same society that creates people like Dylann Roof is the same society that forms us.

Consider the odd conversation that ensued in the wake of the August 2017 "Unite the Right" rally in Charlottesville, Virginia, which was organized to protect a statue of Confederate General Robert E. Lee and resulted in the murder of Heather Heyer, who lived her life in passionate embrace of people who are in any way oppressed. Donald Trump, then the president of the United States, said that there were people on many sides who committed violence. He asked, "George Washington was a slave owner. . . . How about Thomas Jefferson? Because he was a major slave owner. Now are we going to take down his statue?"[47]

There were many who came to the defense of the Founding Fathers. While we can recognize a false equivalency between Confederate leaders who threw the nation into war to defend slavery and the Founding Fathers, too many commentators, including US Catholic bishops, missed a more critical reality: they failed to help people of faith understand the historical roots of white racism in the legacy of slavery and how it implicates all of us today.

The gaping wound that is racism has only festered to a point that is humanly unbearable. Yet too many White people of faith remain blind and ignorant, consciously and unconsciously, of this pernicious reality. Our consciences ought to be stung about how this wound bleeds daily for victims of deadly violence. That the US Conference of Catholic Bishops hesitates to claim that "Black lives matter" only underscores the church's estrangement from Black people and its witness to Eucharistic intimacy. #BlackLivesMatter is far more than a social movement; it is a struggle for full human dignity and sociality that the Catholic Church ought to be embracing intimately and passionately. The Body of Christ in the United States is in profound need of the Catholic Church's leadership to help and protect people and communities torn apart by white supremacy and anti-blackness.

Yet the church's historical complicity in white supremacy sets it in a profound theological, moral, and pastoral bind. If the Catholic Church maintains silence in relationship to its enduring complicity in white supremacy, it denies God's grace, hope, and healing in the Eucharistic memory of Jesus Christ. Through continued silence, the church risks, as theologian M. Shawn Copeland warns, the blasphemy of continued "contempt for Black creatures who share the glory, beauty, and image of the Divine."[48]

On the other hand, practicing love with and for Black people means tak-

---

[47]Kristine Phillips, "Historians: No, Mr. President, Washington and Jefferson Are Not the Same as Confederate Generals," *Washington Post*, August 16, 2017.

[48]M. Shawn Copeland, "Anti-Blackness and White Supremacy in the Making of American Catholicism," *American Catholic Studies* 127, no. 3 (Fall 2016): 6–8.

ing the risk of losing privilege and power, a risk that will alienate people who are comfortable with the status quo. It will involve loss of status and privilege—and, if work for racial liberation seeks reparation for the harms from which White people grotesquely benefit, it will entail real loss of wealth and economic entitlement. If the Catholic Church takes up this risk for the gospel, it likely will lead to loss of funding sources from people who cherish their social standing. It will involve the difficult work of understanding our own inhumanity, blindness, and callousness toward other human beings who also share in the glory of being created in God's likeness. It will mean losing our sense of innocence and taking up the work of becoming authentically responsible for the entire Body of Christ.

The point is not that White sacrifice will lead to Black liberation—that is part of the lie of white supremacy. Rather, people who believe in the myth of whiteness need to recognize and address the plentitude of ways that whiteness is literally killing us.[49] This includes White people supporting politicians whose policies directly harm their own well-being. A case in point is the fact that from 2009 to 2015, "non-Hispanic white men accounted for nearly 80 percent of all gun suicides in the United States, despite representing less than 35 percent of the total population."[50] Nevertheless, the American public remains "largely unaware of the prevalence of white gun suicide" and "the links between gun ownership and gun suicide at all."[51] Michael Eric Dyson laments that the politics of whiteness is "killing us, and, quiet as it is kept, it's killing you too."[52]

That the church hesitates to proclaim that Black lives matter[53] only seems to reveal a certain lack of courage and affirm a blind attachment to a status quo that leaves sinful assumptions of white innocence unacknowledged and unaddressed. And that the church remains largely mute in the face of repeated public acts of racial violence on behalf of public officials and citizens alike only admits deeper internal contradictions between the Catholic Church's public proclamations and where it actually stands in relationship to its members. Perhaps a more frightening and insidious form of violence is that perpetrated by the church in its cowardice to name its own complicity. Blind, cowardly attachment to the racial status quo perpetuates death-dealing racism.

Even nonbelievers like Ta-Nehisi Coates see the profound theological and moral evil of American Christians who "have never betrayed their God,"

---

[49]Jonathan M. Metzl, *Dying of Whiteness: How the Politics of Racial Resentment Is Killing America's Heartland* (New York: Basic Books, 2019).

[50]Ibid., 47.

[51]Ibid., 49.

[52]Michael Eric Dyson, *Tears We Cannot Stop: A Sermon to White America* (New York: St. Martin's Press, 2017), 44. Metzl quotes these words of Dyson in *Dying of Whiteness*, 17.

[53]See Olga M. Segura, *Birth of a Movement: Black Lives Matter and the Catholic Church* (Maryknoll, NY: Orbis Books, 2021).

that is, the god of white supremacy.[54] In his recent work *We Were Eight Years in Power*, Coates reflects deeply upon the unending war America has waged against Black Americans. There were only eight years when African Americans gained power in the halls of state legislatures and Congress—the eight years immediately after the Civil War that ended with white backlash to Emancipation and "slavery by another name" that merged with Jim Crow and lynching. Of course, he also means the eight years President Barack Obama served with extraordinary intellect, patience, and courage in the face of repeated attacks on his character and that of his family. Coates argues that racism is deeper than simple hatred, and more often, is expressed with sympathy for White people and deep skepticism toward others.[55] Perhaps ironically, the deepest fear of White Americans is not that Black people will fail (and thereby fulfill white bias), but that African Americans will practice good governance. By exemplifying good governance African Americans will prove that white superiority and associated black inferiority is plain wrong. Due to the deep racist white skepticism many held of the Obamas, they were admonished "to be twice as good."[56] However, the fact that President Barack Obama and First Lady Michelle Obama were "twice as good" was insufficient, in Coates's analysis, "to cultivate the best" in White Americans. In other words, "acceptance depends not just on being twice as good but on being half as black. And even then, full acceptance is still withheld."[57]

Coates indicts US democracy and Christianity for bone-crushing violence against African Americans and First Peoples in the name of the human values of dignity and equality for all. Some commentators criticize Coates for his atheism. But to blame his atheism is precisely to miss our own atheism, as evidenced by the fact that White Americans have never taken the side of African Americans for dignity and equality against the idolatry of white supremacy. Plainly put, the US Catholic Church and Euro-American Catholics have yet to practice preferential solidarity with and for African Americans and First Peoples. We who claim the benefits of whiteness have never become fully accountable for our idolatry of white supremacy.

Birth of a Colonial Nation

This nation was founded amid the genocide of the First Peoples of the Americas, and it was built on the backs of millions of Africans, stolen from

---

[54]Ta-Nehisi Coates, *Between the World and Me* (New York: Spiegel and Grau, 2015), 6.

[55]Ta-Nehisi Coates, *We Were Eight Years in Power: An American Tragedy* (New York: One World Press, 2017), 123–24.

[56]Ibid., 124.

[57]Ibid.

their place of birth to create unimaginable wealth for White Americans. We have never fully confronted the colonialist roots of white supremacy. We need to confront the ways in which US democracy is built upon anti-black coloniality. Although white supremacy has constantly morphed throughout US history, the fact remains that the nation was built upon the slave labor of Africans and many peoples of color, and people of color have never fully enjoyed freedom and equality.

By white supremacy I do not primarily mean the KKK variety. A fuller understanding and analysis of white supremacy must include the history and historical legacy of colonialism and commodification that endures in at least four dimensions of culture and society.[58] These include how white supremacy functions as a historical mode of white racial class formation and economic ascendancy, constitutes a symbolic hierarchical order of white superiority that feeds upon anti-black bias, serves as a primary socialization process of individual and group white racial identity formation, and organizes a segregated society through "white habitus" that entails a dynamic interplay between both "position—the social geography, location, and power of whiteness—and practice—the ways whites are socialized to perceive and act within the world."[59]

The church tells a story of innocence when it decries racism in society as something separate from its own practice and renders the most basic questioning of white privilege invisible for critical reflection. Whites tend to live by a fantasy of Christian innocence. It strains credulity to claim that the church resists this assumption of white Christian innocence in any meaningful way. Even when the church may affirm universal human dignity, white racial bias is shaped by Christian imagery of good and evil in which white is "innocent" and black is "guilty."[60]

Theologian Jeannine Hill Fletcher explains how "good" White people are complicit in racism even in acts of charity. Relating her experience teaching in a Catholic university in a US urban context, she notices how "good White Christians involved in service work" may do so because they really do want to help people who are less fortunate and struggling. "It is Christlike to help

---

[58]Willie James Jennings, *The Christian Imagination: Theology and the Origins of Race* (New Haven, CT: Yale University Press, 2010), 305–6.

[59]Alex Mikulich, "Where Y'at Race, Whiteness, and Economic Justice? A Map of White Complicity in the Economic Oppression of People of Color," in *The Almighty and the Dollar: Reflections on* Economic Justice for All, ed. Mark J. Allman (Winona, MN: Anselm Academic, 2012), 210. Chapter 2 of the present volume is an extended development of how "white habitus," a racialized socialization process, tends to create conditions that reinforce white ignorance, self-segregation, power, and superiority.

[60]Alex Mikulich, Laurie Cassidy, and Margaret Pfeil, *The Scandal of White Complicity in US Hyper-Incarceration: A Nonviolent Spirituality of White Resistance* (New York: Palgrave, 2013, reissued in paper 2015), 11–12.

those in need," she writes, but after we have completed our service hours "I return to the comforts of my White life. After all, it's *their* problem; I tried to help, but I can't do everything."[61] Fletcher's example points to a subtle and pervasive way in which acts of charity may actually thwart justice while allowing White people to maintain their innocence and position within the status quo.

Overview of the Book

The entire book is organized around two parts that frame unlearning anti-black supremacy in its historical context of modernity/coloniality. We need to understand the historical roots of anti-black racism in modernity/coloniality in order to initiate other ways of living. The central themes of coloniality and decoloniality run throughout the book because, as Walter Mignolo so eloquently wrote, "Coloniality is far from over, so must be decoloniality."[62] Furthermore, quite frankly, our brains are not designed to respond quickly enough to the epochal racial and ecological challenges we now face; we need to focus our attention.[63]

Part I, on coloniality, situates anti-black white supremacy within the broader context of modernity. Chapter 1 focuses on understanding how our historical past endures in the present. Unlearning whiteness is not as simple as turning a switch and becoming human. We need the cold water of history to work through white racial amnesia and denial. Unlearning histories of oppression and resistance is integral to uprooting the deep historical legacies of white supremacy and coloniality. We need to learn how mythologies of individualism, modern progress, and white superiority deform us morally, spiritually, and humanly.

Chapter 2 explores the *where* and *how* of white supremacy. White supremacy thrives in a separate and unequal residential life that fosters a white culture of solidarity and negative views of racialized others. This chapter unpacks the social scientific term "white habitus," which examines Whites' tendency to inhabit the world in a way that normalizes control, possession, and superiority. White habitus reveals how biases of white racial innocence and black criminality are "baked" into American culture and thrive under conditions of white racial segregation.

---

[61]Jeanine Hill Fletcher, *The Sin of White Supremacy: Christianity, Racism, and Religious Diversity in America* (Maryknoll, NY: Orbis Books, 2017), ix.

[62]Walter D. Mignolo, "Coloniality Is Far from Over, So Must Be Decoloniality," *Afterall: A Journal of Art, Context, and Enquiry* 43 (Spring/Summer 2017): 39–45.

[63]Brian Merchant, "Apocalypse Neuro: Why Our Brains Don't Process the Gravest Threats to Humanity," *Vice*, June 10, 2015, www.vice.com.

Chapter 3 investigates the Roman Catholic origins of anti-black supremacy and coloniality. W. E. B. Du Bois's critique of whiteness rightfully relates the dynamic of white supremacy to a nexus of domination structured within colonialism. Christendom itself was an imperial formation that constituted the so-called age of discovery, and, despite the Roman Catholic Church's theological opposition to slavery, helped to facilitate colonial rule of peoples in Africa and the Americas. Roman Catholic theology and papal teaching, I contend, form a primary source of the darker side of Western modernity and the "coloniality of being/power/truth/freedom,"[64] to borrow Sylvia Wynter's enveloping phrase. Assumptions of white innocence and superiority are deeply rooted in Catholic theology, spirituality, and religious practice.

Part II, on decoloniality, comprises chapters 4 through 6 and develops a spirituality for racial liberation. I argue in chapter 4 that one of the ways to unlearn whiteness is to take up the work W. E. B. Du Bois invites through "double consciousness." White engagement of Du Boisian double consciousness suggests a self-critical and compassionate asceticism. An asceticism grounded in double consciousness, I argue, means engaging societal impasse, the reality in which there seems to be no rational way out of multiple, converging breakdowns. I draw upon Carmelite Constance FitzGerald's embrace of impasse as a spiritual path of white disintegration and transformation. Disintegration of white values (superiority, innocence, privilege, and control, among others) through impasse, I argue, is a critical condition of the possibility of unlearning anti-black white supremacy and modernity/coloniality.

Before the Catholic Church can authentically facilitate repair and repent for its role in the historical and cultural evil of white supremacy, it first needs to become a listening community that bends its collective ear to the voices, wisdom, and experience of people who suffer the deadly sting of racism. Chapter 5 discusses the uncanny convergence between decolonial approaches to love and repair with the mystical-political praxis of Black and womanist liberation theologies, especially that of Copeland and Massingale. Second, I suggest a mystical-political praxis as a decolonial process of "p/reparations."[65] A process of p/reparations in the American Catholic ecclesial context begins with becoming a listening church that prioritizes the diverse perspectives of the *damnés*. A listening community of faith that embraces a decolonial p/reparations framework, finally, discerns concrete policies and actions that facilitate decolonial reparations.

---

[64]Sylvia Wynter, "Unsettling the Coloniality of Being/Power/Truth/Freedom: Towards the Human, After Man, Its Overrepresentation—An Argument," *New Centennial Review* 3, no. 3 (Fall 2003): 257–337.

[65]Cecilia Cissell Lucas, "Decolonizing the White Colonizer?" (doctoral dissertation, University of California–Berkeley, Fall 2013), 35 and 45. I draw upon Lucas's elucidation of a "philosophy and praxis of p/reparations" to articulate a decolonial, Christian mystical-political praxis.

Chapter 6 concludes with a call for ecological intimacy. If "there is a way where there is no way" to draw upon African American spiritual wisdom, I believe communities of resistance will need to be formed that reinterpret and reapply ancient spiritual practices of contemplation in new ways that are deeply sensitive to the interpenetrating woundedness of the earth and all people. Drawing upon the encyclical letter *Laudato Si'* and engaging cultural dialogue with Indigenous perspectives, I argue that we need to move away from the neoliberal paradigm of incessant growth to alternative ways of living in harmony with all of our human and nonhuman kin. Then, perhaps, there may be real possibility and hope for a turn to the ecological intimacy that interconnects and invites authentic inclusiveness and intimate belonging.

PART I

The Colonial Context
of Anti-Black White Supremacy

1

The Enduring Presence
of the Past

(Un)learning Anti-Black Supremacy

We Catholics in the United States who believe ourselves to be white have a secret shame that we have kept in the attic for some time. We definitely don't talk about it at the dinner table or in polite company where we tend not to discuss religion and politics. We know, in the recesses of our conscience and being, that we are living the sin of anti-black white supremacy.[1] Drawing upon the wisdom of James Baldwin, I purposefully say "people who believe that they are white." The point is that we have brought the nation to the "edge of oblivion," where we are literally dying of whiteness[2] because our entire view of reality is distorted. This distortion of reality, Baldwin explains, is that the white US community has been "justifying a totally false identity and . . . what must be called a genocidal history," which "has placed everyone now living in the hands of the most ignorant and powerful people the world has ever seen."[3] As to how White people got this way, Baldwin replies, "By deciding they were white. By opting for safety instead of life. By persuading themselves that a black child's life meant nothing compared with a white child's life."[4] "Because they think they are white," becomes Baldwin's mantra:

Because they think they are white, they dare not confront the ravage and the lie of their history. Because they think they are white, they can-

---

[1] Vincent W. Lloyd and Andrew Prevot, eds., *Anti-Blackness and Christian Ethics* (Maryknoll, NY: Orbis Books, 2017). See also Jeannine Hill Fletcher, *The Sin of White Supremacy: Christianity, Racism, and Religious Diversity in America* (Maryknoll, NY: Orbis Books, 2017).

[2] Jonathan M. Metzl, *Dying of Whiteness: How the Politics of Racial Resentment Is Killing America's Heartland* (New York: Basic Books, 2019).

[3] James Baldwin, "On Being White . . . and Other Lies," in *The Cross of Redemption: Uncollected Writings*, ed. Randall Kenan (New York: Pantheon Books, 2010), 137.

[4] Ibid.

not allow themselves to be tormented by the suspicion that all men are brothers.... Because they think they are white, they believe, as even no child believes, in the dream of safety. Because they think they are white, however vociferous they may be and however multitudinous, they are as speechless as Lot's wife—looking backward, changed into a pillar of salt.[5]

The ravage and lie of our history are that we who believe we are white continually justify a false identity that was solidified at the origin of the Atlantic slave trade and the genocide of Indigenous Peoples throughout the Americas. "White being, absolutely," Baldwin declares, is "a moral choice (for there are no White people), for the crisis of leadership for those of us whose identity has been forged, or branded, as black is nothing new."[6] Unmistakably, people who assume or believe that they are white and pursue its benefits of comfort and safety play the ultimate form of identity politics. Baldwin's argument is that the economic and psychological privileges of being white are the consequence of a deeper malaise of white domination:

It is the black condition, and only that, which informs us concerning white people. It is a terrible paradox, but only those who believed that they could control and define black people divested themselves of the power to control and define themselves.[7]

Unlearning the social sin of anti-black white supremacy is a condition of the impossibility of authentically living the gospel. For people who believe they are white to begin to love Black people and Blackness involves two interdependent, interconnected conditions: unlearning how we have internalized anti-black white supremacy and learning how to dwell with and for Black people. Before we can take up a way of dwelling together in love, a problem I take up in chapter 4, a prerequisite is unlearning anti-black white supremacy in the context of white settler coloniality.

The fundamental theological, moral, and spiritual problem for people who believe that they are white is that we lack authentic presence to God, self, or others. Unlearning anti-black white supremacy concerns soul-work we need to do individually and collectively. If we think we are white, we are living in profound absence to God, self, and others. In his analysis of the racial impasse in 1964, Thomas Merton identified three key seeds of destruction: the illusion of white superiority and innocence, the illusion of self-sufficiency and prioritizing profits over people, and white fears and projections, which

---

[5] Ibid.
[6] Ibid.
[7] Ibid., 138.

ultimately result in a false sense of reality, a false sense of self and others, and a false faith. All of these alienate us and destroy society, wound the Mystical Body of Christ, and tear us apart from God and neighbor.

As long as dominant white society remains content with the status quo and sees itself as the only acceptable reality, Merton finds, "then the problem remains without reasonable solution, and there will inevitably be violence."[8] Like Merton, I draw heavily upon James Baldwin to develop my argument. In his famous "Letter to My Nephew on the One Hundredth Anniversary of Emancipation," Baldwin wrote, "But it is not permissible that the authors of devastation should also be innocent. It is the innocence which constitutes the crime."[9] The problem is the way White people tend to think, speak, and act as if we play no role in a racial conflict that is largely of our making. The problem is that over the past five hundred years, dating back to the papacy's initiation of the African slave trade (a point to be developed in chapter 3), the church, as well as US American society since its inception, teaches a narrative of white American innocence that is so deeply ingrained in white American consciousness that it is nearly impossible for us to interrogate the relationship between anti-blackness and white supremacy.

"The real tragedy," writes Thomas Merton to White people who assume innocence and good intentions, is that although "the white man" assumes that he is free, he is really beholden to "the same servitudes which he has imposed on the Negro: passive subjection to the lotus-eating commercial society that he has tried to create for himself, and which is shot through with falsity and unfreedom from top to bottom."[10]

The only way out of this impasse, Merton concludes, is for "everyone to face and accept the difficulties and sacrifices involved, in all their seriousness, in all their inexorable demands."[11] We cannot begin to learn unless we know "the need to learn."[12] Both Baldwin and Merton recognized that unlearning untruth concerns working through the interrelated, interconnected web of "pain and terror" that deforms all of us. We have lost sight of how we are all interrelated in the history of this death-dealing pain, terror, and oppression.

Yet my suggestion may rightfully strike many as ludicrous. How is it possible for people whose identity remains unmarked, invisible, and deceitfully innocent to become present to God, self, and others? Scholar Michael Eric Dyson felicitously names our malady with the acronym "C.H.E.A.T. (Chronic

---

[8]Thomas Merton, *Seeds of Destruction* (New York: Farrar, Straus and Giroux, 1964), 8.

[9]James Baldwin, "My Dungeon Shook: Letter to My Nephew on the One Hundredth Anniversary of Emancipation," in *The Fire Next Time* (New York: Vintage Books, 1993 [1963]), 5–6.

[10]Merton, *Seeds*, 86.

[11]Ibid., 9.

[12]Ibid.

Historical Evasion and Trickery) disorder."[13] Ultimately, the theological, moral, and spiritual problem is that the more we claim white innocence and self-justification in an anti-black society, not only do we "C.H.E.A.T." socially, economically, and politically, we also end up elevating ourselves to a false position of supremacy over God.

Our cultural milieu of white messianic imperialism, writes philosopher George Yancy, "remains invisible to those who inhabit it!"[14] Or, as James Perkinson frames the issue in theological terms, "whiteness has functioned in modernity as a surrogate form of 'salvation,' a mythic presumption of wholeness."[15] Perkinson illustrates the grotesqueness of white performance in how we continually procure a social position of domination that is founded upon always absolving itself. Indeed, we people who believe we are white have been absolving ourselves from the sin of anti-black white supremacy for far too long.

As moral theologian Bryan N. Massingale instructs in his celebration of the classic work of Malcolm X, developing a critical consciousness of who and where we are in historical context is a first step toward liberation. Malcolm X constantly exhorted his followers to instill a discipline of critical self-awareness about their true situation. Massingale quotes one of Malcolm X's associates, Benjamin Karim, on beginning the work of critical self-awareness: "'Untruths had to be untold,' Karim recalls Malcolm telling his students. 'We had to be untaught before we could be taught, and once untaught, we ourselves could unteach others.'"[16]

If Black people need to unlearn untruths of internalizing racial oppression, it is an understatement to say that people who believe that they are white must take responsibility for deeper work of unlearning the sin of white supremacy in heart, mind, and soul.

This chapter invites White people of faith to begin an examination of conscience of anti-black white supremacy in the present. Saint Paul's admonition to people of faith to *not* be conformed to the age of domination in which we live illuminates Baldwin's insight in biblical perspective. I proceed by elucidating the age of domination in which we live: modernity and its hidden legacies of coloniality, slavery, and racial capitalism. The chapter concludes by illustrating a condition of the possibility of taking up the confession that Baldwin, Merton, and Black Catholic faith invite.

[13]Michael Eric Dyson, *Tears We Cannot Stop: A Sermon to White America* (New York: St. Martin's Press, 2017), 72.

[14]George Yancy, *Look, a White! Philosophical Essays on Whiteness* (Philadelphia: Temple University Press, 2012), 6.

[15]James W. Perkinson, *White Theology: Outing Supremacy in Modernity* (New York: Palgrave Macmillan, 2004), 3.

[16]Bryan N. Massingale, "*Vox Victimarum Vox Dei*: Malcolm X as Neglected 'Classic' for Catholic Theological Reflection," *Catholic Theological Society of America Proceedings* 65 (2010): 63–88, at 72.

White people need to take up a contemplative witness of the time and place that inaugurate Atlantic chattel slavery and its afterlife. If we are going to gain historical consciousness of anti-black white supremacy, I believe people of faith—especially those who believe they are white—need to contemplatively, prayerfully enter what the Canadian poet, educator, and activist Dionne Brand envisions as "being a part, sitting in the room with history."[17] I suggest that White people give of themselves to sit in the room with history, as a way of (de)facing anti-black white supremacy, preparing to repent for our sins, and most importantly, becoming humanly present with and for people who strive for life in the midst of the nonstatus and nonbeing of Blackness.

The Presence of the Past

In one of his classic essays published in *Ebony* in August 1965, James Baldwin reflected on how he often "wondered, and it is not a pleasant wonder, what white Americans talk about with one another."[18] Baldwin wonders this, he says, because White people do not have very much to say to him. Baldwin found that he expended a great deal of energy attempting to keep Americans comfortable. This is a futile effort, Baldwin asserts, because White people do see an "appallingly oppressive and bloody history known all over the world."[19] Moreover, he continues, they also see a "disastrous, continuing" present condition for which we White people bear "an inescapable responsibility."[20] Yet Baldwin also perceives a reluctance in White people to address the issue because we do not want to take responsibility for our role in this history.

Indeed, Baldwin is exasperated by the "dazzling ingenuity" and "tireless agility" of White people who are "perpetually defending themselves against charges" of the historical record for which we are responsible. After all, he says, the record is there for all to read. The whole world knows it. Yet White Americans keep defending ourselves against the indefensible. Unless we White people read this history and become accountable for it, argues Baldwin, we will not be able to change ourselves or the enduring history of racism. The failure of White Americans to face our history, warns Baldwin, "menaces this country" and "it menaces the entire world."[21]

Baldwin thus offers people who believe they are white an historic opportunity to take responsibility for anti-black violence. It is certainly no

---

[17]Dionne Brand, *A Map to the Door of No Return: Notes to Belonging* (Toronto: Vintage Canada, 2001), 25.

[18]James Baldwin, "White Man's Guilt," in *The Price of the Ticket: Collected Nonfiction, 1948–1985* (New York: St. Martin's Press, 1985), 409.

[19]Ibid.

[20]Ibid.

[21]Ibid., 410.

easy task. If you believe you are white, Baldwin warns, your entire being is distorted by a lie. Confronting this lie is not a task that can be accomplished in a comforting way. It is, as Baldwin suggests, an opportunity to grow, to become human, and to be liberated from the lie that is whiteness. In order to begin to take up this responsibility, I believe we need to embrace an ongoing task of remembering histories of oppression and of resistance to multiple forms of oppression.

Here is the pearl of wisdom Baldwin eloquently offers:

> White man, hear me! History, as nearly no one seems to know, is not merely something to be read. And it does not refer merely, or even principally, to the past. On the contrary, the great force of history comes from the fact that we carry it within us, are unconsciously controlled by it in many ways, and history is literally *present* in all that we do.[22]

In "White man, hear me!" I hear a witness to truth that resonates with the biblical prophets. I hear a contemporary John the Baptist. I hear a call to be humbly and humanly honest. In other words, "Get real!" Get in touch with the ways we have been molded by the time and space in which we live. History is not merely academic. If we are truly present to ourselves and our culture then we would understand that, indeed, the past is living in us. Being present to ourselves is about being present to our past. Baldwin is fully aware of the mythologies of Western European superiority that deform all of us, which is why he proceeds to illuminate how our identity is predominantly formed by the time in which we live: "It could scarcely be otherwise, since it is to history that we owe our frames of reference, our identities, and our aspirations. And it is with great pain and terror that one begins to realize this."[23]

Baldwin has come to terms with his history because as a man who is despised he has had to struggle, contest, and question it. Being Black in America entails a struggle against believing that as Black people they deserve their history. Baldwin himself struggled with the belief that it would be better to be white than be Black, and he has seen many Black lives "ruined or ended" by the belief that being white is better than being Black. Baldwin acknowledges that he himself carried the seeds of this destruction within himself. This is the experience referred to in racial equity practice as "internalized racial oppression" (IRO).[24] The problem of IRO is not only a negative self-image for Black people. One's negative view of oneself is inextricably tied to the belief that White people "deserve their history and deserve the power and glory which

---

[22]Ibid.
[23]Ibid.
[24]Joseph Barndt, *Understanding and Dismantling Racism: The Twenty-First-Century Challenge to White America* (Minneapolis: Fortress Press, 2007), 124–25.

their testimony and the evidence of my own senses assure me that they have."[25]

If Black people fall into this historical trap, reflects Baldwin—the trap of believing they deserve their fate—then White people fall into the "more stunning and intricate trap of believing that they *deserve* their fate and their comparative safety and that black people, therefore, need only to do as white people have done to rise to where white people are now."[26] The problem for White people is that we tend to be "flattered" by our history and that we like to charm ourselves about US history. Thus, Baldwin writes, White people are "impaled on their history like a butterfly on a pin and become incapable of seeing or changing themselves, or the world."[27] The problem for White people is further compounded by the fact that White people fear that Black people desire to do violence to White people. Moreover, as we who believe we are white ignore or evade our history, we lose touch with reality and the role we play in re-creating the status quo. As Baldwin observes, confronting the illusion and idolatry of whiteness will be no easy task:

In great pain and terror one begins to assess the history which has placed one where one is and formed one's point of view. In great pain and terror because, therefore, one enters into battle with that historical creation, Oneself, and attempts to recreate oneself according to a principle more humane and liberating; one begins the attempt to achieve a level of personal maturity and freedom which robs history of its tyrannical power, and also changes history.[28]

Ultimately, Baldwin believes that White people must make a "personal confession—a cry for help and healing, which is, really, I think, the basis for all dialogues and, on the other hand, the black man can scarcely dare to open a dialogue which must, if it is honest, become a personal confession which fatally contains an accusation."[29]

If we White people are going to make such a confession it will also mean coming to terms with the fact that we are more committed spiritually and practically to the economic priority of capital over human beings, more than we are to anything else. As Baldwin puts it, "White man, you have already arrived at unspeakable blasphemy in order to make money. You cannot endure the things you acquire—the only reason you continually acquire them, like junkies on hundred-dollar-a-day habits—and your money mainly exists

[25]Baldwin, "White Man's Guilt," 411.
[26]Ibid.
[27]Ibid., 410.
[28]Ibid.
[29]Ibid., 412.

on paper."[30] Baldwin sees a white nation that is morally corrupt because we continue to buy things with the flesh we continue to sell.

The Present Domination Age in Biblical Perspective

Saint Paul's Letter to the Romans captures the biblical context of Baldwin's wisdom: "Do not conform yourself to this age but be transformed by the renewal of your mind, that you may discern what is the will of God, what is good, pleasing and perfect" (Rom 12:2). Saint Paul's admonition seems fairly straightforward to North American people of faith who pride themselves on being independently minded. The call appears relatively uncomplicated inasmuch as it addresses the individual in their own time and place; it does not directly address more complex biblical and moral issues, such as love of neighbor. A modern American individualist reading of Saint Paul seems to be the predominant interpretation in US religious culture.

However, the question of location, of the composition of our time and place, may have everything to do with our capacity to even begin to *not* be conformed to the age in which we live. Biblical scholar Walter Wink explains that there are two interchangeable terms for "age" or "time" that are used in sacred texts: *kosmos* and *aiōn*. While the terms are very similar, Wink finds that *kosmos* denotes a spatial concept of time as "System," while *aiōn* indicates a temporal "Epoch." Maintaining the similarity and distinction of the terms is important for grasping the full meaning of biblical texts.

In his exegesis of Saint Paul, Paul uses the word "aiōn," translated as "Domination Epoch," to mark "the intolerable extension of oppression from generation to generation, and century to century, presided over by Satan, the god of the Domination Epoch."[31] Wink translates the first phrase of Romans 12:2 as, "Do not be conformed to this Domination Epoch." Wink warns that healing and liberation become nearly impossible if we conform to the Domination Epoch in which we live. Saint Paul clarifies this difficulty when he warns, "If you think you are wise in the ways of the Domination Epoch, you should become fools so that you may become wise. For the wisdom of the System (kosmos) is foolishness to God" (1 Cor 3:18).

While North American Christians tend to understand that our choices and way of living can thwart God's loving action in our lives, we often miss a larger reality. The biblical perspective of time is that God's ability to intervene is not only circumscribed by individual action; more importantly,

---

[30]Ibid., 413.

[31]Walter Wink, *Engaging the Powers: Discernment and Resistance in a World of Domination* (Minneapolis: Fortress Press, 1992), 59.

and to a much greater extent, God's action is limited by human institutions and systems. For example, the domination system of the Third Reich, Wink explains, wreaked violent havoc and obstructed God's action for twelve years. It certainly seemed like God was impotent in the midst of that genocide. Yet, ultimately, the Third Reich came to an end.

The delay of the in-breaking of God's Beloved Community is not fatal to Christian faith. Wink cites numerous historical examples in which nonviolent faith communities ended oppressive domination systems. These include but are not limited to Mahatma Gandhi's leadership of the Indian independence movement over twenty-six years, the Jewish struggle for an independent state over twenty-six centuries, or Corazon Aquino's leadership of the 1986 People Power revolution that ended twenty-one years of oppressive rule. Through these witnesses and countless others, people of faith have already glimpsed the in-breaking of God's domination-free order, so the people of God should never give up hope and endure in witness to another way of being.

For another example, as we discuss in chapter 6, ecological intimacy with the whole of God's creation has been severely impeded by human overreliance on fossil fuels and systemic abuse of local ecosystems. Pope Francis describes "tyrannical anthropocentrism" as the "irresponsible domination of human beings over other creatures."[32] He explains that rich countries have become enamored of technological mastery without the development of a capacious, responsible use of that power or corresponding growth in human responsibility, values, and conscience. We seem to hand over our freedom to "blind forces of the unconscious, of immediate needs, of self-interest, and of violence."[33] Most importantly, in the context of the legacy of slavery and anti-black white supremacy, African Americans more than any other group have transformed the American republic and Christian faith to reach its highest ideals. We discuss the transformational power of Black Americans later.

The Hidden Domination Age of Western Modernity

We will not understand the domination age of contemporary white American culture until we contend with the legacy of slavery and colonialism. That means taking responsibility for the hidden side of Western modernity. The deeper question is, how do White North Americans resist the violence and inhumanity by which we have been formed since birth? How do we disavow the fundamental assumption that we are innocent human beings superior to all

---

[32]Pope Francis, *Laudato Si': On Care for Our Common Home* (2015), no. 68 and nos. 115–119, http://w2.vatican.va.
[33]Ibid., no. 105.

others? How do we unlearn the untruths of white male superiority, individualism, innocence, and the right to dominate the land and peoples of the earth?

These questions are not rhetorical. The Western, white-settler Christianity where I sit in colonial Massachusetts assumes a normative single consciousness whereby our presence is modern, natural, and right. It also assumes the prerogative of exception above and beyond all of humanity. The question of how to unlearn whiteness is tricky because people who believe that they are white tend not to think of the United States as a colonial power, even though it still maintains three hundred Native American reservations within its borders. We tend not to question the ways that coloniality shapes the ways we think, act, and view the world.

In his cumulative study of Western modernity, cultural anthropologist Walter Mignolo invites a rigorous questioning of the assumption of modernity: that it is only a relentless achievement of progress, development, modernization, and democracy. As Americans, our culture and education train us to forget the histories of colonialism and slavery, which Mignolo terms "the darker side of Western modernity" or the "colonial matrix of power."[34] These unquestioned assumptions are the problem—they hide violence, and they hide the fact that white settlers live on land stolen from First Peoples through genocide. We tend to forget this violence, and when we are reminded of it, we only deny our complicity through self-justification, exacerbating the same violence today. This is why Mignolo refers to modernity/coloniality as constitutive both of good Western achievements and of its history of domination. In brief, we cannot speak about Western modernity without naming its oppressive side. The history and praxis of decoloniality offer a way to become critical of how modernity deforms us socially, morally, and spiritually.

It is important to differentiate the terms "colonization," "decolonization," "coloniality," and "decoloniality." "Colonization" and "decolonization" usually depict historical, geopolitical events or episodes in which, for example, European countries like Spain, Portugal, England, Germany, and the Netherlands procured social, political, and economic control of societies in Africa, Asia, and the Americas. Decolonization, the political action and process of a state or people struggling to gain independence from external colonial rule, is a historical process or event.

By contrast, "coloniality" and "decoloniality" refer to the "logic, metaphysics, ontology, and matrix of power" that were created by the historical processes of colonization and decolonization.[35] In less academic terms, coloniality and decoloniality refer to the entire cultural milieu of Western civiliza-

---

[34]Walter Mignolo, *The Darker Side of Western Modernity: Global Futures, Decolonial Options* (Durham, NC: Duke University Press, 2011), 16.

[35]Nelson Maldonado-Torres, "Outline of Ten Theses on Coloniality and Decoloniality," Foundation Frantz Fanon, October 23, 2016, 10, http://fondation-frantzfanon.com.

tion, modernity, and its constitutive processes of conquest and colonialism. If we speak of Western modernity only in terms of progress, development, modernization, and democracy, we hide its insidious underside of colonial domination and conquest. Modernity and coloniality are constitutive of each other—or, to use the proverbial phrase, two sides of the same coin. We can't speak of modernity without coloniality. If we do speak of modernity without coloniality, we easily fall into the realm of myth.

While Western modernity celebrates itself through a rhetoric of incessant progress, secular salvation, and newness, its "underside" or "hidden agenda" reveals the *"dispensability* (or expendability) *of human life,"* as Western economic practices and "knowledge justified racism and the inferiority of human lives that were naturally considered dispensable."[36] The CMP, referred to earlier, is the logic or framework of colonial domination that "generates, reproduces, modifies, and maintains" interconnected, historical hierarchies of race, class, labor, gender/sex, heterosexuality/homosexuality, spiritual/religious, aesthetic, epistemic, and linguistic categories, and classifies them as natural and right. The CMP constructs the "modern subject" as "the idea of Man," that is, the white, male, heterosexual Christian who "became the model for the Human and for Humanity."[37]

The Bandung Conference of 1955, organized by Indonesia, Burma, Ceylon, India, and Pakistan in order to promote Afro-Asian anticolonial economic and social solidarity, became a watershed moment for decolonial struggles and discourses. Departing from both capitalism and communism, and drawing upon local knowledges and cultural resources, decolonial thinkers and movements created new ways of questioning Western modernity. Through relentless questioning and disobedience to the "rules of the game" set by Western colonialism, decolonial praxis "delinks" from Western prerogatives, assumptions, and rules. Delinking involves continual questioning of modernity and setting different local ways of being that conserve the web of life. If this brief historical review is news to North American ears, it is in no small measure due to the suppression of the Bandung Conference by Western liberal narratives.[38] Such narratives typically feature stories of progress while simultaneously repressing histories of colonialization, conquest, violence, and decolonization.

The idea of the CMP or the "Patron colonial de poder" was first formulated in the 1980s by Anibal Quijano, a professor of sociology at the Universidad de San Marcos in Lima and at the State University of New York at Binghamton. Quijano describes the beginning of the coloniality of power in terms of Euro-

---

[36]Mignolo, *Darker Side of Western Modernity*, 6.
[37]Ibid., 17–19.
[38]Lisa Lowe, *The Intimacies of Four Continents* (Durham, NC: Duke University Press, 2015), 151.

pean conquest and extermination of over 65 million people including Aztec, Maya-Caribbean, and Tawantinsuyana (Inca) in a period of less than fifty years.[39] European colonial domination and its successor, Western imperialism, consists in colonization of the knowledge and imagination of the dominated through a process of physical domination, genocide, and expropriation of labor. The colonial structure of power produced social discriminations that were coded in so-called racial, ethnic, and national terms deemed objective, scientific, rational, and natural categories.

Simultaneously, European culture imposed a mystified image of itself as the source of universal knowledge and power. Knowledge was used both as a tool for the control of authority, mediating the exclusive, optimum way of being in the world, and, once it was conceived as imperially true knowledge, it became a commodity to be exported to those whose knowledge and way of being in the world was deemed deviant or nonmodern according to Western Christian theology and later in secular science and philosophy.

Recall the terms that the Catholic Church and Western society used to refer to nonmodern societies: "traditional" (culturally behind), "barbarian" (savage and primitive), or "heathen" (uncivilized and pagan). By the standard of Western modernity, these societies are inherently backward, uncultured, deviant, and less than fully human. For a specific example, Catholic missionaries used the word "heathen" as a technical term to refer to people who did not believe in the "one true faith." However, as religious studies scholar Matthew Cressler demonstrates in his study of African American Catholicism in Chicago, the history of the word "heathen" is deeply enmeshed in the history of the Atlantic slave trade and colonialism. In the wake of these, the "public meaning of 'Negro' and 'Africa' were finely wedded to 'backward,' 'uncivilized,' and 'heathen.' "[40] Throughout the twentieth century, even after Vatican II, Cressler notes, the fact that Mundelein Seminary and Divine Word missionaries in Chicago "saw no need to distinguish between 'the Negroes' of West Africa and those in the United States is telling."[41] This racist terminology is a case in point of one way that Western modernity/coloniality exerts managerial control of a hierarchy of knowledge and being.

In his original formulation of the colonial matrix, which is the basis for Mignolo's formulation, the Peruvian sociologist Anibal Quijano described four interrelated domains: control of the economy, of authority, of gender and sexuality, and of knowledge and subjectivity. These four domains are supported, so to speak, by two legs: the racial and patriarchal foundations

[39]Anibal Quijano, "Coloniality and Modernity/Rationality," in *Globalization and the Decolonial Option*, ed. Walter Mignolo and Arturo Escobar (New York: Routledge, 2010), 24.
[40]Matthew Cressler, *Authentically Black and Truly Catholic: The Rise of Black Catholicism in the Great Migration* (New York: NYU Press, 2017), 32.
[41]Ibid.

of knowledge. In chapter 3, I address how successive Catholic popes were instrumental in the historical foundation of the colonial matrix of power (CMP). Christian theology made the "blood" distinction between Christians, Moors, and Jews.[42] Although Mignolo notes the long history of conflict between these three religions of the book, the conflict was reconfigured in 1492 when Christians expelled Moors and Jews from the Spanish peninsula and enforced conversion on those who wanted to stay. Simultaneously, conquest of the so-called New World configured race as "blood," and by the eighteenth century the key marker of race was skin.[43]

The hubris of the Western way of thinking and knowledge (epistemology), that is, its totalizing claims that eliminate or subordinate all other perspectives, is what the Colombian philosopher Santiago Castro-Gómez names "zero-point epistemology."[44] This naming is critical because modernity has asserted universal claims and applicability from a very particular, limited point of view. As Mignolo explains, zero-point epistemology asserts "the ultimate grounding of knowledge, which is paradoxically ungrounded," because it obscures the particular geo-historical context in which it was created.[45] In other words, the zero point projects universality from its limited, parochial perspective. In the same way that modernity claims to be the center of time and space as if it were natural, in fact, zero-point epistemology hides its local origination. Every way of knowing and feeling that does not conform to Western epistemology, such as Indigenous or African ways of knowing, is relegated to the status of "myth, legend, folklore, local knowledge."[46] The zero-point assumption of an unlocated, detached, universal, and neutral point of view is the arrogance of a Western, modern way of thinking and being.

Dwelling in the hidden underside of Western modernity, it would be clearly true for Black people and Indigenous Peoples to claim that coloniality corrupts human beings by its assumptions of superiority. Pause for a moment to think about the assumptions that European Americans tend to make about the organization of time and space. As over 130 cities and universities and at least nine states replace Columbus Day with Indigenous Peoples Day, we ought to recognize that Christopher Columbus did not "discover" America, a continental land mass that had already been inhabited by many First Peoples for millennia.[47] We White folks tend to forget how Christian and European conquest of land and genocide of Indigenous Peoples forms the inception of

---

[42]Mignolo, *Darker Side of Western Modernity*, 8.
[43]Ibid.
[44]Santiago Castro-Gómez, *La hubris del punto cero: Ciencia, raza e ilustracion en la Nueva Granada (1750–1816)* (Bogota: Editorial Pontificia Universidad Javerina, 2005).
[45]Mignolo, *Darker Side of Western Modernity*, 80.
[46]Ibid.
[47]Dennis W. Zotigh and Renee Gokey, "Indigenous Peoples' Day: Rethinking How We Celebrate American History," *Smithsonian Magazine*, October 11, 2019, www.smithsonianmag.com.

all of the "Americas." As anti-racism training processes led by Crossroads, the People's Institute, and Pax Christi USA call White people to take up both their histories of oppression and of resistance, I believe a logical next step is to engage the work of decolonial analysis.

The decolonial scholar and activist Andrea Smith outlines three colonial "logics" that interconnect white supremacy and coloniality: "slavery/capitalism," the logic that commodifies people along a racial hierarchy with Black people as the most disposable/slaveable; "genocide/colonialism," the logic that justifies the killing and elimination of Indigenous Peoples in order to seize land for white settlers and corporations (the history of Indian removal and the recent conflict at Standing Rock are prominent examples); and "orientalism/war," the logic that constructs Western civilizations as superior to all others, imagining Asians, Arabs, and Latinx people as dangerous foreigners (tropes that former president Donald J. Trump relentlessly exploited with his political base),[48] and justifying continual threats of war on other nations and peoples.

The Afterlife of Slavery, the 1619 Project, and Racial Capitalism

Within this larger context of the domination age in which we live—modernity and its hidden history of human disposability—people who believe that they are white need to understand the present "afterlife of slavery." As professor of English and comparative literature Saidiya Hartman writes, the "afterlife of slavery" is "skewed life chances, limited access to health and education, premature death, incarceration, and impoverishment. I, too, am the afterlife of slavery."[49] While the logic of the CMP connects interpenetrating hierarchies of power and domination, including colonialism and slavery, here I focus on the enduring presence of slavery and racial capitalism in the United States.

We need to understand the role that slavery played in the historical development of the United States. Historian Edward Baptist exposes three erroneous assumptions about the way the story of slavery is told. The first is that the economy of American slavery was fundamentally different and separate from the rest of the development of the modern economy. The story of American industrialization often features European immigrants and innovative entrepreneurs while leaving out "cotton fields and slave labor."[50] This

---

[48]Tyler Anbinder, "Trump Has Spread More Hatred of Immigrants Than Any American in History," *Washington Post*, November 7, 2019, www.washingtonpost.com.

[49]Saidiya Hartman, *Lose Your Mother: A Journey along the Atlantic Slave Route* (New York: Farrar, Strauss, and Giroux, 2007), 6.

[50]Edward Baptist, *The Half Has Never Been Told: Slavery and the Making of American Capitalism* (New York: Basic Books, 2014), xx.

omission is curious because it fails to recognize how the practice of slavery was indispensable to the economic development of the United States, at least from the American Revolution to the Civil War.[51]

The second assumption is that the political and economic system was primarily oriented to the values of a liberal republic and that the contradictions between slave labor and republican freedom would be resolved, sooner or later, in favor of free labor. The inexorable historical forces of liberal modernity and progress were inevitably bound to overcome the contradictions at some point. This assumption reflects modernity's rhetoric of incessant progress.

The third assumption, implicit in the second, is that the worst thing slavery did was deny slaves liberal rights and subjectivity. It did this and far more, including killing massive numbers of people and stealing everything from those who survived. The acceleration of American industrialization in the nineteenth century would not have happened without the "massive and cruel engineering required to rip a million people from their homes, brutally drive them to new, disease-ridden places, and make them live in terror and hunger as they continually built and rebuilt a commodity-generating empire."[52] And, by minimizing the violence of slavery, Americans would perpetuate the lie that Africans in diaspora refused to fight for their rights during slavery and after Emancipation.

These common and erroneous assumptions hide the true origin of the nation. Pause and reflect, for a moment, if you believe that 1776 is the year of the nation's birth. Award-winning journalist Nikole Hannah-Jones, who initiated the *New York Times* 1619 Project, asks: "What if the assumption that the United States was born in 1776, which is promulgated in our schools and every July 4, is wrong?" What if "the country's true birth date, the moment that its defining contradictions first came into the world, was in late August of 1619?"[53] Although the exact date has been lost to history, on or about August 20, 1619, a ship bearing twenty to thirty slaves arrived at Point Comfort in the British colony of Virginia. The wake of that ship inaugurated the barbaric system of chattel slavery that would last 250 years. The 1619 Project observes that the legacy of chattel slavery is not only the nation's original sin, "it is the country's very origin."[54]

The purpose of the 1619 Project is to reframe US history by regarding 1619 as the birth of the nation. That reframing means placing the "consequences of slavery and the contributions of Black Americans at the very center of the

---

[51]Sven Beckert and Seth Rockman, eds., *Slavery's Capitalism: A New History of American Economic Development* (Philadelphia: University of Pennsylvania Press, 2016), 1.
[52]Ibid., xxi.
[53]Jake Silverstein, "Editor's Note," *New York Times Magazine*, August 18, 2019, 4.
[54]Ibid.

story we tell ourselves about who we are as a country."[55] The project enumerates how "nearly everything that has truly made America exceptional," from its economic power; its industrial strength; its electoral system; its diet and musical traditions; its wealth gap; its inequalities in health, housing, and education; "its astonishing penchant for violence"; its legal system; and the "endemic racial fears and hatreds that continue to plague to this day" are born of slavery and the anti-black white supremacy that legitimated it.[56] The project also reveals how innumerable aspects of contemporary American life, from the development of Wall Street, to the growth of mass incarceration, to rush-hour traffic, to health inequities, and even the business of management are deeply rooted in slavery.

That is not all. Recognizing the origins of the nation in 1619 also means learning how Africans in diaspora transformed the ideals of the Declaration of Independence and the Constitution into reality. In her introduction to the 1619 Project, Nikole Hannah-Jones chronicles bloody struggles for civil rights led by African Americans that paved the way for "every other modern rights struggle."[57] While the Founding Fathers created a demonstrably undemocratic Constitution that excluded women, Indigenous and African people, and men who lacked property, laws created out of Black resistance guarantee voting rights for all, and ban discrimination not only on the basis of race but also on gender, nationality, religion, and ability.

The civil rights movement paved the way for the passage of the Immigration and Nationality Act of 1965 that ended the quotas that attempted to keep the country white European. Nikole Hannah-Jones laments a profound irony in the fact that Asian Americans, among many groups able to immigrate to the United States because of the Black freedom struggle, "are now suing universities to end programs designed to help the descendants of the enslaved."[58] It is time we celebrate the fact that the extent to which the US fulfills its democratic ideals is due to Black struggles. She concludes by quoting the anti-racist sociologist Joe R. Feagin: "Enslaved African-Americans have been among the foremost freedom-fighters this country has produced."[59] Our amnesia of the legacy of slavery also encompasses how Africans in diaspora initiated momentous transformations in faith and the religious moral imagination.

Disentangling the development of capitalism from its racist genealogy in coloniality and slavery is impossible. Western modernity spawned the "conjoined twins" of racism and capitalism, which is rightly called "racial

---

[55]Ibid., 5.
[56]Ibid.
[57]Nikole Hannah-Jones, "Introduction to the 1619 Project," *New York Times Magazine*, August 18, 2019, 16.
[58]Ibid., 26.
[59]Ibid.

capitalism."[60] First, racial capitalism unearths root causes in the history of coloniality and slavery.[61] Drawing upon the work of political scientist Cedric Robinson and historian Walter Johnson's descriptions of racial capitalism, I believe we should engage the history of slavery as "source rather than a subject of knowledge."[62] The problem of viewing the history of slavery as a "subject" of knowledge is the way American culture objectifies history and people. Walter Johnson explains that the common way we talk about the history of slavery is extremely misleading. We tend to talk about it as an era of "dehumanization" of enslaved people. While the language of dehumanization is tempting and popular, it is highly problematic. We rightfully find it difficult to reconcile the commodification of human beings, sexual exploitation, forced labor, starvation, and the systematic torture and measurement of human beings as anything but humane. The problem, however, is that we are separating an aspirational idea of humanity "from the sorts of exploitation and violence that history suggests may well be *definitive* of human beings: we are separating ourselves from our own histories of perpetration."[63]

First of all, the language of dehumanization tends to absolve slave owners of their intention to exploit other human beings for their own satisfaction, living, and superiority. It also denies how enslavers relied upon the human capaciousness of enslaved people. In doing so, not only do we forget the human capacities of enslaved peoples, we also forget their cultures, histories, and human agency. In other words, the way American culture tends to forget the history of slavery and objectify it is also how we deny the reality of the afterlife of slavery. More importantly, the way white culture denies the enduring history of slavery is how we become absent to God, self, and others.

In terms of political economy, that is, racial capitalism, the point is that enslaved people were both capital and labor. Capitalism cannot be separated from racism. Their double economic aspect cannot be separated.[64] And their capital was connected to more than their slave labor. Historian Walter Johnson explains:

> And so, too, were their children: racial capitalism swung on a reproductive hinge. The entire "pyramid" of the Atlantic economy of the nine-

[60] Ibram X. Kendi, *How to Be an Antiracist* (New York: One World, 2019), 156–63.

[61] Cedric Robinson, *Black Marxism: The Making of the Black Radical Tradition* (Chapel Hill: University of North Carolina Press, 2000 [1983]), see chapters 1 and 5. "Black Marxism" is not simply adding Marxism and the Black radical tradition together; rather, it represents a critique of Marxism that eschews its racism and develops a historical account of the overlapping and interpenetrating growth of capitalism and racism.

[62] Walter Johnson, "To Remake the World: Slavery, Racial Capitalism, and Justice," *Boston Review*, February 20, 2018, www.bostonreview.net.

[63] Ibid.

[64] Ibid., 26.

teenth century (the economy that has been treated as the paradigmatic example of capitalism) was founded upon the capacity of enslaved women's bodies: upon their ability to reproduce capital. As Deborah Gray White points out, sexual violation, reproductive invigilation, and natal alienation were elementary aspects of slavery, and thus of racial capitalism.[65]

Cedric Robinson transformed "racial capitalism" from the description of the system in South Africa to a general history of modern capitalism. Robinson is deeply critical of Marx's historical interpretation of capitalism as a revolutionary negation of feudalism. Instead, Robinson argues, capitalism and racialism did not represent a break from the feudal order; rather, they evolved "to produce a modern world system of 'racial capitalism' dependent upon slavery, violence, imperialism, and genocide."[66] Drawing upon the groundbreaking scholarship of W. E. B. Du Bois, Robinson demonstrates how the end of slavery in the United States, far from unleashing capitalism and freedom from the shackles of slavery, evolved into the "generalization on a global scale of the racial and imperial vision of the 'empire of cotton.' "[67] Robinson exhaustively details how the contradictions between American ideals and the reality of slavery and the "distortions of its social structures and political institutions ensued from its dependence on slavery and would resound throughout the system into the twentieth century."[68] While enslaved people's creativity ensured their survival, their creativity was also stolen from them in the development not only of the modern American economy but its underlying social structures and political institutions.

Second, racial capitalism offers a robust intersectional analysis of the multiple levels and ways in which racial, class, gender, and epistemological oppressions are interconnected and interwoven. Too often scholars treat different social identities and forms of inequality as separate and independent from one another, when in fact human life and social categories simultaneously interweave and interact in complex ways in lived experience. The paradigm of intersectionality grew out of the voices of Black and Brown women who taught that their experience of sexism or racism could not be understood in isolation. The history of racial capitalism and coloniality offers a more dynamic way to understand the complex interplay of social identities and relationships between privilege and oppression.

[65]Ibid.

[66]Robin D. G. Kelley, "Introduction," in *Race, Capitalism, Justice*, ed. Walter Johnson and Robin D. G. Kelley, Boston Review Forum 1 (Cambridge, MA: Boston Review, 2017), 7.

[67]Walter Johnson, "To Remake the World: Slavery, Racial Capitalism, and Justice," in Johnson and Kelley, *Race, Capitalism, Justice*, 23.

[68]Robinson, *Black Marxism*, 200.

Analyses of racism by the media and the church too often miss the complexity of white supremacy as a historical mode of class, gender, and sexual formation. A fuller understanding and analysis of white supremacy must include the historical legacy of colonialism, slavery, and commodification that endures in at least four dimensions of culture and society. These include how white supremacy

- functions as a historical mode of white racial class formation and economic ascendancy through expropriation of land, labor, women's reproductive labor, and resources
- constitutes a symbolic hierarchical order of white superiority that feeds upon anti-blackness
- serves as a primary socialization process of individual and group white racial identity formation
- organizes a segregated society through the "positional alchemy" of *white habitus* that entails a dynamic interplay between both "position—the social geography, location, and power of whiteness—and practice—the ways whites are socialized to perceive and act within the world."[69]

Chapter 2 analyzes and develops the reality of "white habitus."

Third, Robinson's development of racial capitalism coheres with Bryan N. Massingale's call to draw upon the wells of the Black radical tradition[70] and the rationality of the oppressed. Robinson criticizes Marx's definition of primitive accumulation,[71] because Marx recognizes no agency in African peoples by failing to realize how "cargoes of laborers also contained African cultures, critical mixes and admixtures of language and thought, of cosmology

---

[69]I draw upon the following resources to develop these four dimensions of white supremacy: M. Shawn Copeland, "Anti-Blackness and White Supremacy in the Making of American Catholicism," *American Catholic Studies* 127, no. 3 (Fall 2016): 6–8; Willie James Jennings, *The Christian Imagination: Theology and the Origins of Race* (New Haven, CT: Yale University Press, 2010), 305–6; Bryan N. Massingale, *Racial Justice and the Catholic Church* (Maryknoll, NY: Orbis Books, 2010); and Alex Mikulich, "Where Y'at Race, Whiteness, and Economic Justice? A Map of White Complicity in Economic Oppression of People of Color," in *The Almighty and the Dollar: Reflections on Economic Justice for All*, ed. Mark Allman (Winona, MN: Anselm Academic, 2012), 189–213.

[70]See Robinson, *Black Marxism*. Robinson describes the Black radical tradition as "a collective consciousness informed by the historical struggles for liberation and motivated by the shared sense of obligation to preserve the collective being, the ontological reality." See 170–71.

[71]Primitive accumulation is basically plunder, violently dispossessing the peasantry of their land in order to create the conditions that reorganize the relations of production and initiate capitalism. See Ben Fine, "Primitive Accumulation," in *A Dictionary of Marxist Thought*, 2nd ed., ed. Tom Bottomore, Laurence Harris, V. G. Kiernan, and Ralph Miliband (Cambridge, MA: Blackwell, 1991), 444–45.

and metaphysics, of habits, beliefs, and morality."[72] The Black radical tradition, Robinson argues, begins in African peoples retaining shared philosophies and cultures developed in their African past that were seeds of rebellion and the contradiction of racial capitalism. The outrage of African peoples against slavery, Robinson concludes,

> was most certainly informed by the Africanity of our consciousness—some epistemological measure culturally embedded in our minds that deemed that racial capitalism we have been witness to was an unacceptable standard of human conduct. It was also the case that the source of our outrage characterized that conduct as inexplicable. The depths to which racialist behavior has fouled Western agencies transgressed against a world-consciousness rooted in our African past.[73]

From the very inception of slavery, the Black radical tradition challenged and confounded European versions of the past by "making history on their own terms," because, after all, "it had been as an emergent African people and not as slaves that Black men and women had opposed enslavement."[74] At the origin and center of the Black radical tradition, Robinson contends, is "the shared sense of obligation to preserve the collective being, the ontological totality."[75] Robinson recounts hundreds of acts of resistance, from seventeenth-century enslaved Africans who rebelled and created their own maroon communities, like that of Nanny Town, Jamaica,[76] to twentieth-century liberation struggles, in order to demonstrate how Black collective resistance reconstitutes collective identities. The Black radical tradition is "antiracist, anticapitalist, and collective-making because it is a name for struggles that arrange social forces for Black survival over and against capital accumulation."[77]

Contrary to the common white refrain "The past is over, so get over it," the history of racial capitalism is critical for understanding the racial wealth gap today. Briefly put, wealth begets more wealth, and lack of wealth begets lack of wealth. In his study of the conditions of wealth inequality at the time of Emancipation (1863), economist T. Kirk White demonstrates that those condi-

---

[72]Robinson, *Black Marxism*, 122.

[73]Ibid., 308.

[74]Ibid., 170–71.

[75]Ibid., 171.

[76]Ibid., 160. Robinson celebrates numerous instances of enslaved Africans who freed themselves from oppression through rebellion and created new communities historically named "maroon" communities. He begins with the example of an enslaved nanny who initiated a rebellion in 1715 that established Nanny Town, Jamaica. He cites the work of Barbara Klamon Kopytoff, "The Early Development of Jamaican Maroon Societies," *William and Mary Quarterly* 35, no. 2 (1978): 287–307.

[77]Jodi Melamed, "Racial Capitalism," *Critical Ethnic Studies* 1, no. 1 (Spring 2015): 76–85, at 80.

tions could dictate current disparity even if "there had been no further bumps in the road." Nearly 100 percent of Black households had zero net worth at Emancipation, having been forced to build wealth for whites for generations.[78]

The historical record demonstrates, however, that African Americans faced multiple bumps in the road after Emancipation. Failing to endow ex-slaves with the promised "forty acres and a mule" after the Civil War, the nation systematically deprived Blacks of property—especially land accumulated between 1880 and 1910—by government complicity, fraud, and seizures by white terrorists.[79]

While some White readers may cringe at the term "terrorist," White Americans curiously and conveniently forget that in 1921, White citizens of Tulsa, Oklahoma, used planes from the local army base to firebomb and destroy Greenwood, the city's prosperous African American neighborhood. And while White Americans often celebrate entrepreneurship, they didn't celebrate then—or mourn now—Greenwood's unparalleled economic success as Black Wall Street.[80] The tendency for White Americans to assume that the events of September 11, 2001, were the nation's first terrorist air attack on US soil, observes literary scholar Jennie Lightweis Goff, "indicates how deeply the term *terrorist* is raced, since white communities are so often protected from the stigma of its application."[81]

Consider, too, that just one hundred years ago, upon their return in 1919 from their service to the nation in World War I, African Americans faced another upsurge in anti-black lynchings. At the National Lynching Memorial, also known as the National Memorial for Peace and Justice, the Equal Justice Initiative (EJI) honors the military service of African Americans throughout our nation's history, including the Red Summer of 1919.[82] As EJI director Bryan Stevenson sees it, "No community is more deserving of recognition and acknowledgment than those Black men and women veterans who bravely risked their lives to defend this country's freedom only to have their own freedom denied and threatened because of racial bigotry."[83]

---

[78]T. Kirk White, "Initial Conditions at Emancipation: The Long-Run Effects on Black-White Wealth and Earnings Inequality," *Journal of Economic Dynamics and Control* 31 (2007): 3370–95. This section is drawn from Mikulich, "Where Y'at Race, Whiteness, and Economic Justice?," 205.

[79]William Darity, "Forty Acres and a Mule in the 21st Century," *Social Science Quarterly* 89, no. 3 (September 2008): 656–65.

[80]The history of Greenwood, Black Wall Street, and the 1921 massacre that destroyed it is enshrined in the Greenwood Cultural Center in Tulsa, Oklahoma. See https://greenwoodcul-turalcenter.com.

[81]Jennie Lightweis Goff, *Blood at the Root: Lynching as American Cultural Nucleus* (Albany: State University of New York Press, 2011), 12–13.

[82]Equal Justice Initiative, "Lynching in America: Targeting Black Veterans," February 2019, https://eji.org/reports.

[83]Ibid.

Returning to the history of the racial wealth gap, African Americans hit more bumps in the road during the 1930s. Too often we forget that the original Social Security legislation of 1935, created at the height of the Great Depression to establish a basic economic security for workers, effectively denied benefits to 75 percent of African Americans by excluding domestic and agricultural workers from this momentous public policy achievement. The Federal Housing Administration's financing structures spurred white suburbanization from the 1940s through the 1970s; during the same time frame, the FHA and banks were utilizing "redlining," the practice of denying mortgage assistance for homes and financing for new businesses, based upon the racial composition of the neighborhood. African Americans bore the greatest burden of lending discrimination. Restrictive covenants (which exclude people of color from white developments), as well as housing and lending discrimination, prevented Blacks from accumulating wealth. All of these practices exacerbated historic racial inequalities rooted in slavery.

As Duke University economist William Darity and his colleagues explain, the racial wealth gap shows no record of abating. Wealth—the difference between the value of what you own and what you owe (net worth)—is a key source of vastly different outcomes in well-being. Wealth is critical for families to provide access to high-quality, debt-free education, as well as to networks connected to well-paid employment, better health care, and entrée into safe, amenity-filled neighborhoods. Darity and his colleagues have demonstrated that the intergenerational transfer of resources and associated benefits are the most profound drivers of the racial wealth gap. Utilizing the most recent data, from the 2016 Survey of Consumer Finance (SCF), they found that the median Black household had $17,600 in net worth while the median White household had $171,000 in net worth.[84] In other words, the typical Black household holds just ten cents of net worth to every dollar of wealth held by the typical white family.

This disparity is projected to expand in the upcoming decades. A combination of racist housing, educational, and tax policies benefitting the hyper-affluent at the expense of the poor, along with a failure to end the school-to-prison pipeline and hyperincarceration, will only dig deeper caverns of inequity. The median wealth of Black households is expected to redline by 2053, and Latinx households will face the same reality by the 2070s.[85] The problem remains that "racial capitalism will live into another epoch of theft and rapacious inequity" unless anti-racists and anti-capitalists collectively fight the conjoined twins of racism and capitalism.[86]

---

[84]William Darity, "Running the Numbers on Closing the Racial Wealth Gap," August 2019, https://socialequity.duke.edu.

[85]Kendi, *How to Be an Antiracist*, 157.

[86]Ibid., 163.

Sitting in History: Decolonizing Faith
and (De)facing Anti-Black White Supremacy

Now is the time for predominantly White churches and people of faith to take responsibility for our enduring role in the afterlife of American coloniality. Drawing upon the wisdom of Africans in diaspora, I suggest that White people give of themselves by becoming conscious of the enduring history of Atlantic chattel slavery, as a way of (de)facing anti-black white supremacy, preparing to repent for our sins, and most importantly, becoming humanly present with and for people who strive for life in the midst of the nonstatus and nonbeing of Blackness.

Giving of ourselves, in terms of faith, concerns how we prepare ourselves for the incarnation, what Pope Francis describes as "[Jesus's] historic coming in the humility of the human condition."[87] Followers who take to heart Jesus's exhortation to "take heed," live "in a full and conscious way, with concern first and foremost for *others*."[88] Preparing to enter the "humility of the human condition," I suggest, means dwelling in the "manger-like" conditions in which the Black Christ is born, to draw upon Kelly Brown Douglas's apt description.[89] The claim that Jesus is born Black means that death is both imminent and immanent for people who are born Black. In other words, ever since the inauguration of the Atlantic slave trade, the nonstatus of being Black means always facing death and living in a world structured for death. Until people of faith who believe that they are white dwell in the reality of Blackness in America, we will not be prepared to become a prophetic counterwitness to the powers that seek to destroy the birth of God's love in the world today.

Taking heed, as a way of preparing for the incarnation, also means understanding how our lives conform to the domination age in which we live. Preparation for the incarnation necessarily involves giving up and relinquishing attachments that block God's grace. Giving of ourselves means giving up our comforts, our insouciant complacence, our need for control, and our need to maintain innocence and deny complicity in an anti-black society. More importantly, giving of ourselves means becoming humble, opening our hearts, minds, and souls to the quotidian death-dealing reality faced by Africans in diaspora. It is within that space of humility, vulnerability, and openness where people who believe they are white may yet be transformed by authentic memory of chattel slavery and "the complex reality within which we remember it," so that our witness is marked by real, intimate solidarity

---

[87] Pope Francis, Angelus, December 3, 2017, http://www.vatican.va.

[88] Ibid., italics in original.

[89] Kelly Brown Douglas, *The Black Christ: 25th Anniversary Edition* (Maryknoll, NY: Orbis Books, 2019), xx.

with and for brothers and sisters who daily suffer anti-blackness.[90] Giving of ourselves means becoming fully present to Black consciousness of the after-life of slavery. A contemplative way of becoming present ought to shape the way we read history, the way we approach prayer, and the way we comport ourselves to prepare the Way of the Lord. This contemplative and prayerful approach to our shared history is integral to preparing to enact reparations, which I address in chapter 5. Becoming contemplative and prayerful to the presence of the past is a way of shaping our lives to become wakeful and conscious.

If we are going to counter the violence of abstraction and gain historical consciousness of "that which is brought forth follows the womb," I believe people of faith—especially those who believe they are white—need to con-templatively, prayerfully enter what the Canadian poet, educator, and activ-ist Dionne Brand calls "sitting in the room with history."[91] For Brand, this means "probing the Door of No Return as consciousness. The Door casts a haunting spell on personal and collective consciousness in the Diaspora. Black experience in any modern city or town in the Americas is a haunting." Echoing Baldwin, Brand finds that "one enters a room and history follows; one enters a room and history precedes."[92] Entering this Door, whether in present-day Ghana or Gorée Island, was the last step for African slaves before walking into the hold of a slave ship.[93] This hallowed ground, Brand asserts, presents a "rupture" for Africans in diaspora.

Rupture means confronting a place where the names, places, and cultures of origin are forgotten. It is perhaps worse than the exile into which Herod thrust the Holy Family. Brand explains that the door is the "end of traceable beginnings" through a "name or a set of family stories that extend farther into the past five hundred or so years." Not only does the Door of No Return represent a historical reality and a geographical place, more importantly, it is a psychic and spiritual reality for Africans in diaspora. Brand rightly insists that a map is not enough to find our way; we also need a cognitive schema and a practical mastery of way-finding.

If people who believe that they are white are going to find a practical mastery to make our way through the racial impasse, then we need to be-come vulnerable with and for Africans in diaspora in their experience and consciousness of slavery and the rupture it created with their cultural roots.

---

[90]M. Shawn Copeland, *Knowing Christ Crucified: The Witness of African American Religious Experience* (Maryknoll, NY: Orbis Books, 2018), 98.

[91]Dionne Brand, *A Map to the Door of No Return* (Toronto: Vintage Canada, 2001), 25.

[92]Ibid.

[93]There are ample pictures of the physical doors of no return whereby we may begin to enter and pray with the historical reality they represent. See, for example, Errol Barnett, "Senegal's Scenic Island Exposes Horrors of Slave Trade," CNN, February 21, 2012, https://www.cnn.com.

This particular vulnerability is a condition of the possibility of not returning to an endless history of domination and violence.

Sitting in the room with history and dwelling in the consciousness of African peoples may be impossible for people who believe they are white. It may be impossible because we have yet to unlearn the myths of whiteness, including our presumed inherent goodness and moral superiority over and above everyone else. Indeed, it may be "easier for a camel to pass through the eye of a needle" (Mt 19:24) than for a white person to prayerfully contemplate how Black people contend with the legacy of slavery. On the other hand, joining Africans in diaspora in their consciousness of the Door of No Return may be the only way people who believe that they are white may become human and prepare to follow in the way of the Lord. If there is a way where there is no way—to draw upon the wisdom of Black Catholics, a way to a shared humanity and healing of the wounds of racial oppression—it will include White people returning to that Door to unlearn anti-black white supremacy and humbly join the human condition.

2

White Habitus

The Ecosystem
of Anti-Black White Supremacy

It is time for White people to take a close look at ourselves. It is time to look at where and how we live. Until White people shift our gaze away from racialized others and examine the ways we create and re-create a segregated society in which we are socialized into white superiority, we will continue to perpetuate anti-black racism. Let me begin by sharing a few stories to set the context for this chapter.

In November 2019 my partner and two friends enjoyed an evening of live rhythms, sounds, and movement through Camille A. Brown & Dancers' performance of *ink*, which celebrates the rituals, gestures, and traditions of the African diaspora. As described in the program notes, "Through self-empowerment, Black love, brotherhood, exhaustion and resilience, community and fellowship, *ink* depicts the pedestrian interactions of individuals and relationships as grounds for accessing one's innate superpowers and finding liberation. The work seeks to reclaim Black American narratives and is the final installment of Brown's dance theater trilogy about identity." Parts of the *ink* performance are available on YouTube.[1] As soon as the performance began, the drumming and dancing brought me back to the rhythms and movements of Maafa,[2] the annual ritual remembering of the holocaust of Africans through the Atlantic slave trade. The beats I heard in the performance of *ink* were reminiscent of the bamboula[3] dance and beat reenacted in New Orleans' Congo Square.

---

[1]See Camille A. Brown's opening to *ink* at https://www.youtube.com/watch?v=V11EfQJd88w.

[2]*Maafa* is a Kiswahili term that means "great disaster" and now refers to annual rituals of remembering the Atlantic slave trade. See the Ashé Cultural Arts Center's website, https://www.ashenola.org/maafa. Maafa rituals are an integral part of the spirituality I suggest in Part II.

[3]For a description of Congo Square and bamboula see Freddi Williams Evans, *Congo Square: African Roots in New Orleans* (Lafayette: University of Louisiana at Lafayette Press, 2011).

Two members of Brown's dance troupe engaged the predominantly White Massachusetts audience in a question-and-answer session after the performance. One White man asked the dancers, "What is your message for white people?" Camille A. Brown immediately ran out from backstage to join her dancers and the discussion. She invited the man to rephrase his question. He repeated, "You must have a message for white people." She kindly coaxed him to think again. He finally arrived at something like, "What might be different messages for different audiences?" Camille A. Brown answered by noting that the performance was created to celebrate the ways African ancestors live in the bodies of Africans in diaspora. The performance was created by Black people for Black people. She stressed, however, that any human being can find ways of connecting with the performance.

This White man's question reminds me of the segregated mind-set in which I grew up. Even though we learned in Catholic worship and school to love everyone, where and how we lived in a segregated community taught us otherwise. Although my parents and extended family were not overt racists, the softer subtlety of our racism precisely fits Dr. Martin Luther King Jr.'s warning about white moderates in "Letter from Birmingham Jail." Dr. King wrote that the biggest obstacle to the "stride toward freedom is not the White Citizen's Counciler or the Ku Klux Klanner, but the white moderate, who is more devoted to 'order' than to justice; who prefers a negative peace which is the absence of tension to a positive peace which is the presence of justice."[4] My family and Catholic parish did not take King's message to heart; in fact, we failed to even consider what he was saying. King was shunned where I grew up and in nearly every predominantly white community throughout the nation.

The way we lived reflected our own sense of innocence, impervious as we were to the experience of our African American neighbors in Lansing and Detroit, Michigan. Although my family discussed a wide range of political and religious issues at every shared meal, our discussions reflected an implicit us/them dualism in which we were always innocent and separate from the racial conflict of the time, including the Detroit rebellions of 1967–1968. I won't repeat the racist language my maternal grandmother and mother often used, except to note that their language frequently disparaged Black people. Yet we assumed the safety of the dominant white cultural environment and enjoyed its comforting semblance of innocence: "race" had nothing to do with us.

I did not begin to become aware of the contradiction between my family's racism and what we learned about universal human dignity in Catholic

---

[4]Martin Luther King Jr., "Letter from Birmingham Jail," in *A Testament of Hope: The Essential Writings of Martin Luther King Jr.*, ed. James M. Washington (San Francisco: Harper and Row, 1986), 295.

elementary school until I played on an integrated basketball team my first year of high school. I witnessed racist hatred against my African American teammates for the first time when Ku Klux Klan members unleashed barrages of rocks on our school bus. I cannot forget how the KKK members' eyes burned with flames of hatred. That was only the beginning of learning how my own family and community were complicit in anti-black white supremacy. These childhood memories inspire my exploration in this chapter of how we are socialized into anti-black white superiority.

As an anti-racism cofacilitator and speaker I repeatedly hear White people reiterate individualistic and racist assumptions. Speaking to faith and justice groups, no matter how much I might unpack the multiple ways White people are complicit in US hyperincarceration, I still get variations of "Am I a racist?" or "Are you calling us racist?" These kinds of questions are a self-serving way to affirm our self-perceived innocence. These questions reinscribe the white American individualistic assumption that racism is only a problem of "a few bad apples." This chapter examines how these questions themselves reflect societal processes of white socialization into superiority and anti-blackness.

For example, speaking to a group of Catholic peace activists in Chicago a few years ago, I argued that we could not be authentic Catholic peacemakers unless we learn from and follow the lead of the Black Lives Matter movement. My message was clear: we can't claim to value all lives until we live in a way that truly values the people who are most undervalued in American society. Nevertheless, no matter how much my cofacilitators or I describe anti-blackness in educational and housing segregation, incarceration, health care, and policing, White people invariably ask: "Why not say 'all lives matter'?" Yet the assumption of "all lives matter" reflects precisely what I learned growing up in East Lansing, Michigan. The message "all lives matter" is not really about universal equality. "All lives matter" is really about the abstract notion of universal equality that enforces the status quo of white domination. This chapter illuminates how the "all lives matter" message really reaffirms white innocence and prevents White people from listening to and really hearing what Black people mean by "Black lives matter."

These stories of the White man's question to Camille A. Brown's dancers; of my childhood in East Lansing, Michigan; and the assumptions of whites affirming "all lives matter" are all examples of white ways of thinking, feeling, acting, and being. As long as White people continue to embody the claim that "I am not a racist," including progressives who claim to be anti-racist, we perpetuate anti-black white supremacy. Our society is permeated with national, regional, and local ecosystems of anti-black white supremacy—ecosystems that foster and promote the ways whites are socialized, leading them to arrive at these kinds of questions and responses. As we will see, these white ecosystems and patterns of socialization are segregated, and they re-create segregated ways of thinking and being. Sociologist Eduardo Bonilla-Silva explains how white socialization cultivates particular white norms, values, feelings, and dispositions—what he calls "white habitus"—that form intragroup identity and cohesion. Bonilla-Silva defines "white habitus" as "a racialized, uninterrupted socialization process that conditions and creates whites' tastes, perceptions, feelings, and emotions and their views on racial matters."[5]

To situate the concept of white habitus in explicitly sociological terms, think of how Americans tend to assume that individuals are relatively free to shape their own identity, unencumbered by the contextual social history, structures, and socialization into which they are born.[6] However, contrary to common assumptions of individualism, the social construction of reality is far more complex. The ways that identities are conferred, rather than subjectively chosen, constitute a basic tenet of sociology. Sociologists find three interrelated ways that identities are formed: groups make people (as when people learn and internalize the values, norms, and habits of those around them); persons make groups (as when persons create new values, norms, habits, and institutions); and groups just exist (as when values, norms, habits, and institutions become objectified, that is, they are just there, so well established that we tend to assume that is the way things have always been).[7] Bonilla-Silva draws upon and develops sociologist Pierre Bourdieu's concept of *habitus* because it interconnects the ways people form their own lives (agency) in the context of the institutions (family, neighborhood, schools, churches, etc.), whereby society forms the way we are socialized into the world. A reader may notice that "habitus" is the Latin root for the English word "habit," which Americans associate with an individual's capacity to shape their own behavior and practices.

Bourdieu's notion of habitus includes an individual's unique capacities and agency, but is also about much more than individual action. Habitus, for Bourdieu, interconnects individual agency with historical social structures like family, school, neighborhood, religious institutions, and government. Bourdieu writes that habitus is a "structured structure,"[8] by which he means that

---

[5]Eduardo Bonilla-Silva, *Racism without Racists: Color-Blind Racism and the Persistence of Racial Inequality in the United States*, 2nd ed. (Lanham, MD: Rowman and Littlefield, 2006), 103.

[6]Robert N. Bellah, Richard Madsen, and William M. Sullivan, *Habits of the Heart: Individualism and Commitment in American Life* (Berkeley: University of California Press, 1985). Bellah et al. trace forms of expressive and utilitarian individualism to the European Enlightenment and American Founding Fathers such as Benjamin Franklin.

[7]Peter Berger and Thomas Luckmann, *The Social Construction of Reality: A Treatise on the Sociology of Knowledge* (New York: Anchor Books, 1966).

[8]Bonilla-Silva, *Racism without Racists*, 279n7. Bonilla-Silva cites Pierre Bourdieu, *Distinction* (Cambridge, MA: Harvard University Press, 1984), 170, and *Pascalian Meditations* (Palo Alto, CA: Stanford University Press, 1997), 138. See also Nick Crossley, "Habitus," in *Key Concepts in Critical Social Theory* (London: Sage, 2005), 104–12.

habitus is not formed by an individual, but by the way individuals internalize social structures through socialization.

Language is a primary example of how individuals internalize structures. Bourdieu's notion of habitus, however, includes the nuances of how language is internalized within diverse social and class contexts. For example, when my family first moved from Michigan to New England, easterners would make fun of our Midwestern way of saying things; simultaneously, we had to adapt to the distinctive language patterns of different parts of New England. Habitus includes the ways we internalize the rules of language, including how we speak in distinctive dialects spawned in particular social and class contexts. Michiganders and New Englanders learn—internalize—American English with different embodied dispositions and dialects.

Bourdieu's concept of habitus interconnects a "structured structure" with the ways our actions reproduce social structures—what he calls a "structuring structure." For example, the car manufacturer Hyundai introduced an ad in early 2020 featuring the Sonata's "smart park" function.[9] The ad, which plays upon the celebrated Bostonian accent by having a neighbor explain the "smaht pahk" feature to his friends on a congested street, features famous Bostonians who make fun of the way the local dialect drops the letter "r." It ends with a famous baseball player calling the parking function "wicked smaht." The ad is an example of a "structuring structure" in the way it reproduces the Bostonian accent by playing with it. Bonilla-Silva extends habitus in terms of race in the way he demonstrates how white habitus shapes particular white embodiment, racial dispositions, tastes, emotions, and perceptions. For example, White people do not perceive how they self-segregate because living in a predominantly White neighborhood is the norm, the status quo that is seen as normal and right. White self-segregation, seen as normal and right, also means that White people don't perceive how excluding Black people from living in their neighborhoods is anti-black and morally repugnant. White people's lack of self-awareness and knowledge of our racial bias and how our arrogant ignorance contributes to both to self-segregation and anti-blackness builds the foundations of housing and school inequalities.

This chapter explores the complexity of white habitus, which is shaped within and contributes to a separate residential and cultural life that fosters a white culture of solidarity and negative views of Black and Brown peoples. I now turn to structural racism and the primary social structures white society has built over the past century to maintain and extend social ecologies of white habitus.

---

[9] See https://www.youtube.com/watch?v=85iRQdjCzj0.

Building Anti-Black White Supremacy
in the Twentieth Century

The initial question that a White man asked of the Camille A. Brown dancers, "What is your message for white people?" exposes an unreflective innocence and a certain dualism or separation in the white mind. It reveals an insouciant segregated mind-set. Similarly, my family's reaction to Black Americans in Harlem reflects the same segregated and racist disposition. Moreover, the White man's question reflects where our minds, bodies, and spirits dwell—our bodily, mental, emotional, moral, and spiritual dispositions do not arise out of nowhere. White racialization reflects the segregated neighborhoods, housing, schools, churches, and institutions in which people are socialized. All of these institutions were built to maintain and perpetuate white dominance. Furthermore, although they may not literally be exactly like the white settler plantation culture upon which the United States was built, these institutions continually adapt to ensure white dominance.

Returning to the presence of our past in chapter 1, where I connected the history of racial capitalism to the development of the racial wealth gap, here I pick up that history to recall how African Americans hit more economic bumps in the road after Emancipation and during Jim Crow from the early twentieth century through the present.

The historical record is brutally clear: not only did the United States fail to endow slaves with the promised "forty acres and a mule"[10] after the Civil War, African Americans were systematically deprived of property—especially land accumulated between 1880 and 1910—by government complicity, fraud, and seizures by white terrorists.[11] The promise of Emancipation and Reconstruction barely lasted ten years before a white backlash extended economic exploitation of former slaves through tenant farming and convict labor, among other means.[12]

Far from fulfilling the promise of equality and justice for African Americans, the post-Emancipation period was the "reconstruction of slavery," as historian Ibram X. Kendi describes it.[13] White people might assume that the

---

[10]"On January 16, 1865, after completing his march to the Georgia coast, General Sherman issued Special Fields Order No. 15 that established the provision 'of not more than (40) forty acres of tillable ground' designated 'for the settlement of negroes now made free by the acts of war and the proclamation of the President of the United States.'" William Darity, "Forty Acres and a Mule in the 21st Century," *Social Science Quarterly* 89, no. 3 (September 2008): 656–65, at 660.

[11]Ibid.

[12]Douglas A. Blackmon, *Slavery by Another Name: The Re-Enslavement of Black Americans from the Civil War until World War II* (New York: Anchor Books, 2009). See also the PBS documentary film *Slavery by Another Name*, https://www.pbs.org/tpt/slavery-by-another-name/home/

[13]Ibram X. Kendi, *Stamped from the Beginning: The Definitive History of Racist Ideas in*

Reconstruction period achieved equality and justice through the passage, right after the Civil War, of the Thirteenth and Fourteenth Amendments to the Constitution. The Thirteenth Amendment prohibits slavery and treating African Americans as second-class citizens, while the Fourteenth Amendment prohibits state and local government from treating people unequally and unfairly.

However, contrary to the notion that the Civil War and Reconstruction achieved freedom and equality for African Americans, Professor Carol Anderson explicates how white rage fueled opposition from the White House in President Andrew Johnson, to the Supreme Court, and to every statehouse in the South. She explains that in "this reconstruction of Reconstruction, with the recision of *Dred Scott*, the exclusion of blacks from the ballot box, and the rescision of forty acres and a mule, African Americans now had neither citizenship, the vote, nor land."[14] President Johnson declared in 1866 that "By God, as long as I am President, it shall be a government for white men."[15] As Johnson pardoned scores of Confederate generals and leaders, they reasserted their power at all levels of government, from Congress to statehouses. President Johnson welcomed former Confederate states back into the Union without any political protection or enforcement of rights for African Americans, and he refused to protect African Americans from emboldened whites who unleashed "a reign of terror and anti-black violence that had reached 'staggering proportions.'"[16] Although Congress passed the Fourteenth and Fifteenth Amendments in 1868 and 1870, respectively, Frederick Douglass lamented a series of Supreme Court decisions that meant that "'in the Southern States, the fourteenth and fifteenth amendments are virtually nullified. The rights which they were intended to guarantee are denied and held in contempt.'"[17]

The United States has failed to fulfill the promises of the Thirteenth Amendment, which prohibits slavery and treating African Americans as second-class citizens, and of the Fourteenth Amendment, which prohibits local governments from treating people unfairly, writes Richard Rothstein, a public policy scholar.[18] The result, he argues, is that we "have created a caste system in this country with African Americans kept exploited and geographically separate by racially explicit government policies."[19] And although many of these poli-

America (New York: Bold Type Books, 2016), 235–60.

[14]Carol Anderson, *White Rage: The Unspoken Truth of Our Racial Divide* (New York: Bloomsbury, 2016), 18.

[15]Ibid.

[16]Ibid., 17.

[17]Ibid., 32.

[18]Richard Rothstein, *The Color of Law: A Forgotten History of How Our Government Segregated America* (New York: Liveright, 2017), viii.

[19]Ibid., xvii.

cies, like redlining and restrictive deed covenants, may no longer be encoded in law, "they have never been remedied and their effects endure."[20]

We forget how a combination of federal, state, and local industrial, housing, education, and transportation policies, combined with business and private interests, built a segregated economy and society. We forget how these policies systemically benefitted White people while exploiting and repressing Black economic development. White people willfully ignore how whiteness literally delivers a "cash value":

> It accounts for advantages that come to individuals through profits from housing secured in discriminatory markets, through unequal educational opportunities available to children of different races, through insider networks that channel employment opportunities to the relatives and friends of those who have profited the most from present and past racial discrimination, and especially through intergenerational transfers of inherited wealth that pass on the spoils of discrimination to succeeding generations.[21]

Too often we forget how local, state, and federal governments instituted policies that delivered this cash value of whiteness. The original Social Security legislation of 1935, created in the throes of the Great Depression to create a basic level of economic security for workers, effectively denied benefits to 75 percent of African Americans by excluding domestic and agricultural workers. The benefits of Social Security, minimum wage protection, and the recognition of labor unions were all denied to domestic and agricultural workers, predominantly African American occupations.[22] The Federal Emergency Relief Administration, the very first national program of the New Deal, "disproportionately spent its funds on unemployed whites," and generally refused to employ African Americans except in the least skilled jobs, and even then "paid less than the officially stipulated wage."[23] The National Recovery Administration established industry-by-industry codes for minimum wages, maximum hours, and product prices. African Americans working in canning, citrus packing, cotton ginning, and other agricultural jobs were denied the NRA's wage and hour standards.[24]

While white workers benefitted from the ability to bargain with management through the 1935 National Labor Relations Act, congressional action

---

[20]Ibid.

[21]George Lipsitz, *The Possessive Investment in Whiteness: How White People Profit from Identity Politics* (Philadelphia: Temple University Press, 2006), vii.

[22]Rothstein, *Color of Law*, 155.

[23]Ibid., 156.

[24]Ibid.

"sanctioned an unconstitutional policy of legally empowering unions that refused to admit African Americans."[25] This policy, which endured until the passage of civil rights legislation, not only denied the privileges of union membership to African Americans; it also segregated them into "janitorial or other lower-paid jobs."[26]

Political and union organizing among industrial workers ignited a white "culture of unity" that broke down old antagonisms between ethnicities and brought together diverse European Americans.[27] Social scientist George Lipsitz explains how a European culture of unity was solidified through the New Deal, which won

> bargaining recognition for industrial workers in mass production in-dustries, but it also secured social security pensions and survivors' ben-efits, federally subsidized home loans, National Labor Relations Board protection for collective bargaining, federal responsibility for welfare, and other direct social benefits. These resources from the state made European Americans less dependent upon separate ethnic identities, and they helped create the standard of living, the suburban neighborhoods, the workplace opportunities, and educational opportunities that enabled the children and grandchildren of immigrants to become middle class and blend together into a "white" identity.[28]

The New Deal legislation of the 1930s and 1940s sealed together a culture of unity through white affirmative action programs.[29] For example, when my father returned from military service in World War II, he benefitted from the 1944 G.I. Bill, which paid for his graduate school education and also enabled my parents to purchase their first home. Unlike returning White servicemen, however, African Americans were denied mortgage subsidies and were "fre-quently restricted by education and training to lower-level jobs," even though many were "qualified to acquire greater skills."[30] The fact of the matter is that White descendants of World War II service personnel accrued advantages that were denied to African American servicemen and women. The nation accepted African Americans' sacrifice and denied them the privileges of that sacrifice. We and millions of White Americans were able to build wealth, ac-cess education and health care, and live in healthier environments because of these federal policies.

---

[25]Ibid., 158.

[26]Ibid.

[27]Lizabeth Cohen, *Making a New Deal: Industrial Workers in Chicago, 1919–1939*, 2nd ed. (New York: Cambridge University Press, 2008).

[28]Lipsitz, *Possessive Investment*, 193.

[29]Ibid., 5.

[30]Rothstein, *Color of Law*, 167.

When I was growing up in East Lansing, Michigan, I recall the Black rebellions of 1967 and 1968. I recall how my parents viewed the 1967 "riots" from the top of the bell tower at the Franciscan seminary Duns Scotus. As I look back, the fact that my family's Franciscan friend and my parents viewed the rebellions[31] from the safe distance and vantage point of the seminary's tower symbolizes the position of privilege we took for granted. I recall how my parents discussed those events as occurring in a kind of vacuum, as if segregation and the rebellions that occurred across the country had nothing to do with the legacy of slavery that produced them. Those rebellions of the late 1960s found new expression from 2014 to 2020 when so-called riots in Ferguson, Baltimore, Milwaukee, Charlotte, and Minneapolis captured national attention. We told ourselves a story that I have heard my entire life and that was taught in graduate school: that these places were "de facto segregated," that is, they were the result of a myriad of unintended private practices. But as Rothstein notes, the far more significant truth of today's "residential segregation in the North, South, Midwest, and West is not the unintended consequence of individual choices and otherwise well-meaning law or regulation but of unhidden public policy that explicitly segregated every metropolitan area in the United States."[32]

The Historical Structures That Created White Habitus

As I describe how supremacy is built into the fabric of white society, it is critical to remember our Catholic Christian biblical and liturgical commitment to solidarity. The clear mark of solidarity is the practice of intimately hearing the cry of the poor and making their cries for dignity, love, justice, and freedom our own. Catholics proclaim through liturgical music and singing that the Lord hears the cry of the poor (Ps 34:15–17) because Scripture and our faith teach that God is close to the brokenhearted and promises that those who mourn will be comforted (Mt 5:4). Yet in the wake of the police shooting of Michael Brown and countless shootings like it, I have heard more homilies about how "blue lives matter" than about the disproportionate levels of violence that African Americans suffer from both vigilante and formal law enforcement. In fact, I have never heard a homily addressing anti-black violence in a predominantly white Catholic parish. Sadly, my experience finds confirmation in a social scientific study

---

[31] I intentionally use "rebellion" to underscore these actions as legitimate responses to oppression. See Ashley M. Howard, "Prairie Fires: Urban Rebellions as Black Working-Class Politics in Three Midwestern Cities," doctoral dissertation, University of Illinois at Urbana, 2012, https://www.ideals.illinois.edu/bitstream/handle/2142/34444/Howard_Ashley.pdf?sequence=1&isAllowed=y.

[32] Rothstein, *Color of Law*, vi–viii.

commissioned by the United States Conference of Catholic Bishops in 2004. Bryan N. Massingale reports how that study found that "most Catholics (64 percent) had not heard a homily on racism or racial justice in the past three years."[33]

Reflecting upon the police shooting of unarmed Michael Brown in Ferguson, Missouri, I wonder whether and how white Christians hear Brown's mother, Lesley McSpadden, when she cried for her son as he lay dead in the street for over four hours.[34] The message of that indignity was clear: Black lives do not matter. Lesley McSpadden is not alone in the annals of American history—we hear the echoes of Emmitt Till's mother in her call for justice when she opened her son's casket on September 3, 1955, so that everyone could see what white terrorists had done to him. Mamie Till Mobley disregarded advice to keep the casket closed because she wanted the whole world to face the violence inflicted upon her fifteen-year-old son. Speaking at his funeral, she proclaimed, "I don't have a minute to hate; I will pursue justice for the rest of my life."[35]

Too many White people complain about crimes against property after shootings like the one in Ferguson, rather than objecting to the fact that a life was taken. Speaking to the Grosse Point, Michigan, high school just three weeks before his death, Dr. Martin Luther King Jr. said, "It would not be enough for me to condemn the riots,"[36] and that he must simultaneously condemn the "intolerable conditions that exist in our society. These conditions are the things that cause individuals to feel that they have no alternative than to engage violent rebellions to get attention. And I must say tonight that a riot is the language of the unheard."[37]

Perhaps White Americans do not hear the cry of Michael Brown's mother or of the protestors because we are not attuned to the lives of the unheard, probably because we are not in close enough physical proximity to hear their cries. Worse, the historical record demonstrates that White people choose to segregate and isolate themselves from people of all other colors.[38] Our failure to hear any of their cries is in no small measure due to where and how our churches and communities form the physical foundations of white domination

---

[33]Bryan N. Massingale, *Racial Justice and the Catholic Church* (Maryknoll, NY: Orbis Books, 2010), 69.

[34]Julie Bosman and Joseph Goldstein, "Timeline for a Body: 4 Hours in the Middle of a Ferguson Street," *New York Times*, August 23, 2014.

[35]See *The American Experience: Mamie Till Mobley*, PBS, https://www.pbs.org/wgbh/americanexperience.

[36]Martin Luther King Jr., "The Other America," speech at Grosse Point High School, Grosse Point, Michigan, March 14, 1968, http://www.gphistorical.org/mlk/mlkspeech/index.htm

[37]Ibid.

[38]Douglas S. Massey and Nancy A. Denton, *American Apartheid: Segregation and the Making of the Underclass* (Cambridge, MA: Harvard University Press, 1993), 45.

in America. In *Jesus and the Disinherited* Howard Thurman clearly named the evil of segregation:

> It is necessary, therefore, for the privileged and underprivileged to work on the common environment for the purpose of providing normal experiences of fellowship. This is one very important reason for the insistence that segregation is a complete ethical and moral evil. Whatever it may do for those who dwell on either side of the wall, one thing is certain: it poisons all normal contacts of those persons involved. The first step toward love is common sharing of a sense of mutual worth and value. This cannot be discovered in a vacuum or in a series of artificial or hypothetical relationships. It has to be in a real situation, natural, free.[39]

The poison of segregation means that we become morally and spiritually insensitive to the plight of the disinherited. A case in point is how people become desensitized to the deaths of African Americans. Isabel Wilkerson explains that an African American is killed almost twice a week, according to data compiled by the Federal Bureau of Investigation from 2005 to 2012.[40] The banality of this reality, she observes, obscures the fact that this is nearly the same rate at which African Americans were lynched during Jim Crow, at a rate of at least one person every four days.[41] In her call to Americans to own up to our violence, Wilkerson details the uncanny similarities between lynching and the shooting of Michael Brown, not the least significant of which is "the fact the lynched body was sometimes left hanging for days or weeks as a lesson to people to not step outside the caste into which they had been born."[42]

Even though White Americans outnumber Black Americans fivefold, she notes, "Black people are three times more likely than white people to be killed by the police in the US, and black teenagers are far likelier to be killed by police than white teenagers."[43] This white American devaluation of black life, Wilkerson writes, is as old as the nation itself and has yet to be confronted. She cites an August 2014 Pew study showing that 73 percent of Black Americans polled believed that the shooting of Michael Brown raised important issues of race. The same Pew study found that only 37 percent of White respondents felt the same way "due in part to *de facto* segregation and

---

[39] Howard Thurman, *Jesus and the Disinherited* (Boston: Beacon Press, 1996 [1949]), 98.

[40] Isabel Wilkerson, "Mike Brown's Shooting and Jim Crow Lynchings Have Too Much in Common: It's Time for Americans to Own Up," *The Guardian*, August 25, 2014, www.theguardian.com.

[41] Ibid. See also Kendi, *Stamped from the Beginning*, 259.

[42] Wilkerson, "Mike Brown's Shooting."

[43] Ibid.

the fact that majority status does not require engagement with those outside their own group."[44] White physical isolation combined with the negative associations with Blackness embedded in American culture create a lack of empathy that "allows otherwise well-meaning people to turn away from the plight of fellow citizens."[45]

We White people must admit that our lack of either empathy or responsibility for many deaths of African Americans is nothing less than grotesque. What happened to Michael Brown in Ferguson, Missouri, fits historical patterns all across the nation. Even the most liberal metropolitan areas, including the San Francisco Bay Area, facilitated labor and housing segregation.[46] White segregation and isolation from African Americans and systemic government and police abuse of African Americans in the twenty-first century have been happening for more than a hundred years. Local and federal officials in the early twentieth century began to promote zoning ordinances that reserved single-family homes for white middle-class neighborhoods that purposely excluded African Americans.[47] The first zoning laws for St. Louis, Rothstein explains, used multiple tools to segregate areas along racial and class lines. St. Louis hired Harland Bartholomew, named the "Dean of City Planning" in his obituary,[48] to develop the first comprehensive categorization of every building and property in the city. Bartholomew's primary goal was to prevent movement into "'finer residential districts . . . by colored people.'"[49] Bartholomew's categories included "single-family residential, multifamily residential, commercial, or industrial," and his planning commission proposed rules and maps that would protect single-family residential areas from being encroached upon by the other categories. The first tool applied in enforcing the law was the issuing of single-family home deeds that excluded African Americans. These neighborhoods were designated "first residential," prohibiting anything but single-family homes that preserved their all-white character.[50]

When the first St. Louis zoning ordinance was adopted in 1919, it also designated land for future industrial development if it was in or adjacent to neighborhoods with significant African American populations. This second tool, called "expulsive zoning," was used to racially segregate cities across the nation.[51] Expulsive zoning is the practice of "siting industrial, semi-industrial,

---

[44]Ibid.

[45]Ibid.

[46]Rothstein, "If San Francisco, Then Everywhere?," in *Color of Law*, 3–14.

[47]Ibid., 48.

[48]Joan Cook, "Harland Bartholomew, 100, Dean of City Planners," *New York Times*, December 7, 1989.

[49]Rothstein, *Color of Law*, 49.

[50]Ibid.

[51]Jessica Trounstine, *Segregation by Design: Local Politics and Inequality in American Cities* (New York: Cambridge University Press, 2018), 32.

or other nuisances into neighborhoods of color."[52] Dating back to the early 1900s, this practice both devalued properties in African American neighborhoods and exposed those neighborhoods to the highest environmental hazards associated with industrialization. For example, consider the similarly sized New Jersey cities of Camden and Cherry Hill, which adjoin each other across the Delaware River from Philadelphia. The history of expulsive zoning means that the predominantly African American Camden is home to two Superfund toxic waste sites, while white Cherry Hill is home to none.[53]

The National Association of Realtors codified segregation in its 1924 code of ethics, which declared that "a Realtor should never be instrumental in introducing into a neighborhood a character of property or occupancy, members of any race or nationality, or any individual whose presence will be clearly detrimental to property values in the neighborhood."[54] Far from being a haphazard individual practice, then, segregationist practices were written into city planning laws and blessed by national ethical codes like that of the National Association of Realtors. Local government ordinances and real estate codes were even more explicit in "excluding 'detrimental' groups from white neighborhoods."[55] For example, following violent White response to Black people moving into an all-White neighborhood, in 1910 Baltimore enacted the first racial zoning law designed to segregate African Americans from Whites.[56] Local governments engineered White enclaves not only through zoning policies that reinforced segregation in the service of business and White single-family neighborhoods, but also by controlling the distribution of public goods like sewer systems and water.[57]

The creation of municipal boundary lines intended to separate white from black neighborhoods were integral to denying public services to African Americans. Drawing upon detailed ward-level data from Baltimore, Chicago, Boston, and Philadelphia, social scientist Jessica Trounstine demonstrates that "sewer extensions were less likely to be built in neighborhoods with higher proportions of African Americans and renting residents."[58] She traces the denial of public goods to African Americans from the early to late twentieth century, showing the "differential rates of access to public sewers in more segregated places in 1970, 1980, and 1990."[59] Explaining that sewer services

[52]Ibid., 32n10.
[53]Ibid., 4.
[54]"Code of Ethics of the National Association of Real Estate Boards," (Chicago: National Association of Real Estate Boards, 1924), Article 34, 7, http://archive.realtor.org/sites/default/files/1924Ethics.pdf.
[55]Lipsitz, *Possessive Investment*, 26.
[56]Trounstine, *Segregation by Design*, 79.
[57]Ibid., 77.
[58]Ibid., 20.
[59]Ibid., 100.

were often built at the behest of white property owners and developers and since very few landowners were "people of color," this meant that "blacks in Birmingham and Mexican and Chinese residents in Los Angeles" lacked the opportunity and power to procure sewer extensions or connections.[60] Yet lack of access to power through land ownership was not the only reason for the unequal distribution of public services like water and sewers. Policy makers in cities like Birmingham chose to ignore sanitation and building codes in African American neighborhoods, while other cities, like Los Angeles, intentionally declined to build sewers in Mexican or Chinese neighborhoods.[61] I discuss in the last chapter how environmental racism was built into segregated cities.

Not only were African American lives and properties devalued because of their proximity to industry and its pollution, early-twentieth-century zoning regulations in St. Louis and other cities permitted taverns, liquor stores, nightclubs, and prostitution houses to open in African American neighborhoods and prohibited these establishments in white residential zones.[62] Residential zones were exclusively single-family in white areas but properties could be subdivided into multiple dwellings and rooming houses in African American and industrial zones. These practices protected the value of white single-family neighborhoods as they simultaneously devalued African American ones.

The federal government developed a program to support existing homeowners who could not make payments in the midst of the Great Depression, and another to enable middle-class families to buy homes for the first time. President Roosevelt's administration created the Home Owners Loan Corporation (HOLC) in 1933 to rescue existing homeowners who were about to default. HOLC purchased existing mortgages and then reissued new mortgages that would be repaid in schedules of fifteen or twenty-five years. These loans were amortized, which means that they included both principal and interest in monthly payments. When the borrower paid off the loan, they owned the home. This new HOLC program enabled White working-class families to own homes, and if a family sold their home, their equity in the home as well as any appreciation would be theirs to keep. Home ownership is a primary way that Whites gain and pass wealth over generations.[63]

HOLC hired local real estate agents to perform appraisals and assess risks to make financing decisions. Unsurprisingly, given the national ethics code of realtors that required them to maintain segregation, the racial composition of neighborhoods became codified into federal financing as well as banking,

---

[60]Ibid., 111.

[61]Ibid.

[62]Rothstein, *Color of Law*, 50.

[63]Edward N. Wolff, "Racial Wealth Disparities: What Are the Causes?," *Indicators* 1, no. 2 (Spring 2002): 68.

insurance, and real estate procedures.[64] The federal government initiated the policy of redlining, whereby the HOLC created color-coded maps of every metropolitan area in the nation. The safest neighborhoods were color-coded green, "still desirable" neighborhoods were blue, "declining" neighborhoods were yellow, and lastly, "hazardous" neighborhoods were red, hence the term "redlining." A neighborhood with African Americans in it was coded red, "even if it was a solid middle-class neighborhood of single-family homes."[65] HOLC's residential security maps for 148 cities are available online.[66]

At a critical historical juncture when the federal government, banks, insurance companies, and real estate agents could have supported existing integration, the practice of redlining isolated and depressed African American neighborhoods while simultaneously advantaging white neighborhoods. Redlining became more deeply entrenched in federal policy with the creation of the Federal Housing Administration (FHA) in 1934. As FHA appraisal standards incorporated a whites-only rule, "racial segregation now became an official requirement of the federal mortgage insurance program."[67] As the volume of applications for home loans increased, Rothstein explains, the FHA created an *Underwriting Manual* to guide real estate appraisers. The first manual in 1935 required class and racial stability and continuity and explicitly prohibited "infiltration of inharmonious racial or nationality groups."[68] In addition to redlining, the FHA discouraged banks from extending loans in existing urban neighborhoods while encouraging lending to newly emerging white suburbs. The FHA further contributed to segregation by "favoring mortgages in areas where boulevards or highways served to separate African American families from whites, stating that 'natural or artificially established barriers will prove effective in protecting a neighborhood and the locations within it from adverse influences, . . . including the prevention of the infiltration of . . . lower class occupancy, and inharmonious racial groups.'"[69]

These zoning practices effectively "rendered African Americans ineligible for such mortgages because banks and the FHA considered the existence of nearby rooming houses," or the existence of commercial or industrial development, to devalue single-family white neighborhoods.[70] Since they were denied federally protected mortgages, African Americans did not have the same resources as White homeowners to keep up their homes. The cost of maintaining African American homes was higher as their homes were more

[64]Rothstein, *Color of Law*, 64.
[65]Ibid.
[66]See https://www.policymap.com/2017/07/holc-historic-lending-guideline-maps-policymap/.
[67]Rothstein, *Color of Law*, 65.
[68]Ibid.
[69]Ibid.
[70]Ibid., 50.

likely to deteriorate, further exacerbating the declining conditions of African American neighborhoods. This higher cost for African Americans is only the tip of the iceberg of what has been called a "black tax" or a "race tax" in which "Black people paid more for the inferior condition of their housing."[71]

The combination of racially structured banking, real estate, and governmental policies created a "political economy of residential segregation [that] not only hastened the conditions of physical decline in urban areas but forever incentivized their perpetuation."[72] The racist presumptions of America's private and public sectors combined not only to segregate housing to the economic benefit of White people but to create a predatory society that extended the plunder of slavery. A century after the Civil War and the abolition of slavery, Ta-Nehisi Coates observes, the "plunder—quiet, systemic, submerged—continued even amidst the aims and achievements of New Deal liberals."[73]

Consider the example of "blockbusting" or "panic peddling," as described by a speculator in 1962. This speculator explains how he "busts" blocks by buying homes from White homeowners and then selling them at inflated prices to Black people:

> I make my money in three ways: 1) by beating down the prices I pay the white homeowners . . . ; 2) by selling to the eager Negroes at inflated prices; and 3) by financing these purchases at what amounts to a very high rate of interest. . . . If anybody who is well established in this business doesn't earn $100,000 a year [they are] loafing.[74]

Yet even as they faced mortgage discrimination, redlining, and other barriers, African Americans still worked toward homeownership. Throughout the period of Black migration in the twentieth century, African Americans organized savings and loan associations to serve their communities. There were seventy-three of these associations in 1930, with assets of $6.5 million, and after consolidation of smaller groups, twenty-nine possessed assets of $18 million in 1950.[75] Sadly, however, some Black lenders "engaged Black customers under predatory terms."[76]

Prohibited from procuring the most beneficial mortgages, Africans Americans turned to land installment contracts (LICs). LICs are essentially

---

[71]Keeanga-Yamahtta Taylor, *Race for Profit: How Banks and the Real Estate Industry Undermined Black Homeownership* (Chapel Hill: University of North Carolina Press, 2019), 11.
[72]Ibid., 54.
[73]Ta-Nehisi Coates, *We Were Eight Years in Power: An American Tragedy* (New York: One World Press, 2017), 189.
[74]Taylor, *Race for Profit*, 48.
[75]Ibid., 49.
[76]Ibid.

rent-to-own schemes in which customers pay higher interest rates and higher overall costs. Whereas White suburban homeowners were enjoying small down payments and low interest rates, African Americans who turned to LICs were paying higher interest rates for older and inferior housing.[77] Higher costs "meant less money to invest in renovations and general maintenance, exacerbating the already deteriorated condition of Black urban properties."[78] A 1961 Urban League study estimated that African Americans in Chicago paid more than $157 million over a seven-year period for the added costs of renting and owning homes.[79] A political economy of racial economic exploitation "had emerged that was structured around the captive African American market."[80] Today, "reverse redlining" has become the new practice of housing and lending discrimination. Reverse redlining occurs in multiple forms, including subprime loans and foreclosures that erase recent gains made by African American and Latino borrowers.[81]

The development of the federal highway system in the 1950s and 1960s intensified policies that built segregation and economic exploitation into neighborhood and urban and suburban divides. The National Interstate and Defense Highway Act of 1956 not only constructed highways, it also literally dismantled formerly healthy and contiguous Black neighborhoods. Although the federal government funded nearly 90 percent of the highway system, local officials were instrumental in steering highways through urban neighborhoods. The interstate system was routinely utilized to "destroy black neighborhoods" and "to keep black and white neighborhoods apart."[82] Throughout the nation, "highway construction displaced Black households and cut the heart and soul out of thriving Black communities as homes, churches, schools, and businesses were destroyed."[83]

The construction of the interstate highway system, which facilitated the economic development of white suburbia,[84] is a physical manifestation both of white privilege and anti-blackness. Whether in Flint, Detroit, Chicago, or New Orleans, or in Orlando, Los Angeles, St. Louis, or Charlotte, "the na-

[77]Ibid.

[78]Ibid.

[79]Ibid.

[80]Ibid., 52.

[81]I explain reverse redlining in greater depth with data from the Center for Responsible Lending in Alex Mikulich, Laurie Cassidy, and Margaret Pfeil, *The Scandal of White Complicity in US Hyper-Incarceration: A Nonviolent Spirituality of White Resistance* (New York: Palgrave MacMillan, 2013), 75.

[82]Kevin M. Kruse, "Traffic," *New York Times Magazine*, August 18, 2019, 49. This essay is part of the original *New York Times* 1619 Project.

[83]Deborah N. Archer, "'White Men's Roads through Black Men's Homes': Advancing Racial Equity through Highway Reconstruction," *Vanderbilt Law Review* 73, no. 5 (2020): 1265, https://papers.ssrn.com/sol3/papers.cfm?abstract_id=3539889.

[84]Kenneth Jackson, *Crabgrass Frontier: The Suburbanization of the United States* (New York: Oxford University Press, 1985), 217.

tion's highway system contributed to the concentration of race and poverty, and created psychological and economic barriers that persist to this day."[85] Legal scholar Deborah Archer explains how the racial intent of building highways was often hidden behind race-neutral language that promised to "clear 'blighted' areas and 'slums.'"[86] Local governments and private developers employed "eminent domain to seize the homes of poor people of color with little payment and no relocation assistance."[87]

"Look, a White!" Exposing the Dynamics of White Habitus

Although white segregation, zoning laws, and a political economy of exploitation are at the source of the deterioration of places like Ferguson, too many White people blame African Americans—as if these historical policies that systemically benefitted White people play no role in the making of similarly situated localities all across the nation. "The penalty of deception," Howard Thurman wrote, "is to *become* a deception, with all sense of moral discrimination vitiated."[88] Nevertheless, White people continue to deceive ourselves that we are racially innocent and have nothing to do with the world that we daily create and re-create in where and how we live.

Recall sociologist Eduardo Bonilla-Silva's explanation of how white socialization cultivates the particular white norms, values, feelings, and dispositions—what he calls "white habitus"—that form intragroup identity and cohesion. Remember how he defines white habitus as "a racialized, uninterrupted socialization process that conditions and creates whites' tastes, perceptions, feelings, and emotions and their views on racial matters."[89] White habitus is nurtured within an ecosystem that interconnects both *position*—the geography, social capital, location, and power of whiteness—and *practice*—the ways White people are socialized to perceive and act within the world.

White habitus is cultivated within the social and moral geography of white segregation. Cardinal Francis George, the former archbishop of Chicago, in his 2001 pastoral letter *Dwell in My Love*, utilized the term "spatial racism" to describe residential hypersegregation. Cardinal George noticed how spatial racism creates a "visible chasm between rich and poor, and between

---

[85] Archer, "'White Men's Roads.'"
[86] Ibid.
[87] Ibid.
[88] Thurman, *Jesus and the Disinherited*, 65.
[89] Bonilla-Silva, *Racism without Racists*, 103.

whites and people of color."[90] Yet we who believe we are white tend to either be unaware of this chasm or to view it as a kind of "second nature" that is normal and natural.

White self-segregation and socialization physically, socially, and morally structure the relationship between privilege and oppression. White habitus socializes us within our provincial, segregated universe to think, act, and believe that segregation is natural and not our responsibility. As theologian M. Shawn Copeland observes, "ordinarily, [non-white] bodies are 'invisible' in the process of historical, cultural, and social creativity and representation, but should these non-white bodies step 'out of place,' they are subordinated literally to surveillance, inspection, discrimination, assessment, and containment."[91] White segregation and ways of thinking and being in the world create the racial dynamic of invisibility/visibility. This dynamic also arises when White people find themselves "out of place" in predominantly African American spaces.

For an example of the dynamic of invisibility/visibility from the perspective of a White person, I recall an occasion in my late teens when my family was visiting my sister, who was a student at a university in New York. We took the subway too far into Harlem (before it was gentrified). As I was walking up the stairwell in the station, I remember seeing fear break across my mom's face as she yelled from the subway platform, "We're in the wrong place!" I recall my own feeling of fear that was relieved by the laughter of dozens of strangers at the top of the stairway. My sense is that people at the subway station were amused by our naked embodiment of being lost; we looked how we felt: embarrassed and alarmed. Of course, we were not in any danger. In fact, the same strangers helped us find our way to our destination. It was a moment in which I began to learn how I had been socialized into anti-blackness and the white association of Blackness with danger. That was one of many experiences in which I began to realize how I had been malformed by white segregation and socialization—the ecosystem of white habitus.

As I reflect back upon my family's experience of getting lost in Harlem, I think about how my mother's vocalized response, as well as my own fear, echo Frantz Fanon's experience of being seen by a White boy who yells to his mother, "Look, a Negro!" The boy continues, "'Mama, see the Negro, I'm frightened!'" Fanon wants to laugh but finds, "Now they were becoming afraid of me. I made up my mind to laugh myself to tears but laughter had

[90]Francis George, OMI, *Dwell in My Love: A Pastoral Letter on Racism,* Archdiocese of Chicago, April 2001.

[91]M. Shawn Copeland, *Enfleshing Freedom: Body, Race, and Being* (Minneapolis: Fortress, 2010), 15.

become impossible."[92] Fanon reflects on how he became a hypersexualized,[93] objectified thing of evil and danger in the collective white gaze.

Looking at white habitus is a way to accept George Yancy's gift of "flipping the script," by turning our collective gaze on whiteness. Yancy observes that the White boy's behavior in Fanon's story fundamentally reflects the ways in which too many White children are "oriented, at the level of everyday practices, within the world, where their bodily orientations are un-reflected expressions of the *lived* orientations of whiteness, white ways of being, of white modes of racial and racist practice."[94] My mother and I in our own ways were echoing Fanon's experience of the White boy yelling, "Look, a Negro!" We who believe we are white need to flip the script into which we have been socialized through white habitus. We need to turn our gaze to ourselves and our social sin of whiteness.

A key problem for White people is how white habitus socializes us to live a lie. When we live in the deception of white habitus, as Howard Thurman warned, we ourselves become a deception. The problem of our deception is compounded when we attempt to live and act as if we were ignorant, as if we had no idea of the roles we learn through white habitus. Ethnographic studies of how White people describe their own experience demonstrate that within White gated communities, White self-perceptions of "niceness" and fear of others is used as a rhetorical way to justify living in residential spaces that exclude racialized others. In his ethnographic studies of White people, Bonilla-Silva found a "social psychology produced by white habitus that leads to the creation of positive self-views ('We are nice, normal people') and negative views of others ('They are lazy')."[95]

More importantly, in terms of white habitus, when White people tell ourselves that we are "nice" and nurture our fear of others, we inscribe white racist assumptions into the landscape. Although through public policy White people constructed the physical landscape over centuries, we socialize ourselves to believe that this is "natural" to the extent that we do not even see it. Thus, within white habitus, a White neighborhood is normal while a Black neighborhood is "racially segregated." The problem of white habitus is that it constitutes a racially biased intellectual and moral horizon that defines, controls, and segregates different, other, Black, and Brown bodies.

Bonilla-Silva finds that White people who claim to be progressive foster

---

[92]Frantz Fanon, *Black Skin, White Masks* (New York: Grove Press, 2008 [Editions du Seuil, 1952]), 112.

[93]Ibid., *135–36*. In his extensive discussion of racism and sexuality, Fanon writes that in the white mind, "Negroes" are seen as "sexually promiscuous" and "sexual beasts," possessing "hallucinating sexual power."

[94]George Yancy, *Look, a White! Philosophical Essays on Whiteness* (Philadelphia: Temple University Press, 2012), 3.

[95]Bonilla-Silva, *Racism without Racists*, 140.

ways of racial nonknowing, or ignorance, in the very act of saying, "I am not a racist" or "I am color-blind."[96] For a more complex example, the claim that "white flight" or suburbanization was merely a result of individual choices is a way White people deploy "strategic ignorance," that is, they deny personal and institutional liability.[97] Ignorance is also deployed as a way of avoiding the costs of taking responsibility for white privilege and power.[98] When we use ignorance in this way, as a rational choice, we reinforce white privilege, power, and dominance.[99] Another way White people employ ignorance is when we deny that we have the capacity to understand the experience of other people. While Bonilla-Silva found rhetorical claims to "color-blindness" among White people, he also found a rhetorical move toward ignorance in the claim "I am not black, so I don't know."[100] Such a statement is a form of rhetorical gymnastics that claims ignorance while recognizing that race might "matter a little bit for minorities."[101]

The normalization of White physical, social, and moral separation from Black people is rooted in the ways White people internalize the history of anti-black white supremacy (discussed in chapter 1) and in the historical policies that segregated the nation. Furthermore, the ways White people—in our tastes, perceptions, feelings, thinking, and way of moving through the world, including how we assume freedom of movement yet avoid predominantly Black localities—carry the history of anti-black white supremacy in our bodies in the ways we segregate and distance ourselves. White self-segregating strategies are part and parcel of an entire ecosystem that nurtures White people's inability to understand or feel empathy for Black people, much less practice the racial intimacy in which Jesus calls followers to "be compassionate as God is compassionate" (Lk 6:36).

Lack of cross-racial empathy becomes apparent in the everyday assumptions by which White people live. Social scientists call this lack of cross-racial empathy "social alexithymia."[102] In other words, this "white frame of mind" has difficulty understanding where people of color are coming from and what their racialized experience may be like. It is critical to understand that where and how White people live, and how White people educate other White people into dispositions and practices of superiority, are cultivated within

---

[96]Ibid.

[97]Jennifer C. Mueller, "Advancing a Sociology of Ignorance in the Study of Racism and Racial Non-Knowing," *Sociology Compass* (May 2018): 5.

[98]Ibid.

[99]Robin DiAngelo, *White Fragility: Why It's So Hard for White People to Talk about Racism* (Boston: Beacon Press, 2018), 51 and 149.

[100]Bonilla-Silva, *Racism without Racists*, 82–84.

[101]Ibid., 84.

[102]Joe Feagin, *Racist America: Roots, Current Realities, and Future Reparations*, 2nd ed. (New York: Routledge, 2010), 89.

an entire social ecosystem. Bonilla-Silva and other social scientists find that White people are not likely to engage in interracial relationships that include a high degree of interaction, interdependence, and closeness, despite their self-professed support for racial equality. Scholars agree that whatever cultural nuances there may be in the meaning of "friendship," it typically involves a high degree of "*interaction, interdependence*, and *closeness*."[103] Regardless of the level of assimilation of Black Americans, white geographical isolation from Black people does not "provide fertile soil upon which primary interracial associations can flourish."[104]

The problem of white habitus is that it offers a cauldron for the reproduction of white dominance in the power dynamics of public policy and public action in the neighborhood, state, and nation. The mechanisms of white habitus include physical, social, and moral distancing from African Americans, along with White people's sense of superiority, fear of racialized others, and intra-white solidarity. Most significantly, profound evil derives from White people's lack of empathy for racialized others, especially African Americans, and from an inability to perceive that we need others in order to become fully human and open to intimate transformation in God's love.

In his reflections titled "The Souls of White Folk" in *Darkwater*, W. E. B. Du Bois warned, "Of them I am singularly clairvoyant. . . . Rather I see these souls undressed and from the back and side. I see the workings of their entrails."[105] We need God's grace to see ourselves as Du Bois sees us. Concluding his reflection on white souls, Du Bois wrote, "I hear a mighty cry throughout the world, 'I am white!' Well and good, O Prometheus, divine thief!" Du Bois exposes our egomaniacal deceit and violence. If you find your finger pointing at the megalomaniac who occupied the White House from 2017 to 2021 pause, and reflect on how he is only symptomatic of a deeper malaise within white culture. As we cry, "I am white and innocent!" within white habitus, we only obscure, as Ta-Nehisi Coates writes to his son, how our racism "dislodges brains, blocks airways, rips muscle, extracts organs, cracks bones, breaks teeth. You must never look away from this."[106] White reader: before you retreat to the safety of self-perceived innocence, stop, quiet yourself, and dwell with the ways our African American brothers and sisters see us. Hear Du Bois and Coates: do not look away from our own violence.

Yet that is precisely what we who believe we are white do: we look away from the problem of violence that is within us. We deny how our way of life destroys the planet. If we do take any time to look at this violence it is only from the security of our own comfort zone. I include myself in these ranks. For

---

[103]Bonilla-Silva, *Racism without Racists*, 124.
[104]Ibid.
[105]W. E. B. Du Bois, *Darkwater* (New York: Washington Square Press, 2004), 21.
[106]Ta-Nehisi Coates, *Between the World and Me* (New York: Spiegel & Grau, 2015), 10.

too long I have attempted to create a kind of safe zone where White people might learn how we perpetuate violence against Black and Brown people and the Earth. No matter how much my anti-racism cofacilitators and I attend to the fragility of White people, invariably, White people resort to evading responsibility, denying complicity, claiming innocence, and minimizing the multiple ways we hurt others and the planet. We believe we can have it both ways; that is, we think we can maintain a foundation of the system—white comfort and safety—while we extend forms of charity that may alleviate some pain but do not change the systemic relationship between privilege and oppression.

Retrieving Du Bois's insights into the "souls of white folk" is a critical way that White people can address our own complicity in racism, a way that we may yet resist white dominance. We need to sit with the soulful gift offered by philosopher George Yancy.[107] Recall that Yancy takes his cue from Frantz Fanon's experience of being marked by a White child telling his mother, "Look, a Negro!" Abhorrently, we White folks say, "Look, a Negro!" every day in where and how we live—we're implicitly saying that when we live in predominantly White neighborhoods and attend largely White churches and schools.

Our white comfort zone is where we White folks embody anti-black white supremacy. That is the segregated area where we massage each other with countless deceptions. Our segregated homes, churches, schools, and minds are where we fail to confront the real problem: ourselves. The point is not to wallow in self-pitying or self-loathing. What we do need is to face reality. We need to face the temptations of our own fragility and comfort that prevent us from seeing and feeling the pain we cause Black and Brown people and the planet. We need to recognize where and how we actually live before we might be able to embrace Jesus's call to the transformative love of neighbors who are Black.

That means seeing ourselves the ways our Black and Brown kin see us. Yancy finds one of the many gifts African Americans have given to whites in a 1963 KQED documentary, *Take This Hammer*, featuring James Baldwin. Listening to the experience of African Americans in San Francisco, which prides itself on its progressive cosmopolitanism, Baldwin says to White people, "But you still think, I gather, that the 'nigger' is necessary. But he's unnecessary to me, so he must be necessary to you. I give you your problem back. You're the 'nigger,' baby; it isn't me."[108] Baldwin is clear that the derogatory term derives from the white mind and reflects the white mind-set. The term

[107]Yancy, *Look, a White!*, 5.

[108]James Baldwin in the KQED documentary *Take This Hammer*, https://www.youtube.com/watch?v=Hy9z_Jo8Du0, quote at 41:53 and following. Quotes in Yancy, *Look, a White!*, 5.

has nothing to do with Baldwin or any Black person. Or, as Yancy describes Baldwin's "incredible psychological insight," another way of framing the question is "'Will the real nigger please stand up?' Ah, yes, 'Look, a White!' "[109] The point is that the source of anti-blackness expressed in the epithet is and has been rooted in white culture for centuries.

It is time we take responsibility for our problem. It is time that we see how we White people create violence in word and deed. We need to feel, see, and hear how whiteness prevents us from taking up Jesus's admonition, "Whoever seeks to protect [their] life will lose it, but whoever loses it will save it" (Lk 17:33). In response, Pastor Lynice Pinkard invites us to practice "revolutionary suicide."[110] She does not mean to literally kill ourselves. Rather, it is a way of grasping the transformation Jesus invites us to undertake. Salvation is not primarily or exclusively an individual matter. Salvation is collective and interwoven within the whole of God's intimate creation. We need to give up everything to save ourselves and the planet (I return to this point in the last chapter). Furthermore, she says, we cannot "return to the bargaining table."[111] The cost of discipleship,[112] the cost of following Jesus in North America today, "is people's willingness to pay with their own lives."[113] Putting Jesus's admonition in other words, to the extent we collectively maintain white privilege and power, we lose our lives. However, when we work with God's grace and our neighbors to unlearn and undo white privilege and power, then we create the condition of the possibility of sharing in collective liberation from a culture of domination.

---

[109]Ibid.

[110]Lynice Pinkard, "Revolutionary Suicide: Risking Everything to Transform Society and Live Fully," *Tikkun Magazine* 28, no. 4 (Fall 2013): 31–41.

[111]Ibid., 32.

[112]Dietrich Bonhoeffer, *The Cost of Discipleship* (London: SCM Press, 1959). Translated from the German *Nachfolge* (Kaiser Verlag München and R. H. Fuller, 1937).

[113]Pinkard, "Revolutionary Suicide," 32.

3

The Roman Catholic Origins
of Coloniality

Taking up the task of unlearning white supremacy necessarily entails the work of tracing the origins of anti-blackness in European Christendom. The Roman Catholic papacy is an originating source of the "darker side of Western modernity," the coloniality of being, and what Walter Mignolo calls the "colonial matrix of power."[1] Recall, in chapter 1, that Mignolo traces the genealogy of coloniality to Catholic Christian theology that "located the distinction between Christians, Moors, and Jews in the 'blood.'"[2] The point is that "The historical foundation of the colonial matrix (and Western civilization) was theological."[3] Mignolo describes the historical shift in which "theology was displaced by secular philosophy and sciences."[4] The social and historical genealogy of the colonial matrix of power involves a very subtle transformation from the theological to the secular foundation of modernity/coloniality. Too often a historical separation, rather than a distinction, is asserted between theology and the "secular." "So, the struggle between *theologism* (I need the neologism here) and secularism," Mignolo explains, "was a family feud. Proponents of both were Christian, white, and male, and assumed heterosexual relations as the norm—consequently they also classified gender distinctions and sexual normativity."[5]

The concepts, ideologies, and classification systems for racism are social, political, and historical products. This chapter contextualizes the historical emergence of one form of racism: anti-black white supremacy. My previous scholarship notes that historical forms of racism are mercurial precisely be-

---

[1] Walter Mignolo, *The Darker Side of Western Modernity: Global Futures, Decolonial Options* (Durham, NC: Duke University Press, 2011), 8, 78.
[2] Ibid., 8.
[3] Ibid.
[4] Ibid., 9.
[5] Ibid. (italics in original).

cause they are not natural, biological, or genetic.[6] This chapter pays attention
to shifting rationalizations and justifications for different forms of racisms[7]
(rather than "racism," as if it were one "natural" thing). Rather, it is "the
struggle for the monopoly of social power that is at stake with racism and
racial theory."[8] Anti-black white supremacy emerged within the historical
struggle of the Roman Catholic hierarchy to monopolize social power and
control of the world.

Catholic theologian M. Shawn Copeland advances five theses to com-
prehend, analyze, and evaluate "the relation of American Catholicism to
anti-blackness and white supremacy."[9] Her first thesis laments the "acute and
painful irony" of the "Catholic sanctioning of the colonization *of* and trade
in flesh."[10] This irony is the fact that at the center of Catholic theology and
worship is the "broken and bruised flesh" of the "person of the Jew Jesus of
Nazareth, God become flesh, lived *with* us and *for* us."[11] In other words, the
Catholic sanctioning of the African slave trade is nothing less than a coun-
terscandal to the gospel of Jesus Christ.

In her second thesis, Copeland laments further that "despite [Catholi-
cism's] reverence for Being and beings; despite its intense sacramental, and,
therefore symbolic character; despite its intimate knowledge of, irrevocable
and essential relation to flesh—

> racialization of flesh has shaped Christianity, and thus Roman Ca-
> tholicism almost from its very origins: women, Jews, people of color
> (especially, indigenous and black peoples) have undergone metaphysi-
> cal violence. . . . In the highly profitable commodification of flesh, this
> specious union of colonial and ecclesiastical power decidedly abused
> religion and the religious.[12]

The term "metaphysical violence" is philosopher Gianni Vattimo's description
of the "attempt to master the real by force,"[13] that is, the Catholic sanctioning

[6]See Alex Mikulich, "Mapping 'Whiteness': The Complexity of Racial Formation and the Subversive Moral Imagination of the Motley Crowd," *Journal of the Society of Christian Ethics* 25, no. 1 (Spring/Summer 2005): 99–122; and "Where Y'at Race, Whiteness, and Economic Jus-tice? A Map of White Complicity in Economic Oppression of People of Color," in *The Almighty and the Dollar: Christian Reflections on* Economic Justice for All, ed. Mark Allman (Winona, MN: Anselm Academic, 2012), 189–213.

[7]Francisco Bethencourt, *Racisms: From the Crusades to the Twentieth Century* (Princeton, NJ: Princeton University Press, 2013), 1.

[8]Ibid., 6.

[9]M. Shawn Copeland, "Anti-Blackness and White Supremacy in the Making of American Catholicism," *American Catholic Studies* 127, no. 3 (Fall 2016): 6.

[10]Ibid. (italics in original).

[11]Ibid. (italics in original).

[12]Ibid., 7.

[13]Ibid. Copeland cites Gianni Vattimo, "Towards an Ontology of Decline," in *Reading Meta-physics: The New Italian Philosophy*, ed. Giovanni Borradori (Evanston, IL: Northwestern

of the colonization and commodification of human beings that enslaved and dehumanized Africans and exterminated Indigenous Peoples. This attempt at best contradicts, if not eviscerates, the central Roman Catholic theological and spiritual claims that all human beings share in the divine likeness (*imago Dei*) within the unity of God's creation.

As Copeland explains in her third thesis, the racialization and commodification of flesh was so deeply attached to and defined against the black body that it "spawned subtle and perverse 'anti-black logics' that took root in cognition, language, meanings, and values, thereby reshaping nearly all practices of human encounter and engagement."[14] This process began with a series of papal bulls[15] in 1444 that sanctioned, legitimized, and authorized the Portuguese to initiate enslavement of people and expropriate the lands of Africa on Catholic theological terms.[16] A critical consequence of these anti-black logics, Copeland explains in her fourth thesis, "repressed the demands of conscience, obscured morality, and eclipsed ethics to induce authority and authorities to kneel before the racialized idol of whiteness."[17] In this context of ecclesial idolization of whiteness and indifference to human beings who are Black, Copeland's fifth thesis celebrates how "God's black human creatures have improvised authenticity of life and worship in struggle, in ways that were and are spiritually defiant, intellectually imaginative, culturally creative, [and] socially interdependent—in *uncommon faithfulness.*"[18]

Against this reality, however, American Catholic priest and US military chaplain Joel Panzer orients his study of the popes and slavery with this question: "When did the Roman Catholic Church condemn slavery?" His question is rhetorical, as he answers it himself this way:

> If it was not 1890, or even 1965, then a great shadow has been cast upon the Magisterium. If, however, it can be shown that the Magisterium

---

University Press, 1988), 64.

[14]Copeland, "Anti-Blackness and White Supremacy," 7.

[15]A papal "bull" is an apostolic letter or brief issued by the Roman Catholic pope that asserts a solemn decree or pronouncement of ecclesial privilege or grants a right or authority. The term "bull" derives from the seal attached to the document, called a "bulla." In the context of the transatlantic enslavement of Black Africans, Pius Onyemechi Adiele refers to "those papal official Decrees issued to the Portuguese Royal Crown granting her right of ownership over the territories discovered in her name in Africa as well as empowering her to drive the natives of those territories into perpetual slavery." See Adiele, *The Popes, the Catholic Church, and the Transatlantic Enslavement of Black Africans, 1418–1839* (Hildesheim, Germany: Georg Olms Verlag, 2017), 250n 94.

[16]Sylvia Wynter, "Unsettling the Coloniality of Being/Power/Truth/Freedom: Towards the Human, after Man, Its Overrepresentation: An Argument," *CR: The New Centennial Review* 3, no. 3 (Fall 2003): 291.

[17]Copeland, "Anti-Blackness and White Supremacy," 7.

[18]Ibid., 8 (italics in original). She cites M. Shawn Copeland, LaReine-Marie Mosely, and Albert Raboteau, eds., *Uncommon Faithfulness: The Black Catholic Experience* (Maryknoll, NY: Orbis Books, 2009).

condemned from the beginning the colonial slavery that developed in
the newly discovered lands, then it may be necessary for some historians and others to revise their opinions of that teaching office, and the
Catholic Church as well.[19]

Panzer does not even raise the possibility that fifteenth-century popes may
have been complicit in, and even bless, the inauguration of the transatlantic
slave trade. *The Popes and Slavery* assumes nearly complete papal innocence
in regard to the slave trade. It is difficult to regard Panzer's book as a critical
study of the popes and slavery when its entire orientation is based upon the
claim that the popes always condemned racial slavery and were never complicit in it. As the historical theologian Pius Onyemechi Adiele writes in his
exhaustive study of the papacy and the initiation of the Atlantic slave trade,
Panzer's book is "a bid to wash the hands of the popes clean from the shame
of the enslavement [and] ignored to mention the many Apostolic Letters with
which the popes of the Church not only called this enslavement into being
but also continued to propagate its existence."[20]

In her otherwise masterful compendium of Roman Catholic social teaching
on racism, tribalism, and xenophobia, Catholic ethicist Dawn Nothwehr raises
a "cautionary note" on the political climate and the power of the papacy in
the Age of Discovery, pointing out that "the Roman pontiffs, as the ultimate
authority in Christendom, established international laws and solidified relationships among nations."[21] She does not intend to call Renaissance imperial
papal power to account for its teaching and practice, however. In her introduction to papal denunciations of slavery, she cautions that "moral teaching
is not necessarily adhered to by the faithful, especially when there are vast
inconsistencies in the teaching, the teachers are of questionable character,
or when obviously political and economic enterprises and favoritism are
involved."[22] I believe she misses the point here—the primary problem is not
that "moral teaching is not necessarily adhered to by the faithful," but rather
the moral teaching itself and the witness the papacy pursued as it asserted
its power over the world. Regrettably, Nothwehr does not discuss how the
Vatican and the papacy sanctioned the racialization and commodification of
human beings. In fact, far from merely propagating "vast inconsistencies" in
magisterial[23] teaching due to the questionable character of individual popes

[19]Joel S. Panzer, *The Popes and Slavery* (New York: Alba House, 1996), 6. Panzer's use of the term "Magisterium" in referring to fifteenth-century popes is anachronistic; see note 23, this chapter.
[20]Adiele, *The Popes*, 6.
[21]Dawn M. Nothwehr, *That They May Be One: Catholic Social Teaching on Racism, Tribalism, and Xenophobia* (Maryknoll, NY: Orbis Books, 2008), 43.
[22]Ibid.
[23]I recognize that it would be anachronistic to use the terms "magisterial" or "magisterium"

or their political or economic favoritism for Portuguese kings, the historical record of papal, theological, and moral teaching and practice initiates, supports, and legitimates enslavement. Panzer's work in particular failed "to mention the many Apostolic Letters with which the popes of the Church not only called this enslavement into being but also continued to propagate its existence."[24]

Catholic historical theologian Pius Onyemechi Adiele laments that Panzer did not discuss how the papal bulls *Dum Diversas* and *Romanus Pontifex* of Pope Nicholas V in 1452 and 1454, respectively, as well as those of Nicholas's successors up to Pope Leo X in 1514, "supported and blessed the Transatlantic enslavement of Black Africans."[25]

Roman Catholic theology and papal teaching, I contend, form a primary source of the darker side of Western modernity and the "coloniality of being/power/truth/freedom,"[26] to borrow philosopher Sylvia Wynter's enveloping phrase. I now turn to the primary theological traditions that set the stage for the Church's leadership in establishing African enslavement.

Setting the Stage for African Enslavement

In his authoritative study examining the leading role of the papacy and the Roman Catholic Church in the transatlantic slave trade, Adiele describes four foundational Church teachings that set the conditions for the role the Church played in the enslavement of Black Africans.[27] Adiele's study is nothing less than a grace-filled gift to the Church; it helps set conditions for the possibility of healing and repairing the colonial wound for which the Church is so deeply responsible. Those conditions include procuring a mature understanding of the depth of the Church's sinfulness and its subsequent responsibility to atone for, repent, and repair this deep historical wound.

The Catholic Church's four foundational traditions that Adiele singles

---

in reference to fifteenth-century papacy, as is done today when referring to the Church's "teaching authority." However, as John Mahoney notes, "The specifically teaching aspect of the term is to be found in reference to the *magisterium* of the Church Fathers, and from [the thirteenth century with] the development of the theological schools, as the title of Master, or *Magister*, was being accorded to those who gave public teaching, so the teaching activity . . . was referred to as their *magisterium*." See John Mahoney, *The Making of Moral Theology: A Study of the Roman Catholic Tradition* (Oxford: Oxford University Press, 1987), chapter 4, "Teaching with Authority," 116–17 and following. I use the terms "magisterial" and "magisterium" in this more limited historical sense of teaching activity in reference to the medieval papacy.

[24]Adiele, *The Popes*, 6.

[25]Ibid. See note 12.

[26]Wynter, "Unsettling the Coloniality of Being/Power/Truth/Freedom."

[27]The extraordinary quality of Adiele's scholarship is grounded in its comprehensiveness and in his enjoyment of "unhindered access" to the Vatican Secret Archives. See Adiele, *The Popes*, xiv.

out are its teaching toward non-Catholics, its concept of worldwide ecclesi-astical authority, the Crusades as missions to regain lost territories, and its position on the right (or lack thereof) of "infidels or pagans to property."[28] We discuss all four traditions in turn, beginning with the Church's stance on those outside its fold.

One of the most basic and consequential teachings of the medieval Church concerned the fate of non-Christians at the end of time. Church member-ship was an absolute condition for the possibility of salvation. The Church always taught that "*extra Ecclesiam nulla salus* (outside the Church there is no salvation)."[29] Saint Cyprian of Carthage (200–258) coined the term; the teaching was reaffirmed by Pope Innocent III in 1215 and Pope Boniface VIII in 1302. Pope Eugene IV, who would be instrumental in establishing the transatlantic slave trade, reaffirmed the teaching in his 1441 bull *Can-tate Domino*, which stated that "none of those existing outside the Catholic Church, not only Pagans but also Jews, Heretics and Schismatics can have a share in eternal life," and that "they will go into the eternal fire."[30] This teaching forms "the very backbone" of how the medieval Church viewed non-Christians, "and served as the prism through which she viewed and treated non-European people especially the Black Africans."[31] The issue is not only that all people who are "outside of the Church" will be damned, but also that they are "classified as enemies of the Church" who must be brought into the Church by "brute force and subjection."[32] The division between who is and is not saved was a "decisive factor" that informed the most critical Church teachings, including the fifteenth-century bulls that initiated "racial slavery in history."[33] This teaching formed one of the foundations for renaissance popes "to give their authority to the various kings of Portugal . . . to carry out war against Black Africans in the form of fighting a religious Crusade."[34]

Supersessionism

One of the critical problems of this teaching concerning nonbelievers, in terms of God's desire that Jesus be the One for the many (Jn 17:21), is its "supersessionism" or theology of replacement. "Jesus is Jewish," observes theologian Willie James Jennings, "and it is a sad and grotesquely ironic reality that the supersessionist moment in Christian theology was enabled

---

[28]Ibid., 215.
[29]Ibid.
[30]Ibid., 216.
[31]Ibid., 217.
[32]Ibid.
[33]Ibid.
[34]Ibid., 218.

through Christian reflection on Jesus Christ."[35] The teaching that there is no salvation outside of the Church is tricky. On the one hand, as Jennings celebrates, it captures the central action of the Church: "seeking and desiring the salvation of all peoples."[36] On the other hand, however, in "supersessionist thinking the church replaces Israel in the mind and heart of God."[37] Jennings describes this teaching as a profound distortion of the Christian theological imagination. Not only does the Church replace "European for Jew," but "the very process of becoming Christian took on new ontic markers" that are aesthetic and racial.[38] A fateful consequence of this teaching was that in the first Crusade in the 1010s, Jews were massacred in "Rouen, Orleans, and Limoges as well as in Mainz and other cities of the Rhine."[39] Crusaders "pillaged and murdered" thousands of Jews throughout cities in western and central Europe (current France and Germany) and "led to massive forced conversions."[40] The ultimate consequence of this teaching and its crusading mission meant that only "the white body would be a discerning body, able to detect holy effects and saving grace."[41]

But the Church's supersessionist turn was neither necessary nor inevitable. The patristic theology of Gregory of Nyssa and the Cappadocians, theologian J. Kameron Carter explains, expresses an ecclesiology in which "the church, in being the social space that is humanity—a Jewish, covenantal humanity—of Jesus of Nazareth, must be conceived of inside of Israel's covenantal relationship with YHWH."[42] In other words, writes Carter, "ecclesiology is Israelology, but only by means of the mediation of Jesus of Nazareth, the Messiah of Israel who is Head of the Church."[43] Put in metaphorical musical terms, patristic theologians articulated a melody of divine unity in which our human "riffing within it [w]as the transformation of our mode of existence beyond divisions of self-enclosure and into the ecclesial or churchly harmonics of Israel-Christ. To be attuned to the divine harmonics is to play Israel's covenantal song."[44] A Christ that is severed from his Jewishness and Israel is not only "deeply mistaken" for Christology, concludes Carter, but also

---

[35]Willie James Jennings, *The Christian Imagination: Theology and the Origins of Race* (New Haven, CT: Yale University Press, 2010), 259.

[36]Ibid., 26.

[37]Ibid., 32.

[38]Ibid., 33.

[39]Bethencourt, *Racisms*, 30–31.

[40]Ibid., 31.

[41]Jennings, *Christian Imagination*, 33–34.

[42]J. Kameron Carter, *Race: A Theological Account* (New York: Oxford University Press, 2008), 420n25. Carter cites the scholarship of historical theologian Brian E. Daley, "Nature and 'Mode of Union': Late Patristic Models for the Personal Unity of Christ," in *The Incarnation: An Interdisciplinary Symposium on the Incarnation of the Son of God*, ed. Stephen T. Davis, Daniel Kendall, and Gerald O'Collins (New York: Oxford University Press, 2002).

[43]Carter, *Race*, 420n25.

[44]Ibid., 166–67.

delivers "deleterious consequences" that move toward "making whiteness and Western civilization coeval with Christianity."[45]

Papacy as Empire

The second constitutive teaching revealing the Church's quest for power and its role in African enslavement is closely tied up with the first. If the seed of this teaching and inauguration of Christian empire were not inaugurated in the fourth century with Emperor Constantine's affirmation of Christianity, they definitively were by Pope Leo III on Christmas Day 800 CE at Saint Peter's Basilica in Rome, when he consecrated Charlemagne as emperor of the Holy Roman Empire.[46] "It was by this brilliant gesture," asserts historian Brian Tierney, "that papal coronation was essential to the making of the emperor, and thereby implanted the germ of the later idea that the empire itself was a gift to be bestowed by the papacy."[47] The germination of this idea, whereby the pope would be synonymous with empire, becomes a cornerstone for the Church's use of brute force and subjection against nonbelievers. A Constantinian, imperial approach to Christianity is evidenced, for example, in the argument that in "union with her husband and head, the church is a warrior bride, called to carry out wars in and with him."[48]

Pope Gelasius I (492–496), in a dispute with the Byzantine emperor Anastasios I, was the first pope who claimed superior authority due to his sacred role.[49] Later, two medieval canonists played a critical role in advancing the universal authority of the pope to rule the "Orbis Christianus" (the Christian world). Italian canonist Tancred of Bologna (1185–1230) asserted in his "De Translatione Episcopi" that "whatever is done by authority of the Lord pope is done by the authority of God."[50] Archbishop and canonist Niccolo Panoramitanus (1386–1445) articulated the same point from a divine angle: "The pope can do whatever God can do."[51] Papal authority was not merely ecclesiastical and spiritual; canonists, theologians, and popes established the pope as a political and spiritual world emperor directly overseeing "all men and their affairs irrespective of religion, time, and place."[52]

---

[45] Ibid., 420–21.

[46] Adiele, *The Popes*, 221.

[47] Ibid. Adiele quotes Brian Tierney, *The Crisis of Church and State, 1050–1300* (Englewood Cliffs, NJ: Prentice-Hall, 1964), 18.

[48] Peter Leithart, *Defending Constantine: The Twilight of Empire and the Dawn of Christendom* (Downers Grove, IL: InterVarsity Press, 2010), 335.

[49] Adiele, *The Popes*, 218–19.

[50] Ibid., 219.

[51] Ibid.

[52] Ibid.

Adiele's comprehensive historical scholarship underscores how seven popes from the early eleventh century to the fourteenth century formalized and instituted a hierocratic concept of global papal jurisdiction. Intimately connected to the Catholic Church's view of nonbelievers, the pontiff's supreme authority over the entire world meant that the Church must save souls and bring nonbelievers into the fold. The Church justified war against Africans and their enslavement "based on this concept of authority that non-Catholics (pagans) were denied their fundamental rights to lordship, dominion, and to possess private belongings," and because "they do not belong to the Church under command of the pope."[53] Consequentially, when popes issued fifteenth-century bulls authorizing the kings of Portugal to invade West Africa and enslave its inhabitants, the kings believed "they were backed up by the unchallengeable authority of the popes, upon which they heavily relied in establishing the Transatlantic slave trade."[54]

The Crusades

The Roman Catholic crusading mission to reconquer former Christian lands forms the third foundational teaching for African enslavement. However, the notion of "a holy war as a personal and collective duty was alien to the Christian tradition."[55] The initiation of the Crusades thus constituted a major turning point in Christendom, both because they "gave ideological expression to an enormous process of expansion and conquest," and because they "unleashed new forms of religious persecution and new concepts of ethnic hierarchy."[56] Catholic Crusades were a way to practice papal dominion and to bring nonbelievers into the fold.

Augustinian and Thomistic just war teaching provided an integral theological justification for reconquering the Holy Land. In just war terms, the Crusade was a religious holy war in which the pope ruled the world as *vicarius Dei*. Therefore, papal power "extended even 'to all places irrespective of whether they were once under Christian dominion or not.' "[57] The religious character of the Crusade was expressed by the preacher John of Abbeville in 1217 as the capture of "our inheritance" of the Holy Land, and that this place "where Christ was buried and suffered is our home. And this inheritance is seized, the Holy places profaned, the holy cross is made a captive."[58] One of the

---

[53]Ibid., 226.
[54]Ibid., 227.
[55]Bethencourt, *Racisms*, 19.
[56]Ibid., 20.
[57]Adiele, *The Popes*, 230.
[58]Ibid.

most influential clergy of the medieval Church, Saint Bernard of Clairvaux, employed the imagery of two swords that joined the religious and political missions to summon Pope Eugene III (1145–1153) to Crusade:

> Now will Christ endure a second passion where He endured His first, both swords, the material as well as the spiritual must be unsheathed. And by whom but thee? For the two swords are Peter's, to be drawn whenever necessary, the one by his own hand, the other by his authority.[59]

Utilizing the power of these "two swords," Pope Urban II called upon French kings and all the faithful to rise up and take up the cross in defense of God and their brethren in the Holy Land on November 27, 1095.[60] Urban II declared that anyone who died in the Crusade "shall have immediate remission of sins."[61] While Urban II's appeal to Christians inspired passion and fury "in the hearts of his hearers," he also inflamed "seeds of hatred" and "resentment" between Catholics and Muslims that linger to this day.[62] Adiele illustrates how these "negative portrayals of the Saracens in the preaching of the first Crusade" were "later transferred over to the pagan natives of West Africa in the fifteenth and sixteenth centuries."[63]

Dispossession of Unbelievers

The fourth teaching, which is also integral to the previous three, declared that the pope "has authority to declare war on infidels and pagan territories and can order their inhabitants to be dispossessed of their lands and personal belongings."[64] Adiele describes an exhaustive debate among canonists in the thirteenth century who did not see dispossession of pagan lands and property as a foregone conclusion. The significance of that debate, briefly stated, is that some canonists applied natural law to argue that nonbelievers possessed the right to private property, meaning the Church could not dispossess non-Christians of their land or property. Fatefully, the Church did not follow the teaching of Saint Thomas Aquinas, who argued that heathens and Jews "are by no means to be compelled to the faith" because the "lack of faith is not sinful provided that it is a product of a lack of knowledge, and in this case, it is not justified to make wars against them."[65] This debate was also tempered

---

[59]Ibid., 232.
[60]Ibid., 233.
[61]Ibid., 234.
[62]Ibid., 235.
[63]Ibid., 236.
[64]Ibid., 240.
[65]Ibid., 242. Adiele cites Thomas Aquinas, *Summa Theologiae*, II, iiae, q.x. Art 8.

by the precepts of universal love and charity, "which militated against the expulsion of non-Christians from their lands."[66] Sadly, however, upon the inauguration of the Atlantic slave trade, love and charity did not become the operative precepts that oriented the practice of the Roman Catholic hierarchy.

The canonist Giles of Rome (1243–1316), a contemporary and student of Thomas Aquinas, rejected his master's teaching. In his treatise on papal power, "De Ecclesiastica Poteste," Giles argued that even though unbelievers received their possessions from God, "They are unjustly in possession of all that they possessed because they have not subjected themselves to God."[67] Two contemporaries of Giles, Bishop Guilelmus de Amidanis (1270–1356) and Cardinal Petrus Bertrandi (1280–1349), upheld that unbelievers had no right to land or property unless they submitted to the pope. Pope Innocent IV (1243–1254), a canon lawyer himself, developed the just war argument by contesting "the occupation of the Holy land by Muslims by force" and "justified the Crusades as a defensive war," claiming "the western lands of the Roman Empire as the rightful inheritance of the papacy."[68] Cardinal Bertrandi bluntly stated the position that fifteenth-century popes would assert against Africans and their lands: "The pope was the rightful and lawful owner of the whole world."[69]

In summary, these four theological positions that interconnected the Church's teachings—toward non-Catholics, of worldwide ecclesiastical authority, on Crusades as mission to regain lost territories, and on rejection of the right of infidels or pagans to property—were foundational for the "medieval papacy's quest for control over all mankind—Christians and non-Christians alike."[70] This constellation of teachings, Adiele demonstrates, established

> the Transatlantic slave trade, which totally changed the normal course of events in the world and drastically affected millions of lives of men, women and children of Black African origin. It was therefore the aforesaid traditions of the Catholic Church that paved the way for this trade in humans. And the Church's very role in this slave trade traces its root first and foremost back to her justification of slavery based on the Aristotelian cum Thomistic ideas of slavery as well as to these traditions discussed above.[71]

[66]Bethencourt, *Racisms*, 40.
[67]Adiele, *The Popes*, 246–47.
[68]Bethencourt, *Racisms*, 40.
[69]Adiele, *The Popes*, 247.
[70]Ibid., 248.
[71]Ibid., 248–49.

The Papal Bulls That Inaugurated African Slavery

There were possibilities other than intolerance, hatred, and violent conflict between Judaism, Christianity, and Islam in medieval Europe. In her exploration of medieval Andalusian culture (the Islamic name for Spain), linguistic scholar María Rosa Menocal illuminates seven centuries from the 700s to the 1400s when these three major traditions all thrived together. She describes "a chapter of Europe's culture when Jews, Christians, and Muslims lived side by side, despite their intractable differences and enduring hostilities, [and] nourished a complex culture of tolerance."[72] For example, Qur'anic injunction demands that all Islamic polities do not harm and "tolerate the Christians and Jews living in their midst. But beyond that fundamental prescribed posture, al-Andalus was, from these beginnings, the site of memorable and distinctive interfaith relations."[73] These memorable relations included a tenth-century caliph who "had a Jew as his foreign minister."[74] Perhaps a more distinctive and vital dimension within Andalusian identity was "fruitful intermarriage among the various cultures that was cultivated over the first centuries."[75] That Christians adopted Arabic in their faith and liturgy[76] was seen by some as entirely appropriate and by others as a travesty. An example of the latter is the ninth-century Christian scholar Alvarus of Cordoba, who viewed Arabization as a betrayal of Christianity and lamented that "young men in the Christian community could not so much as write a letter in Latin but wrote (or aspired to write) odes in classical Arabic to rival those of the Muslims."[77] A critical point here is that in the complex context of conflictual and thriving interfaith relations, reconquering non-Christian lands was not the only option available to the Church.

Nevertheless, the Church sought a "Padroado Real" (Royal Marriage) with Portugal, and later Spain, as a means to defeat Islam and eventually to gain control of the African slave trade. Far from being a brief, incidental relationship of convenience, a whim of licentious popes, or an anomaly, the Portuguese Royal Crown's "request from the popes and its granting was as old as the institution of the first Portuguese Royal dynasty itself. It traces its origin to back to the time of the first king of Portugal Alfonso Henriques I (reigned 1128–1185) . . . who linked the Crown of Portugal

---

[72]Maria Rosa Menocal, *The Ornament of the World: How Muslims, Jews, and Christians Created a Culture of Tolerance in Medieval Spain* (Boston: Little Brown and Company, 2002), 11.
[73]Ibid., 30.
[74]Ibid.
[75]Ibid.
[76]Ibid., 69.
[77]Ibid., 29.

with the papacy during his reign precisely in 1143."[78] Pope Alexander III (1159–1181) granted Alfonso the protection of the Holy See, recognized Portugal as an official kingdom separate from that of Castile, and praised the king for his success in fighting Iberian Muslims.[79] This Royal Marriage not only approved of the Crusade against Islam on just war grounds, "the Crusade of Africa was carried out by the Portuguese Royal Crown with the authority of the renaissance papacy."[80] Following the consensus of ecclesiastical historians, Adiele defines the "renaissance papacy" as the period that began with the pontificate of Martin V (1417–1431) and lasted until Pope Clement VII (1523–1534).[81]

The Crusade of Africa, unlike Crusades to the Holy Land, had little concern for individual Christian life and practice. Rather, the enslavement of Black Africans "presented a new opportunity for the papacy to make a comeback on the international stage of exercising a universal and unlimited papal authority over the whole world," which it had lost under the "Babylonian exile" in Avignon (1305–1377) and the great Western schism of 1378–1417.[82] The Church played a major, primary role in colonizing and commodifying African peoples and lands.

Adiele locates the beginning of the Portuguese business monopoly in Africa in 1415, in the attack on the strategic port of Ceuta (now an autonomous Spanish city bordering Morocco), also known as "Septa" (city of seven hills, under Roman rule). According to historian John Ure, Ceuta was "a Terminal for the African trading caravans which came both along the Libyan coast from Egypt and Baghdad, and across the Sahara from the fabled Sudan and Timbuktu."[83] In other words, control of Ceuta constituted a strategic channel between the northern and southern Mediterranean through which gold "reached the Christian world from the distant and mysterious mines of Black Africa."[84]

"It was from this point forward," argues Adiele, that "Portugal began to make claims of ownership over the Atlantic Ocean and the whole region of West Africa."[85] Pope Martin V (1417–1431) gave papal authority to Portugal to invade Africa in his bull *Sane Charissimus* on April 4, 1418.[86] *Sane Charis-*

---

[78]Adiele, *The Popes*, 251.

[79]Ibid., 254.

[80]Ibid., 258.

[81]Ibid.

[82]Ibid., 258–59.

[83]Ibid., 263. Adiele quotes John Ure, *Prince Henry the Navigator* (Edinburgh: Constable, 1977), 54.

[84]Peter Russell, *Prince Henry "the Navigator": A Life* (New Haven, CT: Yale University Press, 2001), 14.

[85]Adiele, *The Popes*, 268.

[86]Ibid.

simus declared war and legitimized the Portuguese military raids on Africa, which were economically and politically motivated. Pope Martin V wrote,

> Therefore, we wish to communicate to you through this apostolic letter, patriarchs, archbishops, the chosen ones, administrators and prelates of the Church, that king John of Portugal intends to raise a strong and powerful army to fight against the unbelievers. If it is our wish to support this enterprise of king John as long as he lives, then it requires some armament in order to carry out successfully such a responsible and salutary enterprise.[87]

Pope Martin V appealed to all Christians to fast, pray, and give financial assistance to King John in the Crusade to Africa. In doing so, he became the "first pope of the Holy Roman Catholic Church who not only sanctioned but blessed the Portuguese plan of territorial expansion and business monopoly in Africa under the cover of spreading the gospel of salvation to Africa."[88]

Martin V reaffirmed this endeavor in his bull *Cum Charissimus* in 1419, admonishing all Christians to maintain financial support for Portugal in their "war against the so-called 'enemies.' "[89]

However, in the mid-1430s, when Prince Henry was planning to inaugurate a crusade by attacking Ceuta, powerful figures within the Portuguese court were questioning the legitimacy of the proposed crusade "in terms of canon law, [and] thus, by implication, also calling into question the right of the Portuguese to be in Ceuta."[90] In his discussion of King Duarte's deliberations on the matter of sanctioning Prince Henry's attack on Morocco, the scholar of Spanish and Portuguese studies Sir Peter Russell explains that the king was aware of "a body of international opinion, ecclesiastical and lay, which denied the unrestricted right of the papacy to authorize, or Christian princes to undertake, wars of conquest against infidel or pagan states because these did not belong to the Christian community."[91] As Russell notes, we see from examining deliberations within the Portuguese king's court and within the Vatican that it was far from a foregone conclusion that the papacy ought to sanction a Portuguese crusade in Africa, or even if it was legal to do so.

The historical documents in the Vatican archives show that Pope Eugene IV provided King Duarte with formal consultations written by the best-known canon jurists of the day, Antonio Minucci da Pratovecchio and Antonio de Rosellis, both professors of civil law at Bologna. Their scholarly *consulta*

---

[87]Ibid., 271.
[88]Ibid., 272.
[89]Ibid.
[90]Russell, *Prince Henry*, 136.
[91]Ibid.

were lengthy—thirty-four and twenty-two pages in the Vatican register, respectively—and reveal a century of debate that undermined the assumption that "the spiritual and temporal powers of the papacy were unlimited."[92] In Prince Henry's point of view, Russell reports, these scholarly perspectives were "decidedly disconcerting" precisely because they "were not members of the anti-papalist camp but were advisors to the curia."[93] These jurists found that the papacy did not have the right to dispossess Muslims of their territories just because of their religion. On the contrary, according to the law of nations (*jus gentium*), Muslims were entitled to their lands because "'dominion, possession and jurisdiction are permitted to infidels since they have been created not only for the benefit of faithful but for all rational creatures.'"[94] The papacy did possess de jure authority, these jurists argued, but not de facto jurisdiction of all peoples on earth because the pope is "Christ's vicar on earth." Exceptions to *jus gentium* would include instances in which infidels offended against natural law, or in which non-Christians "refused to allow missionaries to enter their lands to preach the gospel."[95]

More importantly, against an unlimited assertion of papal power, de Rosellis argued that infidels had "an indisputable right to rule themselves and resist force against anyone seeking to deprive them of that right," according to both natural law and divine law.[96] Only lawful just war causes, such as defense against a direct attack on the common good, would grant legitimacy for Christian princes or the pope to declare war on infidels. Pratovecchio made this point unambiguously in his argument that "proclaiming the intention to convert infidels to Christianity by force or simply to make them better persons did not constitute a just cause."[97] This contemporaneous debate provides a deeper context within which to evaluate the role of the papacy in the emergence of the Atlantic slave trade. Canon lawyers, *magistra*, the curia, and popes themselves were aware of an emerging body of moral teaching—from the writings of Ambrose of Milan, Augustine, Gratian, Aquinas, and Francisco de Vitoria in particular—that limited both the use of force by Christian princes and the papacy itself.

Simply stating that the Roman pontiffs are "the ultimate authority in Christendom" and that they "established international laws and solidified relationships among nations"[98] beginning in the fifteenth and sixteenth

---

[92]Ibid., 162.

[93]Ibid.

[94]Ibid. Russell cites the opinions written by the jurists in the fifteen-volume *Monumenta Henricina*, a comprehensive annotated collection of all known documents "bearing on Prince Henry's life and career." Here he cites *Monumenta Henricina*, 5:301, no. 140.

[95]Russell, *Prince Henry*, 162.

[96]Ibid., 163.

[97]Ibid.

[98]Nothwehr, *That They May Be One*, 43.

centuries precisely misses how the pontiffs asserted and claimed power over the world, and different actions they could have taken. Nothwehr writes that due to the immense papal power when the slave trade was initiated in the fifteenth century, "national leaders and powerful people" sought "the popes' legitimatization of their actions and explorations."[99] The implication of Nothwehr's argument is that the popes were passive agents as national leaders pursued geo-strategic priorities of no interest to the popes. Contrary to these assumptions, Adiele demonstrates a long history of popes actively sanctioning and participating in the Atlantic slave trade even when they may have been articulating moral arguments against it. For example, Pope Eugene IV's papal bull *Sicut Dudum* (1437) forbade the enslavement of Canary Islanders who were converting or had converted to Christianity but did not universally forbid slavery. This was due in part to the bull *Romanus Pontifex* (1436), in which Pope Eugene IV "granted to Portugal the exclusive right over the Canaries [that] were populated by the infidels so that Portugal could work 'for the propagation of the Christian name.' "[100] A second example of a contradiction in the medieval papacy's evaluation of slavery is Pope Paul III's *Sublimis Deus* (1537), which condemned enslavement of Indians who became or who were becoming Christian.[101] As Adiele observes, while Pope Paul III underscored the humanity and rationality of Indians, "his silence on the hot issue of the humanity of Black Africans is ipso facto his rejection of their humanity pure and simple."[102] The contradiction between papal condemnations of slavery, including popes throughout the fifteenth and sixteenth centuries, and their active complicity in condoning the Atlantic slave trade makes it difficult to imagine these popes were ignorant and unwilling participants in African enslavement.

Pope Eugene IV's bull *Dudum Cum* (1436) is a prime example of the papacy's ongoing assertion of its authority in order to dominate international affairs. *Dudum Cum* addressed complaints by King Eduard of Portugal about the king of Magazan (Castile in Spain), who felt "unjustly cheated" by the rights and grants over Africa given to King John I of Portugal in 1418 and 1419 by Pope Martin V.[103] While the Castilian king may have had a legitimate complaint, and although we know that Prince Henry constantly provided successive popes with "misleading information to help them help him," it is

---

[99]Ibid.

[100]John T. Noonan Jr., *A Church That Can and Cannot Change: The Development of Catholic Moral Teaching* (Notre Dame, IN: University of Notre Dame Press, 2005), 243. Noonan cites Charles Martial de Witte, "Les Bulles Pontificales et L'Expansion Portugaise au XV siècle," *Revue d'histoire ecclésiastique* 48 (1953): 703.

[101]Adiele, *The Popes*, 408.

[102]Ibid., 410.

[103]Ibid., 275.

difficult to portray Eugene IV as a passive or unwitting accomplice.[104] *Dudum Cum* reconfirms the papal grants and rights of ownership of the Atlantic islands (the Canaries) given to Prince Henry in the Royal Charter of 1433, which is a highly significant landmark in the development of the initial Portuguese monopoly in the African slave trade. Not only did the colonization of the Canary Islands serve Prince Henry's interest in securing geo-strategic control of the Atlantic slave trade, both Adiele and Russell argue that this charter initiated the colonial form of government that would become the norm in all of the Atlantic islands.[105]

In 1442, Eugene IV's bull *Etsi Suscepti* reconfirms Prince Henry's economic mission in the Atlantic islands and establishes Henry as the administrator of the Military Order of Christ,[106] whereby he was granted authority to exercise both temporal and spiritual power in all Portuguese islands in Africa.[107] Prince Henry and Portugal were thereby "totally in charge of the Church within his kingdom," including the power to appoint priests and bishops and to send missionaries to all Portuguese territories. *Etsi Suscepti* also granted these powers to the Military Order of Christ and Portugal to carry out this mission in Africa beyond the life of Prince Henry. Even more consequentially, Eugene IV issued another bull in 1442, *Illius Qui*, which granted the Military Order of Christ "the right to organize military raids and expeditions in Africa and gave blessing for indulgence for the forgiveness of sins of their members and all those who might lose their lives in the course of slave raids viewed as a Crusade against Africa by Prince Henry."[108] The pope closes *Illius Qui* with a warning of "excommunication and the eternal wrath of Apostles Peter and Paul" on all who would "venture to weaken or nullify the authority and grants of this Apostolic letter." This legitimated military raids and the enslavement of prisoners in Africa on just war grounds. Adiele concludes that *Illius Qui* bestowed "perpetual assurance" upon the Military Order of Christ that the papacy was fully behind their involvement in the slave trade and that they "had nothing to fear even in danger of death in the course of carrying out slave raids against the Saracens and other unbelievers in Africa."[109]

In August 1444, Prince Henry inaugurated the first ritual sale of African

---

[104]Ibid., 276.

[105]Ibid., 278.

[106]The Military Order of Christ, a "clerico-military order" composed of "monk-knights who made vows of poverty, chastity, and obedience and served as soldiers in the fight against the Infidel," replaced the international Order of Knights Templar that Pope Clement V disbanded in 1312. The Military Order of Christ gained the properties of the Knights Templar and most of its members. See Francis A. Dutra, *Military Orders in the Early Modern Portuguese World: The Orders of Christ, Santiago, and Avis* (Aldershot: Ashgate, 1988), 228.

[107]Adiele, *The Popes*, 282.

[108]Ibid., 283.

[109]Ibid., 288.

slaves in the port of Lagos, Portugal. Although privateers had previously sold slaves in Lagos, Prince Henry's chronicler, Gomes Eannes Azurara (known as Zurara), circulated detailed documentation and defense of this inaugural event of the Atlantic slave trade, in *The Chronicle of the Discovery and Conquest of Guinea*, to the royal court as well as to scholars, investors, and captains who read and circulated it throughout Portugal and Spain.[110] Zurara credits Lançarote da Ilha, one of Henry's primary henchmen and the royal tax collector, as the primary leader and organizer of Portugal's first slave-raiding expedition of six ships on Arguin Island (just off the coast of present-day Mauritania) in June 1444. Portugal utilized caravels, a unique ship, because they carried forty to fifty tons each and had the agility to move quickly to evade hostile craft.[111] Through the history of the slave trade, caravels and other ships were named *Our Lady of Mercy* or *Our Lady* (over 1,100 ships), *Jesus* (over 180 ships), or *St. Michael* and other Catholic male saints (over 1,100 ships).[112]

In early June 1444, the Portuguese mercilessly attacked the economically poor Sanhadja fishermen, one of the largest North African tribal confederations at that time, killing anyone who resisted without regard to age or sex in order to intimidate others into surrender.[113] About 235 men, women, and children were captured and carried to the caravels where they were bound and chained at the feet.[114] While some were kept in the hold, others were exposed to the worst weather on the long trip back to Portugal. Upon their arrival in August, Prince Henry decided to make a "major public spectacle"[115] of the disposal of these newly captured slaves in the port of Lagos. Prior to auctioning them, Prince Henry ritualized the event by providing one slave to the principal church in Lagos and another to the Franciscan convent on Cape Vincent as thanksgiving to God and "to give force to the claim that it was concern for the salvation of souls" that motivated his mission and service to the Church.[116]

---

[110]The following historians critically corroborate the major details of Zurara's account of the "Great Event" of 1444: Adiele, *The Popes*; Charles Raymond Beazley, *Prince Henry the Navigator: The Hero of Portugal and of Modern Discovery* (New York: G. P. Putnam & Sons, 1901); John Ure, *Prince Henry the Navigator* (London: Constable, 1977); M. Saunders, *A Social History of Black Slaves and Freedmen in Portugal: 1441–1555* (Cambridge: Cambridge University Press, 2010); Russell, *Prince Henry*; and Ibram X. Kendi, *Stamped from the Beginning: The Definitive History of Racist Ideas in America* (New York: Bold Type Books, 2016), 23.

[111]Russell, *Prince Henry*, 227.

[112]Thomas Hugh, *The Slave Trade: The Story of the Atlantic Slave Trade, 1440–1870* (New York: Simon and Schuster, 1997), 305.

[113]Russell, *Prince Henry*, 240.

[114]Ibid.

[115]Ibid., 241.

[116]Ibid., 242.

Perhaps most notably, and unexpectedly to the prince and his hench-men, was how the "common folk were enraged by seeing the separation of families of slaves," and how the chronicler Zurara himself was moved to tears.[117] Zurara describes the terrifying scene of families being separated as the auction was carried out:

> These people, assembled together on that open place, were an astonishing sight to behold. Among them were some who were quite white-skinned, handsome and of good appearance; others were less white, seeming more like brown men; others still were as black as Ethiopians, so deformed of face and body, that, to those who stared at them, it almost seemed that they were looking at spirits from the lowest hemisphere. But what heart, however hardened it might be, could not be pierced by a feeling of pity at the sight of that company? Some held their heads low, their faces bathed in tears as they looked at each other; some groaned very piteously, as if they were calling on the father of the universe to help them; others stuck their faces with their hands and threw themselves full length on the ground; yet others lamented in the form of a chant, according to custom of their native land, and though the words of the language in which they sang could not be understood by our people, the chant revealed clearly enough the degree of their grief. To increase their anguish still more, those who had charge of the division arrived and began to separate one from another. . . . As soon as the children who had been assigned to one group saw their parents in another they jumped up and ran towards them; mothers clasped their children in their arms and lay face downwards on the ground, accepting wounds with contempt for the suffering of their flesh rather than let their children be torn from them.[118]

In his discussion of "Zurara's tears," Willie James Jennings highlights a rare chapter in Zurara's chronicle that is set in the form of a "penitent prayer":

> O, Thou heavenly Father—who with thy powerful hand, without al-tercation of thy divine essence, govern all the infinite company of thy Holy City, and control all the revolutions of the higher worlds. . . . I pray Thee that my tears may not wrong my conscience; for it is not their religion, but their humanity that make mine weep in pity for their suf-ferings. And if the brute animals, with their bestial feelings, by a natural

---

[117]Saunders, *Social History of Black Slaves*, 35.
[118]Zurara, *Chronicle of Guinea*, quoted in Russell, *Prince Henry*, 242–43.

instinct understand the suffering of their own kind, what would Thou have my human nature to do on seeing before my eyes that miserable company, and remembering that they too are of the sons of Adam?[119]

Jennings observes that Zurara and his leader, Prince Henry, were not converted to the plight of the Africans—that is, they did not perceive and were not moved to end the injustice they were experiencing. However, Zurara's description "draws life from the pathos of those slaves."[120] Although Zurara and subsequent colonial masters might recognize the humanity of people whom they enslaved, his prayer seeks a "clear sign of God-ordained preeminence over black flesh."[121] Zurara employs "divine immutability to new use" to make it "work at the slave auction."[122] Zurara concludes his chronicle thus:

> The Infante [Henry] was there, mounted upon a powerful steed, and accompanied by his retinue, making distribution of his favors, as a man who sought to gain but a small treasure from his share; for of the forty-six souls that fell to him as his fifth, he made a speedy partition of these for his chief riches lay in his purpose; for he reflected with great pleasure upon the salvation of these souls that before were lost. And certainly his expectation was not in vain; for ... as soon as they understood our language they turned Christians with very little ado; and I who put together this history into this volume, saw in the town of Lagos boys and girls ... as good and true Christians as if they had directly descended, from the beginnings of the dispensation of Christ, from those who were first baptized.[123]

Jennings reveals how Zurara "wrote a passion narrative" that "reads the gestures of slave suffering inside the sufferings of Christ."[124] While many have given a lifeless description to this event as one of the originating moments of the Atlantic slave trade, Jennings observes that "something more urgent and life altering is taking place in the Christian world, namely, the auctioning of bodies without regard to any form of human connection."[125] This event is carried out "inside" of Christian society, "as part of the *communitas fidelium*."[126] Jennings describes how this moment distorts the Christian imagination and practice from that moment forward:

---

[119]Zurara, *Chronicle of Guinea*, quoted in Jennings, *Christian Imagination*, 17.
[120]Jennings, *Christian Imagination*, 17.
[121]Ibid., 18.
[122]Ibid.
[123]Ibid., 19. Jennings quotes the end of Zurara's *Chronicle of Guinea*.
[124]Ibid., 20.
[125]Ibid., 22.
[126]Ibid.

The auction will draw ritual power from Christianity itself while mangling the narrative it evokes, establishing a distorted pattern of displacement.

Christianity will assimilate the pattern of displacement. Not just slave bodies, but *displaced* slave bodies, will come to represent a natural state. From this position they will be relocated into Christian identity. The backdrop of their existence will be, from this moment forward, the market. Zurara narrates this horror of displacement within a strange new soteriological orientation. Divine immutability yields Christian character—an unchanging God wills to create Christians out of slaves and slaves out of those black bodies that will someday, the Portuguese hope, claim to be Christian.[127]

This theological, moral, and spiritual distortion and displacement inaugurate "a new creation" in which "Zurara invokes a scale of existence, with white at one end and black at the other end and all others placed in between."[128] This "new creation"—a worldwide hierarchy of being—was not established by the Portuguese alone, however.

Adiele indicts Pope Nicholas V's crowning of anti-black logic. In his bulls *Dum Diversas* of 1452 and *Romanus Pontifex* of 1454, Nicholas V employs the Aristotelian theory of natural slavery to assert that Africans "were slaves of nature whose enslavement was justified on the grounds of their barbarity and lack of enough wisdom to rule themselves and as such should be ruled and governed by the stronger and wiser Portuguese folk."[129] First, in *Dum Diversas*, Nicholas V not only affirms that Prince Henry is motivated by religious zeal but positively permits Portugal and Prince Henry "to invade, search out, dispossess the Saracen, pagans and other unbelievers . . . of all their kingdoms, possessions, lands, locations, villas and all movable and immovable properties and make them their own."[130] Nicholas V wrote "authoritatively" in *Dum Diversas* to King Alfonso V of Portugal:

> We grant to you by these present documents with our Apostolic authority, full and free permission to invade, search out, capture and subjugate the Saracens and pagans and any other unbelievers and enemies of Christ wherever they may be, as well as their kingdoms, duchies, counties, principalities, lands, towns, villas and other properties . . . and to reduce their persons to perpetual slavery. And appropriate all their kingdoms, commands, retainers, dominance, and other possessions, lands, towns, villas, and any possessions to yourself and to your successors on the

---

[127]Ibid.
[128]Ibid., 22–23.
[129]Adiele, *The Popes*, 315.
[130]Ibid., 312.

throne of Portugal in perpetuity. By reason of our apostolic authority, we allow you and your successors to use and enjoy these assets fully and freely.[131]

Adiele points to a geographical ambiguity in the text in that it seemingly does not specify where the "possessions" begin or end. Adiele cites the scholarship of historians Richard Raiswell and Werner Stein, who contend that the pope's references to "pagans" and "other enemies of Christ" were "applicable to the newly discovered lands of the West coast of Africa," and that "the ambiguity of the text" was intended to encourage "the Portuguese to extend their explorations further afield."[132]

Pope Nicholas V does much more than reaffirm *Dum Diversas* with his bull *Romanus Pontifex* in 1454. He acknowledges and reaffirms the papal grants of Popes Martin V and Eugene IV and the Royal Charter made to Prince Henry in 1443, and "raised its status to international law having binding force of law on all Christian kings, kingdoms and nations the world over."[133] Given that Portugal's business monopoly was a "source of irresistible economic interest" to kings and merchants, and as Prince Henry and Portugal flaunted their newfound success in the trade of African slaves, Adiele finds it unsurprising that the Venetian merchant Alvise Cadamasto (1432–1483) "quickly bought a license from Prince Henry" to engage in the slave trade himself.[134] Meanwhile, King Juan II of Spain (r. 1406–1454) "gave license to the duke of Medina Sidonia in 1449 to explore and exploit the land facing the Canary Islands south of Cape Bojador with the claim that his ancestors had earlier been in possession of this region of Africa."[135] In this context, as other European states and commercial interests were working to exploit "African gold and slaves," Nicholas V gives monopoly rights over African territories to Portugal.[136]

Enslavement by military force, rather than peaceful conversion, is "unmistakably" asserted by Nicholas V in *Romanus Pontifex*. The 1454 bull praises the Portuguese king and Prince Henry, noting that for a quarter-century,

with the greatest labor, danger, and expense, in very swift ships . . .[they] had explored and taken possession of very many harbours, islands, and seas, [and] they came at length to the province of Guinea. . . . Thence also many Guinea-men and other Negroes, taken by force, and some by

---

[131]Ibid.
[132]Ibid., 313–14.
[133]Ibid., 317.
[134]Ibid., 316.
[135]Ibid.
[136]Ibid., 317–18.

barter of unprohibited articles, or by other lawful contact of purchase have been sent to said kingdom [Portugal]. A large number of these have been converted to the Catholic faith, and it is hoped, by the help of divine mercy, that if such progress be continued with them, either these peoples will be converted to the faith or at least many of them will be gained for Christ.[137]

Adiele laments how the pope is "more concerned with the victimizers themselves and regretted the loss in human and material goods which Prince Henry suffered in the course of his slave-raids in Guinea."[138] More disconcertingly, not only does the papal legacy of depriving the peoples of West Africa of all rights, possessions, and freedom exacerbate "hatred against Islam," it also "crowned all the legacies and anti-black attitudes of the Church,"

> which ranged from her viewing Black African race as an accursed race of Ham punished with blackness of skin-color and perpetual enslavement, as a barbarous and an inferior race of people, that is good for nothing and synonymous with sin and all sorts of abominations, and worst of all, to her viewing the Black Africans as children of the evil One, enemies of the Christian faith, whose existence in this life should be extinguished like a wild fire by the Christians. This is the tradition which pope Nicholas V was fostering and implementing in this Bull by decreeing in the above citation that the Black Africans should be invaded, raided, deprived of all possessions and be forcefully held by the Portuguese Christians as slaves in perpetuity.[139]

Adiele documents, in exhaustive detail, how Pope Nicholas V was "no lone ranger"—his sanctioning of the colonization of Africa is in fact reaffirmed and reasserted by his successors from 1456 through 1514. The bull *Inter Caetera* (1456) of Pope Calixtus III confirms the rights given by Nicholas V, grants new requests, and supports Portugal's business monopoly in African enslavement.[140] Since the bulls of Nicholas V and Calixtus III failed to settle the disputes between Spain and Portugal, Pope Sixtus IV adjudicated a treaty between the two powers in 1479 and issued the bull *Aeterni Regis* in 1481. Sixtus IV reasserted papal authority as judge and arbiter of international law by inserting the full texts of the bulls of Nicholas V and Calixtus III in favor of Portugal's enslavement of Africans into *Aeterni Regis*. The bull unequivocally threatens all "who contravene our confirmation . . . and mandate" with

---

[137]Ibid., 322.
[138]Ibid.
[139]Ibid., 325.
[140]Ibid., 336–44.

"the wrath of Almighty God and of the blessed Apostles Peter and Paul."[141]

After Christopher Columbus made his so-called discovery of the "New World" in 1492 under the directives of the Spanish king and queen, Pope Alexander VI issued a series of bulls in 1493 that affirmed both Portugal's right to Africa and Spain's right to the lands and peoples of the "New World." The bull *Eximiae Devotionis* bestowed the same kinds of grants and privileges to Spain in the "New World" that Portugal had been granted over Africa by Nicholas V, Callixtus III, and Sixtus IV. This bull exacerbated the conflict between Portugal and Spain, and the Portuguese king "protested against" its "contradictory nature."[142] Alexander VI then attempted to adjudicate the conflict through the 1493 bull *Inter Caetera* and the subsequent Treaty of Tordesillas.

The Catholic imperial partition of the world begins with the Treaty of Tordesillas in 1494, argues Walter Mignolo, in which the pope draws a line that divides the north and south of the Atlantic to settle the dispute between Portugal and Spain. The pope's assertion of global authority is both political and epistemic, that is, it establishes the "modern" assumption that this division of the world is natural and right. Through this act of sovereign authority, Mignolo argues, the papacy plays a fundamental role in establishing the origin of international law and the constitution of modernity/coloniality and Western civilization. He explains:

> For the act of tracing a line dividing the Atlantic means that there is an epistemic sovereign: God has the knowledge backing up the legality of the decision, and He is also in control of the rules and acts of knowing. Although by the mid-sixteenth century the authority of the popes and monarchs began to be disputed by a group of legal theologians in Salamanca . . . the fact remains that global linear thinking . . . goes hand in hand with the origin of international law.[143]

Drawing upon Valentin Mudimbe's explication in *The Invention of Africa*, Sylvia Wynter explains how the series of papal bulls described above essentially conceded all non-European lands to the Portuguese king because these lands were defined as "not belonging to a Christian prince, were terra nullius (the 'lands of no one'), and so legitimately expropriated by Christian kings."[144] By naming an entire continent the "lands of no one," the papacy inflicted a theological, political, moral, and spiritual wound from which the world has yet to heal. The significance of this "large scale accumulation of

---

[141]Ibid., 349.

[142]Ibid., 354.

[143]Mignolo, *Darker Side*, 79.

[144]Wynter, "Unsettling the Coloniality of Being/Power/Truth/Freedom," 291.

unpaid land, unpaid labor, and overall wealth expropriated by Western Europe from non-European peoples," writes Wynter, "was to lay the basis of its global expansion from the fifteenth century onwards, [and] was carried out within the order of truth and the self-evident order of consciousness, of a creed-specific conception of what it was to be human."[145]

Today, Crossroads Anti-Racism Ministry, which trained Pax Christi USA's Anti-Racism Team (PCART), typically begins its anti-racism program by immersing participants in the history of racial oppression and resistance to oppression. One exercise invites participants to create a visual history or timeline by marking dates and key events on a wall of paper in a classroom. The exercise enables participants to see and learn the history of both racial oppression and resistance to it. That historical exercise typically begins with 1492, the year in which Columbus "discovers" the "New World" and the "Doctrine of Discovery" establishes colonialism.[146] Undoubtedly, "under this legal cover for theft," Euro-American "wars of conquest and settler colonialism devastated Indigenous nations and communities, ripping their territories away from them and transforming the land into private property, real estate."[147] This historical timeline, which Crossroads calls the "Wall of History," I believe, should also include the role the renaissance papacy played in the early fifteenth century and the Great Events of 1444 that inaugurated the African slave trade. The Roman Catholic papacy and Church bears undeniable responsibility both in the African slave trade and in the theft and destruction of Indigenous Peoples and lands throughout the Americas.

Against its teaching of the equality of all people before God, Adiele summarizes the Church's résumé on the enslavement of Africans. First, the Church was wholly complicit in establishing the African slave trade primarily due to its political interest in reestablishing universal papal authority over the whole world.[148] Second, the renaissance papacy judged as a just war the Crusades against Islam and Saracens in Africa as they viewed title to African lands and peoples as just.[149] Third, the central theological justification for granting just war and title rights to Portugal, then Spain, was the teaching of *extra ecclesiam nulla salus* (outside the church there is no salvation).[150] Fatefully, however, against its own teaching of universal equality, the Church employed the "curse of Ham" and the symbolism of black as the devil to further justify the use of force and enslavement against Africans. Adiele cites Portuguese

[145]Ibid.

[146]Joseph Brandt, *Understanding and Dismantling Racism: The Twenty-First-Century Challenge to White America* (Minneapolis: Fortress Press, 2007), 15. Brandt is the founder of Crossroads Anti-Racism Ministry in Chicago, Illinois.

[147]Roxanne Dunbar-Ortiz, *An Indigenous Peoples' History of the United States* (Boston: Beacon Press, 2014), 198.

[148]Adiele, *The Popes*, 469.

[149]Ibid., 469–70.

[150]Ibid., 470.

manuscripts from the fifteenth century stating that "Black Africans were blackened in their bodies because they descended from Ham, the accursed son of Noah."[151] He also cites an 1873 Vatican prayer in the Decree of the Sacred Congregation of Rites for the conversion of "Wretched Ethiopians."[152] Adiele speculates that the papacy may have gotten "cold feet" in condemning slavery because of its history of purchasing and utilizing "galley slaves" who served as rowers for the papal naval fleet from the fifteenth century until the nineteenth century.[153]

More egregiously, perhaps, is the way the Church made "huge material profits" through the "dues she collected for the baptism of slaves."[154] The papacy benefitted financially from this practice at least until 1831.[155] Not until 1839, nearly four hundred years after Prince Henry captured the first slaves in 1444, did Pope Gregory XVI condemn the transatlantic slave trade as an evil against humanity.[156] Adiele concludes his historical study of the Roman Catholic papacy with a call for a thorough confession by the papacy and for the Church to initiate reparations for the Atlantic slave trade. I return to the necessity of reparation in chapter 5, but next I turn to a way of unlearning anti-black white supremacy.

---

[151]Ibid., 420.
[152]Ibid., 419.
[153]Ibid., 420–21.
[154]Ibid., 471.
[155]Ibid., 478.
[156]Ibid.

PART II

Living Decolonially

4

Engaging Impasse

The First Will Be Last

The Roman Catholic Church and people who believe they are white stand at a historical crossroads where we can no longer evade the legacy of modernity/coloniality[1] and its cornerstones of patriarchy and anti-black white supremacy. We stand at a crossroads where people of faith—especially those who enjoy any form of racial, patriarchal, gender, sexual, or ableist privilege and power—must make a choice regarding where and for whom we stand. We face a reckoning in the current crisis of modernity/coloniality: either strive to maintain the comfort, power, and privilege of supremacy within the colonial matrix of power or cross over to the side of Black and colonized peoples. That may seem practically impossible, especially for people who live within a mythology of whiteness that denies the enduring presence of the past and who are deformed emotionally, socially, morally, and spiritually by coloniality and white habitus. In *Seeds of Destruction*, Thomas Merton recognized the great difficulty that otherwise good and well-intentioned White people face in taking responsibility for our own role in racism. He wrote that White people "must dare to pay the dolorous price of change, *to grow into a new society.* Nothing else will suffice!"[2] He continued,

> The only way out of this fantastic impasse is for everyone to face and accept the difficulties and sacrifices involved, in all their seriousness, in all their inexorable demands. This is what our society, based on a philosophy of every man for himself and on the rejection of altruism

---

[1]As noted in chapter 1, modernity and coloniality are constitutive of each other—they are two sides of the same coin. Thus, we can't speak of modernity without coloniality.

[2]Thomas Merton, *Seeds of Destruction* (New York: Farrar, Strauss and Giroux, 1964), 9.

and sacrifice (except in their most schematic and imaginary forms), is not able to do. Yet it is something which it must learn to do.[3]

It is time for people who believe they are white to take up the politically impossible call of the gospel to social, political, and spiritual racial intimacy.[4] Embracing mystical and political intimacy means embodying freedom *on the side of* Black and colonized peoples.[5] Prioritizing Blackness and Black people is not another form of exclusivity; rather, it is the option Jesus makes for anyone deemed the "the least of these" (Mt 25:40). The gospel question is this: For whom and what do you lay down your life (Jn 15:13)? If there is a way where there is no way, it is embodying a "blues transcendental hope,"[6] lamenting with and for people afflicted by anti-black violence, and following the lead of African American Catholics that we may yet glimpse the possibilities of new birth in God's "beloved community."[7] Yet White people siding with and for Black people is nearly impossible in the context of the Roman Catholic Church's social-historical role in the genesis of the transatlantic slave trade, modernity/coloniality, and anti-black white supremacy.

I contend that unlearning anti-black white supremacy is a critical condition of the possibility of people steeped in white habitus to enter a collective process of embracing racial intimacy. Such a collective process, however, depends upon White people becoming open to listening to, and learning from, criticism and protest from Black people. A key test of moral conversion is the degree to which individuals and communities learn from criticism and protest.[8] A basic historical marker of internalized superiority is White people who refuse to learn from Black people's criticism and protest—for example, white backlash to Reconstruction, rolling back civil rights achievements, or negative white reaction to the election of the first African American president.[9] W. E. B. Du Bois's articulation of double consciousness, I believe, offers a spiritual gift whereby White people may yet see ourselves the way Black people see us. Du Bois describes double consciousness as "always feeling his twoness, an American, a Negro; two souls, two thoughts, two un-reconciled strivings; two warring ideals in one dark body, whose dogged strength alone keeps it

---

[3] Ibid.

[4] Alex Mikulich, "Time to Live the Politically Impossible Art of the Gospel," *National Catholic Reporter*, February 8, 2019, https://www.ncronline.org.

[5] M. Shawn Copeland, *Enfleshing Freedom: Body, Race, and Being* (Minneapolis: Fortress Press, 2010).

[6] M. Shawn Copeland, "Theology at the Crossroads: A Meditation on the Blues," in *Uncommon Faithfulness: The Black Catholic Experience* (Maryknoll, NY: Orbis Books, 2009), 103.

[7] A term popularized by Martin Luther King Jr. See https://thekingcenter.org/king-philosophy/.

[8] Bernard Lonergan, *Method in Theology* (New York: Seabury Press, 1979 [1972]), 240.

[9] Carol Anderson, *White Rage: The Unspoken Truth of Our Racial Divide* (New York: Bloomsbury, 2016); see chapter 1 ("Reconstructing Reconstruction"), chapter 4 ("Rolling Back Civil Rights"), and chapter 5 ("How to Unelect a Black President").

from being torn asunder."[10] If White people enter contemplative silence and humbly listen to Du Bois and the Black radical tradition, both secular and religious, a spirituality of double consciousness creates conditions favorable to the possibility of unlearning white supremacy.

A full embrace of double consciousness—intellectually, emotionally, practically, and morally—means co-sensing an epoch of societal impasse structured by the colonial matrix of power. "We are all in the matrix," Walter Mignolo poignantly explains, and the "colonial matrix of power is the very foundational structure of Western civilization."[11] We live in a time of "societal impasse," an epoch in which citizens of a dominant nation—the United States—"can find no escape from the world we have built, where the poor and oppressed cry out, where the earth and the environment cry out, and where the specter of nuclear waste haunts future generations."[12] The world "we have built" and rebuild daily is modernity/coloniality. Recall that modernity/ coloniality is not a totalitarian concept but rather the hidden agenda and project of modernity—that is, coloniality that "emerged with the European invasions of Abya Yala, Tawantinsuyu, and Anahuac; the formation of the Americas and the Caribbean; and the massive trade of enslaved Africans."[13] A critical part of a pedagogy of unlearning modernity/coloniality and anti-black white supremacy is understanding how "the logic of coloniality [is] driving all of us to collective death dressed under the triumphal growth of a global economy."[14] There is no rational way out of this societal impasse because modernity/coloniality is all around and inside each and every one of us.

The claim that "we are all in the matrix" does *not* mean that people socialized into Eurocentric white modernity—that is, all of us everywhere—do not have agency or options. For example, some Christian ethicists contend that arguments that utilize "white complicity" or "white supremacy" language pay little attention "to what sort of individual agency might be required to overcome complicity and supremacy."[15] I am arguing for decolonial options,

---

[10]W. E. B. Du Bois, *The Souls of Black Folk* (New York: Barnes and Noble Classics, 2003 [1903]), 9.

[11]Walter Mignolo, *The Darker Side of Western Modernity: Global Futures, Decolonial Options* (Durham, NC: Duke University Press, 2011), 16.

[12]Constance FitzGerald, "Impasse and Dark Night," in *Living with Apocalypse: Spiritual Resources for Social Compassion*, ed. Tilden Edwards (San Francisco: Harper & Row, 1984), 105.

[13]Mignolo, *Darker Side*, 2.

[14]Ibid., 117.

[15]See, for example, David Cloutier, "Cavanaugh and Grimes on Structural Evils of Violence and Race: Overcoming Conflicts in Contemporary Social Ethics," *Journal of the Society of Christian Ethics* 37, no. 2 (2017): 59–78, here 69. Cloutier does not discuss how Margaret Pfeil, Laurie Cassidy, and I contend that White people do have choices and options in how we live, namely, that agency begins with naming our participation in a privileged group and taking steps to critique and dismantle that participation. Cf. my essay "(Un)learning White Male Ignorance," in *Interrupting White Privilege: Catholic Theologians Break the Silence* (Maryknoll, NY: Orbis Books, 2007); and Mikulich, Laurie Cassidy, and Margaret Pfeil, *The Scandal of*

which include among their primary features "an analytic of the construction, transformation, and sustenance of racism and patriarchy that created the conditions to build and control a structure of knowledge, either grounded on the word of God or the word of Reason and Truth."[16] "Decolonial options" is plural because "breaking the Western code," that is, analysis and critique of racism and patriarchy, begins from particular localities[17] that have been "configured by the colonial matrix of power."[18] The assertion that "I am where I do and think" is a geopolitical movement away from modernity, creating conditions for people to exist and thrive on their own terms. Mignolo offers the example of Évelyne Trouillot, who opened her "intervention in the Sixteenth International Conference of the Academy of Latina in Lima" by stating, "'I am a woman, I am Black, and I am Haitian.'"[19] These seemingly simple declarations inaugurate her "confrontation" with patriarchy (I am a woman), racism (I am Black), and imperial geopolitics (I am Haitian). She is not claiming universal knowledge to speak for all women, Blacks, or Haitians; rather, "I am telling you that I am speaking as a Black woman and, by so doing, breaking the Western code that has denied women and Blacks both humanity and intelligence."[20] Her declaration, however, is not begging for recognition within the dominant Western epistemology. Instead, she is "disengaging" and "breaking away" from the Western code in order to "engage in rebuilding what was destroyed and build what doesn't yet exist."[21]

I am arguing for decolonial options as a way of creating conditions for the possibility of forming people of faith who are breaking away from the Western code in order to embody a "lived transformation" of "discipleship" as the practice of solidarity with, beside, and among 'the least.'"[22] As Mignolo notes, decolonial options "does not mean 'decolonial missions.' Missions imply projects of conversion, of achieving an end programmed in the blueprint. Options are the antithesis of missions."[23] In other words, decoloniality does not mean going out on a mission "to convert and promote our form of salvation";[24] it is not on a mission to reject Eurocentrism and replace it with

---

White Complicity in US Hyper-Incarceration: A Nonviolent Spirituality of White Resistance (New York: Palgrave Macmillan, 2013). Sadly, Cloutier also completely ignores or is perhaps ignorant of the realist perspective of the Black radical tradition, both secular and religious, and its historical account of how Black people have demonstrated creative agency within an antiblack white supremacist world.

[16]Mignolo, *Darker Side*, xv.

[17]See Walter Mignolo, *Local Histories / Global Designs* (Princeton, NJ: Princeton University Press, 2000).

[18]Mignolo, *Darker Side*, xvi.

[19]Ibid.

[20]Ibid.

[21]Ibid., xvii and 109.

[22]Copeland, *Enfleshing Freedom*, 6.

[23]Mignolo, *Darker Side*, xxviii.

[24]Ibid.

another universal paradigm or blueprint. Thus, for example, John Milbank's critique of the secular reason of the social sciences "is not enough," because his questioning does not shift away from Western imperial reason.[25] Decoloniality does not seek the "demolition of modern, secular social theory,"[26] as that would be yet another form of domination.[27] Rather, decoloniality involves changing the "rules of the game" imposed by Western parochialism, and doing so from the plural, "multiple memories and colonial wounds inflicted by racism, ways of life, languages, beliefs, and experiences connected to the West, but at the same time not subsumable to it."[28]

Rather than another mission of domination, I suggest a decolonial option (in the last section of this chapter) as a way of engaging the deeper reality of "dark night and societal impasse"[29] as a divine path of education in contemplative transformation. I am suggesting the decolonial option because of the way it facilitates creating conditions for the possibility of radical openness to God and building communal futures whereby all persons and communities may thrive. I draw upon M. Shawn Copeland's approach because it is wholly oriented to reality as a way of "being in love with God [that] reorients us and all that we desire, even in the thick of 'dark night and societal impasse.'"[30] In the midst of this predicament, the Carmelite mystic Constance FitzGerald finds that logical solutions rooted in Western rationality, however attractive they may be, do not yield or facilitate transformation. I draw deeply upon the work of FitzGerald, Bryan N. Massingale, and Copeland in this chapter because I find deep resonance in their respective analyses of Western epistemology, patriarchy, and racism with decoloniality and its relentless questioning and critique of modernity/coloniality and the colonial matrix of power. Specifically, their articulation of the need for people of faith to engage "dark night and societal impasse" offers, I believe, a way of learning how "God makes a way where there is no way."[31]

[25]Madina V. Tlostanova and Walter D. Mignolo, *Learning to Unlearn: Decolonial Reflections from Eurasia and the Americas* (Columbus: Ohio State University Press, 2012), 66. Mignolo criticizes John Milbank, *Theology and Social Theory: Beyond Secular Reason* (Oxford: Blackwell, 1990).

[26]Milbank, *Theology and Social Theory*, 1.

[27]Mignolo, *Darker Side*, 21.

[28]Ibid., 330.

[29]Copeland, *Enfleshing Freedom*, 27. Copeland cites Constance FitzGerald, "Impasse and Dark Night," in Joann Wolski Conn, ed., *Women's Spirituality: Resources for Christian Development* (New York: Paulist Press, 1986), 299.

[30]Copeland, *Enfleshing Freedom*, 27.

[31]I first learned this phrase from African American women in a biblical prayer group at Sacred Heart Parish in San Francisco in the early 1990s. Their prayer, lament, and way of wrestling with God witnessed to me how "God makes a way where there is no way."

Engaging Double Consciousness:
A Way of Unlearning Anti-Black White Supremacy

For White Americans to become present to the colonial wound of anti-black white supremacy, we need to pray incessantly to *"see ourselves as others see us."*[32] We need to listen to the criticism and protest of Black people, welcome the gift of double consciousness, and unrelentingly name whiteness—"Look, a White!"—and expose its contradictions and inhumanity.[33] The virtuous seeing I am suggesting is not remote and removed, nor is it a rapacious gaze; rather, it humbly co-senses the fully embodied experience of how colonized peoples perceive White people. Too often throughout history, as Part I extensively discusses, White people employ intellectual, emotional, and/or physical distancing strategies to segregate so that White people do not perceive, in any way, the plight of Black, Brown, or Indigenous Peoples. We discussed these distancing strategies within the rubric of "white habitus" in chapter 2. Recall that within the context of geographically segregated White neighborhoods, schools, and professional associations, white habitus maintains white social comfort and reestablishes that social comfort when other people do not act in familiar and acceptable ways. For example, white fragility is a "state in which even a minimal amount of racial stress in the habitus becomes intolerable, triggering a range of defensive moves."[34] These defensive moves, education scholar Robin DiAngelo explains, might include feelings of anger, fear, and guilt and become manifested in actions like argumentation (insisting that one is "color-blind"), silence as avoidance, and physically leaving the situation where White people feel racial stress.[35]

Among many diverse ways that White people might contemplatively and with humility begin to co-sense how Black and Brown people may perceive us, I suggest W. E. B. Du Bois's self-aware and critical way of autobiography, which connects his personal experience of "double consciousness" to wider cultural and structural realities within which he and all people are embedded. I describe in greater detail below Du Bois's critical way of telling his own story (autobiography) and double consciousness.

My children's experience offers an example of the difference between

---

[32]Alex Mikulich, "(Un)Learning White Male Ignorance," in Laurie Cassidy and Alex Mikulich, eds., *Interrupting White Privilege: Catholic Theologians Break the Silence* (Maryknoll, NY: Orbis Books, 2007), 170, emphasis in original.

[33]George Yancy, *Look, a White! Philosophical Essays on Whiteness* (Philadelphia: Temple University Press, 2012), 10.

[34]Robin DiAngelo, *White Fragility: Why It's So Hard for White People to Talk about Racism* (Boston: Beacon Press, 2018), 103.

[35]Ibid., 103–4.

white fragility within a white habitus and double consciousness. Du Bois's experience of feeling and perceiving two separate worlds resonates with our Black children's experience of inhabiting a white culture, from our extended family to the wider world. After an extended family Zoom call during the 2020 pandemic, my daughter lamented how her White relatives either do not perceive, or are incapable of engaging, her experience as an African American woman. Never did our extended family members ever broach the topic of how we might be experiencing the recent spikes in police and vigilante violence against African Americans. Our relatives' failure or inability to discuss the topic suggests that either they do not want to acknowledge it or that they may not even perceive how Black people experience police and vigilante violence. In terms of DiAngelo's description of white fragility, perhaps my relatives do not have the capacity to engage racially stress-inducing situations. In contrast, Black people cannot avoid living in a trauma-inducing world dominated by an insouciant whiteness. Not unlike W. E. B. Du Bois, our children are critically conscious of both Black and White worlds. This is only one instance of my children's experience of visibility/invisibility within our extended family and of double consciousness. Other examples include our children's formal education and our son's experience of abusive policing. Our experience as parents includes being called a "nigger family" and being threatened with deadly violence, but also learning how to parent from peers within Black Catholic parishes. This lived experience illuminates both the depth of my (and our) white privilege and power and has opened us to welcome the wisdom and insight of Black Catholics. Certainly, Du Bois is not the only resource available for initiating the decolonial shift to bodily co-sensing the experience of Black and colonized peoples. Other possibilities include, and are not limited to, Gloria Anzaldua's *Borderland / La Frontera: The New Mestiza*, Frantz Fanon's entire body of work, Rigoberta Menchú's *Me Llamo Rigoberta Menchu y asi me nacio la conciencia*, and Ottobah Cugoano's *Thoughts and Sentiments on the Evil of Slavery.*[36]

Du Bois invites White Americans to co-sense with him and to recognize how we White people collectively embody oppression. Yet my prayer and hope of bodily co-sensing with Du Bois seems like an impossibility in a white supremacist world where white Americans blithely claim without an ounce of data, and without any grounding in the experience or reality of another, that oppression is a myth.[37] As one theologian recognizes, "White people do

---

[36]I purposefully write Menchú's title in Spanish because the English translation inserts a meaning she did not intend. As Mignolo notes, the English translator or publisher "trumpeted Benjamin Franklin's exultation of the first person: 'I, Rigoberta Menchú.'" See *Darker Side*, 108.

[37]Dan Fagan, "The Myth of Oppression Holds Americans Back," *The Advocate*, October 1, 2017, 6B.

need to de-center themselves and listen to people of color," but she fails to actually demonstrate *how* White people might listen and become accountable to Black and Brown communities.[38]

Heralded as the first African American graduate of Harvard University (cum laude in 1890), the first social scientist to publish a study of African Americans (the *Philadelphia Negro* in 1899), a cofounder of the NAACP in 1909, and the first editor of the NAACP's journal *The Crisis*, Du Bois was a historian, social scientist, pioneering civil rights activist, and pan-Africanist who died at the age of ninety-five in Ghana on August 27, 1963, one day before the March on Washington. He was born February 23, 1868, in Great Barrington, Massachusetts.

While many people of color have critically engaged double consciousness in multiple and diverse fields of study, I believe Du Bois offers an approach to spiritual transformation that white America has largely missed. The most celebrated sentence in Du Bois's nonfiction (he also wrote novels)—"The problem of the twentieth century is the problem of the color line,"[39] which begins the second chapter of *The Souls of Black Folk*—must be read within the context of the first chapter.

Every chapter of *Souls* begins with at least one stanza of poetry above one bar of a spiritual hymn, which Du Bois calls the "sorrow songs." Chapter 1, titled "Of Our Spiritual Strivings," centers the deep desire of both Du Bois and African people to be free. His chapter starts with a quotation from Arthur Symons's poem "The Crying of Water," which expresses Du Bois's incessant suffering and mourning, and his insatiable thirst for freedom within the experience of the oppression of the slave trade. The voice of his heart "in his side" is nearly indistinguishable from the voice of the sea that wells up incessantly "all night long the water is crying to me."[40] Like the poet's "voice of my heart" that merges ambiguously with the "voice of the sea," Du Bois's mourning will not rest until "the last moon droop and the last tide fail."[41] And not unlike the great slave spiritual "Nobody Knows the Trouble I've Seen," Du Bois expresses through the poet the unyielding terror and sorrow of the troubled waters of the Middle Passage. The voice of the narrator and the voices of a people cry without end, with unquenched thirst, for liberty and life. Opening one's heart to Du Bois's sorrow is critical for entering his exploration of his experience of double consciousness, for without it, the reader might get easily caught in

---

[38]Julie Hanlon Rubio, *Hope for Common Ground: Mediating the Personal and the Political in a Divided Church* (Washington, DC: Georgetown University Press, 2016), 42. Other than drawing upon two womanist scholars in her discussion of abortion, Black people are strangely silent in Rubio's discussion about creating common ground.

[39]Du Bois, *Souls of Black Folk*, 16.

[40]Ibid., 7. Du Bois quotes "The Crying of Water" by the Welsh poet Arthur Symons (1900).

[41]Ibid.

a grim philosophical dualism with no outlet. He invites the reader to enter his bodily, emotional, and intellectual experience by embracing the poem's biblical imagery, symbolism, and message. By beginning the chapter in this way, Du Bois suggests that readers put themselves in the place of slaves on a slave ship and to imagine the pain of thirst for life and liberty in the midst of the endlessly swelling sea.

As James Baldwin expresses, an honest cry for help and healing "is the true basis of all dialogues."[42] Claiming that there is no oppression is one of the myriad ways white Americans refuse to hear the cry of the oppressed. Put in terms of the beatitude, "Blessed are they who mourn" (Mt 5:4), the refusal to mourn with another is a refusal to join another in shared vulnerability and need for God's love. To the extent that White people ignore this cry and refuse to mourn with Black Americans, we not only cut ourselves off from connection and dialogue with Black brothers and sisters but also from our own humanity and God.

Immediately after quoting the Symons poem, Du Bois addresses the issue of the denial of his existence and predicament by White people. "Between me and the other world," says Du Bois, White people hold on to an "unasked question."[43] Sometimes the question "How does it feel to be a problem?" is not raised by some "through feelings of indelicacy," and by others through the difficulty of "rightly framing it."[44] Du Bois laments how White people say, "I know a colored man," or "I fought in the Civil War," or criticize southern racism instead of directly asking the question "How does it feel to be a problem?"[45] To that "real question" Du Bois replies, "I answer seldom a word."[46]

While we may hear the prophet Job pleading when Du Bois cries, "Why did God make me an outcast and a stranger in my own house?" he knows that the Negro is neither condemned to be a stranger nor soulless. In fact, the "Negro is a sort of seventh son born with a veil and gifted with second sight in this American world—a world which yields him no true self-consciousness, but only lets him see himself through the other world."[47]

As historian Edward J. Blum explains in his biography of Du Bois, the use of the biblical number seven—God rested on the seventh day of creation and Jews honored the seventh child born into a family—marked Negroes as a chosen people with the gift of second sight.[48] This second sight enabled

---

[42]James Baldwin, "White Man's Guilt," in James Baldwin, *The Price of the Ticket: Collected Nonfiction, 1948–1985* (New York: St. Martin's Press, 1985), 412.

[43]Du Bois, *Souls*, 7.

[44]Ibid.

[45]Ibid., 7–8.

[46]Ibid., 8.

[47]Ibid., 9.

[48]Edward J. Blum, *W. E. B. Du Bois: American Prophet* (Philadelphia: University of Pennsyl-

African Americans to see the myth of American white supremacy. Or, as Du Bois would later say about "the souls of white folk," "Of them I am singularly clairvoyant."[49] Even when whites "clutch at rags of facts and fancies to hide their nakedness," he still sees "them ever stripped—ugly, human."[50] Until White people look at ourselves in the mirror of double consciousness, and see in ourselves what Black people see in us, we will not know the role we play in perpetuating the wound of American racism.

Recall that Du Bois describes his experience of double consciousness as "always feeling his twoness, an American, a Negro; two souls, two thoughts, two un-reconciled strivings; two warring ideals in one dark body, whose dogged strength alone keeps it from being torn asunder."[51] Having been ripped from his ancestral home and forced across the ocean into a white world that only looks on in "amused contempt and pity," white supremacy puts his Americanness and Africanness at war against each other and against his very humanity. And the violent dualism that pits White against Black and American against African exposes the problem of bad faith.

The Problem of Bad Faith

If you (the reader) find your heart and body quaking in sorrow with Du Bois, perhaps you have experienced the grace of bodily co-sensing Black double consciousness. Perhaps you are beginning to understand that all of us are implicated—that is, all of us are deformed by racism and deconstructing it begins with "seeing through" whiteness for what it is: a complex of superiority. On the other hand, if you do not see yourself implicated in Du Bois's critique of White culture, that might suggest the tendency to disavow or deny one's culpability in white superiority. This may be an opportunity to begin to understand Du Bois's experience of the question "How does it feel to be a problem?" as an insight into the religious bad faith of modernity, a "perpetual question" that Nelson Maldonado-Torres describes as "a manifestation of the Manichean misanthropic skeptical attitude toward Black people, Indigenous people, and people of color that entered Western modernity perhaps most clearly through the distinctions between having religion (and a soul) and not having religion."[52] Echoing C. S. Lewis's *The Screwtape Letters*,

---

vania Press, 2007), 79.

[49]W. E. B. Du Bois, *Darkwater* (New York: Washington Square Press, 2004, with an introduction by David Levering Lewis [1919]), 21.

[50]Ibid.

[51]Du Bois, *Souls of Black Folk*, 9.

[52]Nelson Maldonado-Torres, "Religious Studies and/in the Decolonial Turn," Contending Modernities, March 3, 2020, https://contendingmodernities.nd.edu.

Maldonado-Torres likens this particular skepticism to "a worm at the very heart of modernity."[53] That "worm" raises an insidious rhetorical question (really an assumption) about the humanity of Black and Indigenous people and other people of color. The question is posed from the "imperial attitude" of the "*ego conquiro*," where the idea of progress "always meant progress in modernity for a few" and that "the Rights of Man do not apply equally to all," among many other contradictions.[54] The imperial attitude, ultimately, "promotes a genocidal attitude in respect to colonized and racialized people. Through it colonial and racial subjects are marked as dispensable."[55]

The Roman Catholic Church played a primary role in spawning this "worm" of racism. In the wake of the Church's deep complicity in the origination of the African slave trade, its participation in human trade for at least four hundred years, and its inability to effectively counter the scandal of anti-black white supremacy, especially in North America, the Church and people of faith perpetuate an existential problem of bad faith.[56] That problem is that institutions and people who assume they are white are living a lie that institutions, including the Roman Catholic Church, encourage in an anti-black white supremacist society.[57]

Recall, too, that taking the political side of Black people is not as simple as merely invoking the notions of human dignity, equality, and solidarity. As Frantz Fanon put it, it is easy to prove equality as privileged folks tend to do, "But my purpose is quite different: what we are striving for is to liberate the Black man from the arsenal of complexes that germinated in a colonial situation."[58] The papacy played a key role in establishing the "arsenal of complexes" with which we must contend today, including the mundane reality of anti-black white supremacy that makes reaffirmation of white superiority "superfluous."[59]

Merton recognized the problem of inviting White people to identify fully with Black people: "Most of us [White people] are congenitally unable to think Black, and yet that is precisely what we must do before we can even hope

[53]Nelson Maldonado-Torres, "On the Coloniality of Being: Contributions to the Development of a Concept," in *Globalization and the Decolonial Option*, ed. Walter D. Mignolo and Arturo Escobar (London: Routledge, 2010), 100.

[54]Ibid.

[55]Ibid.

[56]Lewis R. Gordon, *Fanon and the Crisis of European Man: An Essay on Philosophy and the Human Sciences* (New York: Routledge, 1995), 38.

[57]M. Shawn Copeland, "White Supremacy and Anti-Black Logics in the Making of U.S. Catholicism," in *Anti-Blackness and Christian Ethics*, ed. Vincent W. Lloyd and Andrew Prevot (Maryknoll, NY: Orbis Books, 2017), 61–62.

[58]Frantz Fanon, *Black Skin, White Masks*, trans. Richard Philcox (New York: Grove Press, 2008 [1967]), 14.

[59]Gordon, *Fanon and the Crisis of European Man*, 38.

to understand the crisis in which we find ourselves."[60] Therein lies another layer of the problem. We who maintain the comforts and privilege of white superiority are unwilling to take the social, political, economic, and spiritual risk of siding with people who are always already living in the wake of slavery, facing the fact of premature death. We who believe we are white either fail to perceive the need to change, refuse outright, or tentatively embrace the Black Lives Matter movement because transformation necessarily involves giving up and relinquishing our power, dominant position, privilege, and indeed our whole way of thinking and being in the world. We tend not to see—or even refuse to see—our own "soul sickness,"[61] both individually and collectively. Historically, we who enjoy white privilege and power have been unwilling to pay the price that must be paid to begin a process of undoing and unlearning anti-black white supremacy—namely, we must relinquish the social, political, economic (material), and psychological benefits of the anti-black white supremacy that has existed for generations.

This is the existential problem of bad faith: hiding from one's role in oppression. The most egregious example of bad faith, perhaps, is the unwillingness of the Roman Catholic hierarchy and magisterium to fully acknowledge its own role in initiating the trade in African peoples, an issue I address in the next chapter on reparations. A more immediate example in the US Catholic Church is its inability to implicate itself in anti-black white supremacy and to take full responsibility for its role in maintaining the status quo. Statements condemning racism by the United States Conference of Catholic Bishops, for example, too often reinforce the reality of bad faith. For example, while the 1986 pastoral letter *Economic Justice for All (EJA)* acknowledges that Blacks, Latinos, and Native Americans bear disproportionate burdens in every sphere of economic life, "At best the document leaves undone the work of critiquing the relationship between white advantage and racial oppression; at worst, *EJA* reinscribes the dominant white cultural perception that people of color are the problem and that white advantage is 'normal' and 'natural.' "[62]

In his prescient analysis of the situation of bad faith in the mid-1960s, Merton recognized that the achievement of civil rights legislation "is not the end of the battle but *only the beginning of a new and more critical phase in the conflict.*"[63] That "more critical phase" arrived in the context of the assassination of President Kennedy and the refusal of White Americans and

[60]Thomas Merton, *Seeds of Destruction* (New York: Farrar, Strauss, and Giroux, 1964), 60.

[61]Bryan N. Massingale, "Racism Is a Sickness of the Soul: Can Ignatian Spirituality Help Us Heal?," *America*, November 20, 2017, www.americamagazine.org.

[62]Alex Mikulich, "Where Y'at Race, Whiteness, and Economic Justice? A Map of White Complicity in the Economic Oppression of People of Color," in *The Almighty and the Dollar: Reflections on Economic Justice for All,* ed. Mark Allman (Winona, MN: Anselm Academic, 2012), 201.

[63]Merton, *Seeds,* 4.

politicians to undertake the kind of radical change necessary for racial justice. Merton gave the example of southern politicians who knew that White constituents would respond to civil rights legislation by becoming "more deeply and grimly entrenched in its refusals."[64] That kind of refusal in 2020 is, perhaps, most evident in police unions that refuse to change even in the face of massive national protests against widespread police brutality against African Americans. The violence of anti-black white supremacy, however, may be more deeply secured not only by the refusal of the church to embrace the ideas of the Black Lives Matter movement but by local dioceses and parishes that choose indecision in the face of a crisis that demands action for "the least of these" (Mt 25:40). Whether by outright refusal or passive indecision, Merton described the crisis of the 1960s as seemingly "insuperable," because "As long as white society persists in clinging to its present condition and to its own image of itself as the only acceptable reality, then the problem will remain without reasonable solution, and there will inevitably be violence."[65]

Frantz Fanon exposed the obscenity of the violent crisis of European colonialism and anti-black white supremacy. His insight is that it is obscene to expect that master and slave, or colonizer and colonized, or White people and Black people to be well adjusted to racism.[66] In the contemporary US context, in the wake of massive protests against the brutal police murder of George Floyd, such obscenity is manifest in police brutality against peaceful protestors, in the president ordering the removal of protestors in order to stage a photo-op[67] holding the Bible—looking more like he was holding a lottery ticket than venerating sacred scripture—and in statements from predominantly white institutions, such as the 2018 US Catholic bishops' conference statement "Open Wide Our Hearts," which "contorts into passive voice and platitudes of kindness; it speaks of the sin of racism, but never names the sinner."[68] Moral theologian Bryan Massingale has repeatedly demonstrated the failure of the US bishops to effectively combine passion for racial justice with an analysis of "how deeply affected US Catholics are by a cultural ethos of White racism."[69]

An individual example of this is a White theologian arguing "that the

---

[64]Ibid., 6.

[65]Ibid., 8.

[66]Lewis R. Gordon, *Fanon and the Crisis of European Man: An Essay on Philosophy and the Human Sciences* (New York: Routledge, 1995), 41.

[67]See, for example, Diana Butler Bass's op-ed, "As a Christian and as a Human Being, I Was Appalled by Trump's Photo Op," CNN, June 4, 2020, www.cnn.com.

[68]Daniel P. Horan, "When Will the US Bishops Address the Evil of Systemic Racism Head-On?," *National Catholic Reporter*, June 10, 2020, www.ncronline.org.

[69]Bryan N. Massingale, "James Cone and Recent Catholic Episcopal Teaching on Racism," *Theological Studies* 61, no. 4 (December 2000): 700–747, here 728.

starting point of [white] complicity is too broad, too overwhelming."[70] The privileging of whites being "overwhelmed" is a case in point of "white fragility," that is, the need to maintain white comfort by "leaving a stress-inducing situation."[71] The privileging of whites being too overwhelmed gives no consideration to how diverse people of color, including W. E. B. Du Bois, have expressed being overwhelmed by their experience of mourning oppression, of the slave trade, of Indian removal and extermination, of living constantly with the threat of death, and of always being treated as less than human. Regrettably, the experience of being "overwhelmed" is not generally perceived as a way of engaging double consciousness, that is, as a possible point of compassionate, intimate connection with people who are overwhelmed with the burden of anti-blackness every day.

Bad Faith and the Loss of Lament

A deeper spiritual obscenity of the sin of anti-black white supremacy is loss of the desire and capacity to lament with and for people who struggle to live in an anti-black culture. Du Bois invites a shared, bodily, spiritual lament that Catholics ought to recognize as central to our faith. Catholics proclaim through liturgical music and singing how "the Lord hears the cry of the poor" (Ps 34) because scriptures and our faith teach that God is close to the brokenhearted and that those who mourn will be comforted (Mt 5:4). Authentic Christian solidarity is marked by the intimate presence of reciprocal recognition, lifting the burden of racism by making African American cries for life, justice, and freedom our own. Sadly, however, at least since the civil rights movement of the 1960s, predominantly white churches, including the Roman Catholic Church, seem to have no desire to lament the disproportionate burdens, sorrows, pain, and losses endlessly endured by African Americans as well as Latinos, First Peoples, and other vulnerable communities.

Not unsurprisingly, lament goes to the depth of faith of the people and God of Jesus Christ, Israel. Biblical scholar Walter Brueggemann explains that the loss of lament implies a loss of authentic praise and thanksgiving to God.[72] Authentic praise of God arises out of experiences and expressions of lament. In fact, the cry of Israel initiates salvation history (Ex 2:23–25). God hears the cry of the afflicted and acts with mercy (Ps 107); Israel responds with praise and thanksgiving. Brueggemann writes that the "proper [biblical] setting of praise is as lament resolved."[73] By "setting," Brueggemann refers

---

[70] Rubio, *Hope for Common Ground*, 42.

[71] DiAngelo, *White Fragility*, 103.

[72] Walter Brueggemann, "The Costly Loss of Lament," in *The Psalms: The Life of Faith*, ed. Patrick D. Miller (Minneapolis: Fortress Press, 1995), 98–111.

[73] Ibid., 99.

to the social construction of reality and what Catholic social thought has practiced in "reading the signs of the times" since Vatican II.[74] Understanding a people's experience in a particular setting is critical; recall that the setting of Israel was bondage under Pharaoh, and that in the last five hundred years living in slavery and its aftermath is when Africans in diaspora articulated lament in blues music, a point to which I return.

Examining the loss of lament in scripture, Brueggemann contends that Israel loses an authentic relationship with God and covenantal interaction that is genuinely concerned with economic and social injustice.[75] He finds three movements in Israel's relationship to God in the pattern of lament in the Psalms. These movements begin with crying out in hurt, anger, and pain; then submitting to hurt, pain, and anger to God in prayer; and finally, if a growth of mature faith develops, moving to ritually, liturgically, rhetorically, and emotionally relinquishing power, privilege, and economic advantage in favor of restoring justice and covenantal relations devoted to caring for the most vulnerable first. That relinquishment is expressed in thanksgiving and praise to God. Conversely, where the cry of lament "is not voiced, heaven is not moved, and history is not initiated. The end is hopelessness."[76]

Lament makes a difference in Israel's life because it "shifts the calculus" of the status quo of power and ignites a transformation in the distribution of power. The crucial question that Brueggemann asks is, "What happens when the appreciation of lament is lost in our time?" He answers,

It shifts the calculus and *redresses the distribution of power* between the two parties, so that the petitionary party is taken seriously and that the God who is addressed is newly engaged in a way that puts God at risk. As the lesser petitionary party (the psalm speaker) is legitimated, so the unmitigated supremacy of the greater party (God) is questioned and made available to the petitioner.[77]

However, Brueggemann contends, loss of lament in contemporary society reinforces "docility and submissiveness"[78] before the powers that be, engendering social practices that consolidate the political and economic monopoly of the status quo. Not unlike times when Israel reinforced the status quo of unjust covenantal relations with neighbor and God, so in our own times predominantly white churches and congregations have not only lost a desire to lament the unjust loss of life, including George Floyd and Breonna Taylor,

[74]Ibid., 100.
[75]Ibid., 100n9.
[76]Ibid., 111.
[77]Ibid., 101.
[78]Ibid., 102.

among too many others; we white Catholics also tend to foster a silence that only affirms the social, political, and economic status quo. That silence itself gives life to the yes men and women who dare not discourage Pharaoh—in this case not only Donald Trump but an entire culture—from fomenting more violence and inequality.

Bad Faith and God's Gratuitous Love

The gratuitous gift of God's love, especially through the presence of *les damnes de la terre*[79]—"the least of these" (Mt 25:40)—exposes perhaps the deepest theological, moral, and spiritual dimension of the bad faith of anti-black white supremacy. Du Bois underscores this reality by stressing that the "end of [African American] striving" is "to be a co-worker in the kingdom of culture, to escape both death and isolation, to husband and use his best powers and latent genius."[80] The dualism of white supremacy, "its double aims" of affirming white superiority and condemning Blackness, sends people "wooing false gods and invoking false means of salvation."[81]

Being a colonized and raced person is, by definition, "to be incapable of giving."[82] Being constructed as incapable of giving is being less than human. In the "theo-politics"[83] initiated in the Atlantic slave trade by the Catholic papacy and imperial states in the fifteenth century, being Black means lacking the gift of humanity and God's grace as a person made in the image and likeness of God. And that is not all—that imperial epistemology also initiated the idolatry of whiteness and White people's blindness to the giftedness of Black, Brown, and First Peoples.

However, that does not mean that colonized peoples have not given their exploited labor to their oppressors, their own labor, or that of their children. Anna Gordon asks rhetorically, "Is not being a person to be involved in the give and take of the most basic of social forms, as well as of the more com-

[79]I purposefully employ the original French title of Frantz Fanon's *Les Damnes de la terre* (Paris: Maspero, 1961) because the English translation—*The Wretched of the Earth*—is not true to Fanon's intent. The English word "wretched," defined as "very unfortunate in condition or circumstances; miserable, pitiable," misses Fanon's meaning of colonized peoples being designated by the colonizer as racially inferior. "Wretched" also misses Fanon's description of colonial segregation and violence; the word is also ambiguous inasmuch as it leaves open the possibility that the wretched may be to blame for their own condition. The ambiguity of "wretched" contradicts Fanon's critique of the source of violence: colonizers and colonial institutions, such as the state, which enforce racism through physical segregation and police violence.

[80]Du Bois, *Souls of Black Folk*, 9.

[81]Ibid., 10.

[82]Jane Anna Gordon, "The Gift of Double Consciousness: Some Obstacles to Grasping the Contributions of the Colonized," in *Postcolonialism and Political Theory*, ed. Nalini Persam (Lanham, MD: Lexington Books, 2007), 143.

[83]Mignolo's term to describe the source of coloniality in theological epistemology in the sixteenth century. See Mignolo, *Darker Side*, 15.

plex kinds of exchange that structure and buttress a human world? There is no doubt that colonized peoples engaged precisely in such acts."[84] Being colonized, enslaved, and raced within a colonial world means "living within a political economy in which one has no option but 'to give' to the colonial world."[85] Historical theologian Pius Onyemechi Adiele articulates this point theologically—the perversity of the Roman Catholic papacy's approval of African enslavement rests upon the assumption that African people are wholly lacking in humanity and that "their enslavement will bring them civilization and teach them to know bread and wine, housing and clothing," and ultimately, "make them become good Christians" and redeem them.[86]

Embracing Impasse and "Dark Night"

In her poetic "meditation on the blues," M. Shawn Copeland invites people of faith to a historical, theological, transformational, and spiritual crossroads where we can no longer evade the persistent relationship between white supremacy and anti-black oppression.[87] In the midst of a global pandemic, the nation stands at a historical juncture where we could easily descend into deeper violence and despair that threatens the fabric of the US constitutional republic, or we could seize epochal transformation. Drawing upon Robert Johnson's "Cross Road Blues," Copeland explains that, in Africa, "The cross is of two roads intersecting to flow into each other, to nourish each other."[88] She invites people of faith before the cross of Jesus, where our hearts, souls, and relationships may experience graced retuning, individually and collectively.[89] Aware that some readers may miss the universal message of her Black and Catholic theology, she writes, "The blues recount Black struggle to cross the river of racism, certainly, but as that river rushes over the rapids of imperial domination all of us—irrespective of cultural, racial-ethnic identity, or religion—are caught in its current."[90] We stand at a crossroads filled with the danger, chaos, and disorientation expressed by African American blues music even before enslaved Africans first gathered in the early 1700s in Congo Square.[91] As Cornel West eloquently put it in his reflection on the

---

[84]Gordon, "Gift of Double Consciousness," 143.

[85]Ibid., 153n1.

[86]Pius Onyemechi Adiele, *The Popes, the Catholic Church, and the Transatlantic Enslavement of Black Africans, 1418–1839* (Hildesheim, Germany: Georg Olms Verlag, 2017), 474.

[87]Copeland, "Theology at the Crossroads."

[88]Ibid., 97.

[89]Ibid., 105.

[90]Ibid., 100.

[91]See the thorough retrieval of African musical, dance, and cultural roots in Freddi Williams Evans, *Congo Square: African Roots in New Orleans* (Lafayette: University of Louisiana at

meaning of 9/11, when Americans were feeling vulnerable in a way that African Americans always have felt, "It is time for a blues nation to learn from a blues people."[92] Perhaps the deepest way White people might embrace double consciousness and help repair the colonial wound of anti-black white supremacy is by embodying with every ounce of our individual and collective being a "blues hope," in Copeland's felicitous phrasing of prophetic and mystical wisdom rooted in the cross of Jesus Christ.

However, a key problem is that the condition of the possibility of such transformation is not something we can achieve through our own will, intellect, and power. In their respective womanist and liberation theologies, Copeland and Massingale both draw deeply upon the Carmelite mystic Constance FitzGerald's public education for contemplation and transformation, especially in the way FitzGerald reinterprets "impasse and dark night" in the works of Saint John of the Cross and Saint Teresa of Ávila. In preparation for the 2009 Catholic Theological Society of America convention, Copeland and Massingale invited FitzGerald to address the conference theme of "impasse." In their letter of invitation to FitzGerald, Massingale wrote,

> Yet I do believe that Shawn and my experiences give us a "connatural affinity" to the reality of impasse [and the dark night] which compel us to engage it forthrightly and fruitfully—not only for ourselves but for the sake of the Church.[93]

Massingale invites Catholic scholars and the Church to "re-examine their familiar constructs through an encounter with the Black experience, that is, the experience of carving out meaning, purpose, and identity amid the crushing ordinariness of coping with white racial supremacy."[94] The "dark night," he explains, "looks different when examined from the perspective of the marginalized and despised."[95]

I find an uncanny resemblance between decoloniality, FitzGerald's interpretation of societal impasse, and Copeland's articulation of a "blues hope." The problem of impasse, FitzGerald finds, is far more than personal, because its historical roots are global in scope. FitzGerald, Copeland, and decolonial

Lafayette, 2011).

[92]Toni Morrison and Cornel West, "We Had Better Do Something," *The Nation*, May 4, 2004, www.thenation.com.

[93]Bryan Massingale shares a part of this letter to Constance FitzGerald in his essay honoring M. Shawn Copeland, "The Dark Night(s) of Malcolm X: Apophatic Mysticism and African American Spirituality," in Robert J. Rivera and Michelle Saracino, eds., *Enfleshing Theology: Embodiment, Discipleship, and Politics in the Work of M. Shawn Copeland* (Lanham, MD: Lexington Books, 2018), 227.

[94]Ibid., 226.

[95]Ibid.

scholars and activists all find interwoven roots of global domination in Western epistemology, patriarchy, and racism. Our dominant nation, FitzGerald contends, exacerbates the problem of impasse because it only teaches us "illusion, minimization, repression, denial, [and] apathy," through the "social, economic, and political forces of our time."[96]

Impasse is a limit situation in which there is "no way out, no way around, no rational escape from what imprisons one, no possibilities in the situation."[97] Ironically, FitzGerald explains, impasse is experienced, both personally and societally, as the problem itself in the attempt to respond rationally. Logical solutions provide no way out and feel dissatisfying. She notices how the "whole life situation suffers a depletion" in which suffering seems to take over one's entire life. Impasse may feel like physical and spiritual imprisonment. The most dangerous temptation is giving into despair "in the face of the disappointment, disenchantment, hopelessness, and loss of meaning that encompass one."[98]

As Americans, FitzGerald argues, "We are not educated for impasse, for the experience of human limitation that will not yield to hard work, studies, statistics, and rational analysis. We stand helpless before the insurmountable problems of our world."[99] Perhaps worse, we dare not engage impasse, as we will not allow it to come to full consciousness as it is too destructive of US national esteem. The problem religiously, spiritually, and morally is that collectively we do not allow ourselves to be totally challenged by anyone who is oppressed or "by the unjust, unequal situation of women in a patriarchal, sexist culture; by those tortured and imprisoned and murdered in the name of national security; [or] by the possibility of the destruction of humanity."[100]

Paradoxically, FitzGerald explains, impasse itself may provide the condition of the possibility of bodily co-sensing the cries of the earth and people who are oppressed everywhere. However, that means embracing impasse and dying to false images of self and society. Left to our own devices, we lack the capacity to free ourselves from our attachments to wealth, privilege, and power. To face the challenge of impasse, she writes, we need the kind of radical faith, hope, and love that "can endure the death-dealing touch of God's hand," the only touch that facilitates an "emptying of our isolated self-sufficiency, on the one hand, and our unfree dependence and fear of transformation and change, on the other."[101]

---

[96]FitzGerald, "Impasse and Dark Night," in *Living with Apocalypse*, 105.

[97]Ibid., 94.

[98]Ibid.

[99]Ibid., 105.

[100]Ibid., 106.

[101]Constance FitzGerald, "Transformation in Wisdom: The Subversive Character and Educative Power of Sophia in Contemplation," in *Carmel and Contemplation: Transforming Human Consciousness*, ed. Kevin Culligan, OCD, and Regis Jordan, OCD (Washington, DC: ICS

We need to bring personal and societal impasse to prayer and into the presence of Sophia-Wisdom. FitzGerald purposefully employs feminine imagery of God as Sophia-Wisdom, based upon feminine grammatical gender in Greek *sophia*, Hebrew *chokmah*, and Latin *sapientia*. There are more important reasons than grammar for using feminine imagery of God, however. First, the biblical depiction of wisdom in pre-Christian Judaism "is invariably female," because biblical wisdom is not an "it" but rather someone whom scripture describes as "sister, mother, spouse, female beloved, teacher, chef and hostess, preacher, judge, liberator, establisher of justice, and numerous other female roles."[102] Second, the Carmelite mystics John of the Cross and Teresa of Ávila draw deeply upon the feminine biblical wisdom tradition, FitzGerald explains, which offers great potential for spirituality today. This is "a time when [the] long dominant masculinity [of the Western tradition] has become so apparent to us," with its stifling dualism and patriarchy, that "Sophia is a God image capable of moving humanity into the next evolutionary era when the universe will be experienced not as a collection of objects for human use and mastery but rather as an intimate, interconnected, and diverse communion of subjects."[103]

Bringing personal and societal impasse to prayer is the only way "society will be freed, healed, changed, and brought to paradoxical new visions, therefore, for community on this earth."[104] FitzGerald warns that the indwelling of Sophia-Wisdom involves death—"dying in order to see how to be and act on behalf of God in this world."[105] Impasse itself may provide the conditions of the possibility of transformation "if the limitations of one's own humanity and human condition are squarely faced and the sorrow of finitude allowed to invade the human spirit with real, existential powerlessness."[106]

In times of impasse—when we do not feel faith, hope, and love—we need to maintain a contemplative posture of acceptance in our prayer and life, precisely when it is most difficult to do so. This seems so contradictory, says FitzGerald, because it is faith itself that "causes darkness in our power to understand."[107] She reminds us that dark night "is not primarily *something*" like an abstract, impersonal darkness causing "a distressful psychological condition." Rather, dark night "is *someone*, a presence leaving an indelible imprint on the human spirit and consequently on one's entire life."[108] That

Publications, 2000), 322.
[102]Ibid., 283.
[103]Ibid., 283–84.
[104]FitzGerald, "Impasse and Dark Night," in *Living with Apocalypse*, 107.
[105]Ibid.
[106]Ibid., 96.
[107]FitzGerald, "Transformation in Wisdom," 323.
[108]Ibid., 310.

someone is the indwelling Jesus-Sophia who transforms all of the destructive values of Western mastery, patriarchy, and racism.

Jesus-Sophia is the one who draws us into intimacy with God. As we become aware of our limitation and finitude, Jesus-Sophia teaches us that our mind, heart, memory, and imagination are vast "caverns" that reveal our infinite capacity for divine love and transformation.[109] John of the Cross uses the term "caverns" to elucidate his theological anthropology that perceives how the human person has an infinite capacity for God.[110] Jesus-Sophia purifies these caverns of the human knowledge, loves, and memories that fail to fulfill infinite longing for God and transforms them into intimate longing and relationship. Jesus-Sophia subverts how we see reality, including how we tend to see reality through Western individualism, dualism, patriarchy, and racism.

Thus, in her elucidation of the "dark night" in John of the Cross, FitzGerald describes three levels that the indwelling Jesus-Sophia subverts our self-image, our image of God and Christ, and our relationship to the world, including "unveiling our cultural violence."[111] Ultimately, Sophia-Jesus draws us away "from domination, control, anxiety, competition, and exploitation to receive Wisdom in mindless, playful joy, and delight."[112]

Through surrender in faith and trust to the unfathomable Mystery that transforms human desire in the midst of societal breakdown and impasse, "When the pain of human finitude is appropriated with consciousness and consent and handed over in one's person to the influence of Jesus' spirit in the contemplative process, the new and deeper experience gradually takes over, the new vision slowly breaks through, and new understanding and mutuality are progressively experienced."[113] The process of transformation within impasse and dark night facilitates an entirely new way of seeing and sensing that draws us into a "more genuine intimacy with God [and] with the 'other.' "[114]

---

[109]Ibid., 303.
[110]Ibid., 351n46. FitzGerald quotes John of the Cross's commentary on his poem "Living Flame of Love," stanza 3, paragraph 22: "The capacity of these caverns is deep because the object of this capacity, namely God, is profound and infinite. Thus in a certain fashion their capacity is infinite, their thirst infinite, their hunger is also deep and infinite, and their languishing and suffering are infinite death." Saint John of the Cross, "Commentary on *The Living Flame of Love*," stanza 3, paragraph 22, in *The Collected Works of St. John of the Cross*, rev. ed., trans. Kieran Kavanaugh, OCD, and Otilio Rodriguez (Washington, DC: ICS Publications, 1991), 681.
[111]FitzGerald, "Transformation in Wisdom," 312.
[112]Ibid., 329.
[113]FitzGerald, "Impasse and Dark Night," in *Living with Apocalypse*, 103.
[114]Ibid., 100.

Embracing a Blues Hope

How do white colonial settlers in North America even begin to sense our geopolitical and historical situation? And what would it mean for a white colonial settler body "to give" in a way that inhabits—dwells within—a disobedient, decolonial way of being in the world? Such a movement, I argue, would be marked by a cluster of at least five moral and spiritual practices. The order in which I present these practices is not intended to be linear or progressive; rather, the way God draws us into transformation in the midst of societal impasse is unique for each individual and community. These interconnected practices include taking sides with and for Black and colonized peoples; epistemic and civil disobedience; lament; radical dispossession of land and wealth, an issue I address in the next chapter; and ecological intimacy, an issue integral to transforming racial and social consciousness that I address in the closing chapter.

Crossing Over to Take Sides

A key ingredient and marker of double consciousness and decolonial dwelling, I believe, is choosing sides with and for racially oppressed peoples in the midst of a societal conflict that is historically integral to European Christianity and the founding of the United States. A deeper level of mystical and political intimacy is decolonial dwelling with and for Black and colonized peoples. In her meditation on the blues, M. Shawn Copeland explains that the "blues come from the brutal realities of the underside of the Enlightenment, an underside distorted by uncritical commitment to autonomy, power, acquisitiveness, control, and indifference."[115] The gifts of double consciousness derive not only from public intellectuals like Du Bois, but from enslaved people

> who teach us a love-ethic that commands us to love ourselves and our own people, yet not to love others or ourselves uncritically. The dangerous memories and dark wisdom of the enslaved people teach us how to be defined by commitment to the here-and-now to the realization of the reign of God, rather than victimization. The dangerous memories and dark wisdom of enslaved people join ethos and cosmos to teach us not how to avoid or deny suffering, but how to suffer suffering.[116]

---

[115] Copeland, "Theology at the Crossroads," 102.

[116] M. Shawn Copeland, "Knowing Christ Crucified: Dark Wisdom from the Slaves," in *Missing God? Cultural Amnesia and Political Theology*, ed. John K. Downey, Jurgen Manemann, and Steven T. Ostovich (Berlin: Lit Verlag, 2006), 77–78.

In the context of societal breakdown and impasse post-9/11 and during a global pandemic, who would be a better guide for working through "impasse and dark night" than a people whose experience of God's wisdom was forged in the midst of the source of our current impasse: modernity/coloniality? At this historical, moral, and spiritual crossroads I believe that standing with and for Black and colonized people is where we find God's wisdom and the transforming power of love of God and neighbor.

"The acid test of authentic solidarity," Massingale argues, "is how it is lived in the midst of reality, that is, in the midst of social conflict."[117] The root of racial violence is in the minds, hearts, and souls of White people who accept the structure, culture, and habitus of whiteness as a way of life. Massingale quotes a similar challenge from Malcolm X: "Where the really sincere white people have got to do their 'proving' of themselves is not among the Black victims, but out in the battle lines where America's racism really is—and that is in their own home communities; America's racism is among their own fellow whites."[118] One of the critical ways people who believe they are white can stand with and for Black people is by (de)facing whiteness:

> (De)facing whiteness implies a double movement: facing whiteness, in all of its horror, without resorting to white flight; and (de)facing whiteness, both in the sense of destroying it and in the sense of de-facing it, i.e., undoing the notion that whiteness is human.[119]

Massingale explains how Malcolm X would judge the solidarity advocated by too many Catholics, including theologians and scholars, as "unrealistic, if not ideologically complicit in its assessment of the difficulty of achieving social change."[120] The problem I have been describing in this book is that White people tend to view racism as something beyond us, as in the distant past, or as something only committed by overt white supremacists, but definitely not something that deforms us systemically and culturally through the colonial matrix of power and white habitus. With these widely held assumptions of white individuality, racial innocence, and moral superiority (which the ecclesial hierarchy does not expose or confront), addressing racism then becomes a kind of nice add-on to living the gospel rather than an issue that directly impinges on our image of God, how we practice faith, and how we

---

[117]Bryan N. Massingale, "*Vox Victamarum, Vox Dei:* Malcolm X as a Neglected 'Classic' for Catholic Theological Reflection," in *Proceedings of the Catholic Theological Society of America* 65 (2010): 63–88, here 83.

[118]Ibid.

[119]Cecelia Cissell Lucas, "Decolonizing the White Colonizer?," PhD dissertation, University of California–Berkeley, 2013, 2, https://digitalassets.lib.berkeley.edu/etd/ucb/text/Lucas_berkeley_0028E_13606.pdf .

[120]Massingale, "*Vox Victamarum, Vox Dei,*" 83.

live out our lives. People formed by coloniality and white habitus have great difficulty developing a critical consciousness that pierces the illogic of the dominant way of being and knowing.

Again, Massingale quotes Benjamin Karim, one of Malcolm X's close associates, who expressed development of a critical consciousness as understanding how "untruths had to be untold." Karim continued to explain that Malcolm X would teach his students, "We had to be untaught before we could be taught, and once untaught, we ourselves could unteach others."[121] Just as Black people and other people of color may need to unlearn internalized inferiority, so White people need to unlearn internalized superiority, as a spiritual discipline. The work of unlearning internalized white superiority demands a life commitment internally, interpersonally, and within communities, to delinking from modernity/coloniality. The work of unlearning internalized domination learned within white habitus is integral to a process of transformation into a way of life characterized by racial intimacy.

Epistemic and Civil Disobedience

Taking sides with and for Black and colonized people is a way of taking up epistemic and civil disobedience. Disobeying the rules of the game through epistemic and civil disobedience is a condition of the possibility of delinking from modernity/coloniality's hegemony and setting the conditions for authentic liberation. Far more profound than resistance to the colonial matrix of domination, Constance FitzGerald's contemplative praxis, drawing upon the life-giving well of Sophia-Wisdom, underscores the need for unlearning the untruths in which we are humanly, spiritually, and morally deformed everyday through white settler coloniality. FitzGerald's acoustic ethic of hearing the cries of the oppressed suggests reexisting—that is, reorienting one's entire way of knowing and being—on grounds other than modernity/coloniality that create conditions whereby women, people of all colors, and *les damnes de la terre* may fully thrive through ways of living that give life to planetary biodiversity.

The main goals of decolonial aesthesis as disobedient conservatism include delinking from modernity in order to reexist and relinking with the "legacies one wants to preserve in order to engage in modes of existence with which one wants to engage."[122] Reexisting on terms that are disobedient to modernity means discerning how to live life in one's local context, "instead of giving our time and bodies to corporations, our attention and intelligence

---

[121]Ibid., 72.

[122]Walter Mignolo, "Coloniality Is Far from Over, and So Must Be Decoloniality," *Afterall: A Journal of Art, Context and Enquiry*, no. 43 (Spring/Summer 2017): 38–45, at 40–41.

to mainstream media, our energy to banks, which are constantly harassing us to obtain credits to pay high interest."[123] However, Mignolo argues that this is not a call to delinquency. Rather, disobedient conservatism entails both epistemic disobedience and Gandhi-like civil disobedience in order that people deemed "untouchable" may reexist and thrive on their own terms. Reexisting means that African American, Caribbean, Latino, and Indigenous people relink with and conserve their own memories and legacies and live in ways that conserve the life and energy of the entire community and the earth itself.

Lament

A third critical way of embracing double consciousness, societal impasse, and racial intimacy is lament. Copeland explains that "lament protests, pushes against that calculus of power by which the weak and the vulnerable suffer oppression and abuse."[124] Recall biblical scholar Walter Brueggemann's discussion of the way lament goes to the depth of faith of the people of Israel. He recounts how Israel's cry of distress initiates salvation history (Ex 2:23–25); God hears the cries of the afflicted and acts with mercy (Ps 107); and Israel responds with praise and thanksgiving. In this biblical and theological context, Copeland urges lament not only as dialogue but as a way of "boxing" with God that "questions, argues, and rebukes."[125] It is precisely through our questioning, argumentation, and rebuke of God that "lament takes seriously God's compassionate love and care in the midst of suffering and privation even as it 'refuses to accept a view of the world where God fixes everything, although God has not done so' in the past."[126] Lament is a practice of justice that prophetically names injustice "in the here-and-now"[127]—listening, hearing, and crying with and for our mothers, fathers, brothers, sisters, and all of our kin whose lives were taken by death-dealing violence. As Sybrina Fulton, mother of Trayvon Martin, wrote in an open letter to the family of Michael Brown, "Feeling us means feeling our pain; imagining our plight as parents of slain children. We will no longer be ignored."[128] When we lament with people in a way in which we see others as "we," as "us," then we not only practice double consciousness and embrace Sophia-Jesus in the midst of

---

[123]Ibid., 41.

[124]M. Shawn Copeland, "Presidential Address: Political Theology as Interruptive," in *Catholic Theological Society of America: Proceedings of the Fifty-Ninth Annual Convention*, Weston, Virginia, June 10–13, 2004, 81.

[125]Ibid.

[126]Ibid. Copeland cites Kathleen O'Connor, *Lamentations and the Tears of the World* (Maryknoll, NY: Orbis Books, 2002), 131.

[127]Ibid.

[128]Sybrina D. Fulton, "If They Refuse to Hear Us, We Will Make Them Feel Us," *Time*, August 14, 2014, www.time.com.

impasse, we enter into the intimate neighbor-love at the heart of the gospel. Then we might yet become "friends of God and prophets, 'the body of Christ broken together, the sacrament of healing for our world.' "[129] Then we, as the people of God, may yet find our shared desire for God in the revelation of the cross's "radical risk—the resurrection in its audacious, ironic, blues-transcendental hope."[130] I now take up the practices of radical dispossession as reparations in chapter 5. Then I address embracing ecological intimacy in the final chapter.

[129]Copeland, "Presidential Address," 81.
[130]Copeland, "Theology at the Crossroads," 103.

5

Reparation

So the Last Will Be First

It is time for a reckoning. It is time to pay restitution to African Americans to end five hundred years of racialized plunder. In his encyclical on social friendship, Pope Francis calls people of faith to "form a new society" and "write a new page of history" that "changes social conditions that create suffering" for our neighbors.[1] Writing a new history means restructuring society so that our neighbor does not find herself in oppressive conditions; this is "an indispensable act of social love."[2] Restructuring society, rightly rooted in love and justice, means paying restitution that establishes equality. As defined by Saint Thomas Aquinas, restitution "denotes the return of the thing unjustly taken; since it is by giving it back that equality is re-established."[3] In terms of the US constitutional republic, "If true justice and equality are ever to be achieved in the United States, the country must finally take seriously that it owes Black Americans."[4] When we, as a church and society, acknowledge the history of racialized plunder and redress this injustice by instituting reparations, we can rightly claim that Black lives matter—indeed, all lives.

Decolonial repair means embodying epistemic disobedience of modernity/coloniality, as well as a counterimagination in our entire way of thinking, feeling, and being. Sharing in the struggle of Black Lives Matter within concrete communal praxis is integral to nurturing epistemic disobedience that subverts the history of coloniality. This subversion begins with memory of the "scourged Christs of America," of "memory of the Christ who is pres-

---

[1] Pope Francis, *Fratelli Tutti, On Fraternity and Social Friendship*, Vatican, October 3, 2020, nos. 229 and 231.

[2] Ibid., no. 186.

[3] Saint Thomas Aquinas, *Summa Theologica* II-II, q.62, a.2, ad (Westminster, MD: Christian Classics, 1981 [1911]), 1450.

[4] Nikole Hannah-Jones, "What Is Owed," *New York Times Magazine*, June 28, 2020, 30–35, 47, 50–53, here 30.

ent in every starving, thirsting, imprisoned, or humiliated human being, in the despised minorities, in the exploited classes (Mt 25:31–45)."[5] This is a memory of a Christ who "not only freed us, he meant us to remain free (Gal 5:1)."[6] Gustavo Gutiérrez describes the subversion of history—that is, the "rereading of history"—in a way that focuses the work of decolonial repair taken up in this chapter:

> But *rereading* history means *remaking* history. It means repairing it from the bottom up. And so it will be a *sub*versive history. History must be turned upside-down from the bottom, not the top. What is criminal is not to be *sub*versive, struggling against the capitalist system, but to continue being "*super*versive"—bolstering and supporting the prevailing domination. It is in this subversive history that we can have a new faith experience, a new spirituality—a new proclamation of the gospel.[7]

A liberating decolonial vision and framework for rereading, remaking, and repairing history are critical for all people who desire to be human. Too often, White "reparations" discourse in the North American context tends to be reduced to a one-off event with a myopic focus on the cost of a one-time reparation payment—this is a distinctly capitalist, egocentric approach that maintains the matrix of domination. Such fixation on a one-time cost and payment will fail precisely because:

- Reparation is framed from within the dominant consciousness of coloniality.
- It does not begin with hearing the voices and perspectives of people who have carried the burden of death-dealing racism for five hundred years.
- It is in the short-term immediate interest of maintaining the status quo, rather than in the longer-term effort to discern and address the social and moral issues at stake.

Decoloniality invites a different framework and counterimagination as a long-term process that facilitates an enduring exodus to life-giving ways of being in the world. In short, I suggest engaging a decolonial Christian praxis of healing with and for Black Lives Matter as a different framework and counterimagination. A communal praxis of decolonial love invites innovative

---

[5] Gustavo Gutiérrez, *The Power of the Poor in History* (Maryknoll, NY: Orbis Books, 1983), 21.
[6] Ibid.
[7] Ibid.

ways of rereading and remaking history with and for diverse perspectives of the *damnés*, including Black, Indigenous, and Latinx communities, and other communities of color. Grounded in love of neighbor (Jas 2:1–8), it is possible to make a different world—cocreating a world in order that Black lives may thrive.

I begin this chapter by discussing the uncanny convergence between decolonial approaches to love and repair with the mystical-political praxis of Black and womanist liberation theologies, especially that of M. Shawn Copeland and Bryan Massingale. Second, I suggest a mystical-political praxis as a decolonial process of "p/reparations."[8] P/reparations, I explain, means prayerfully preparing ourselves as people of faith for entering an open, long-term process of repairing the damage and trauma of slavery and racism. Such a process is needed to begin to undo a five-hundred-year legacy of coloniality. A process of p/reparations in the American Catholic ecclesial context begins with becoming a listening church that prioritizes the diverse perspectives of the *damnés*. A listening church is one whose Eucharistic memory is informed and reformed by those most impacted by the historically distorted witness and life-denying effects of the church. Truthful remembering is integral to reorienting the people of God to Sophia-Wisdom's preferential love for the *damnés* and embodying and enacting the Eucharistic welcome table of the *basileia tou theou*. A listening community of faith that embraces a decolonial p/reparations framework, finally, discerns concrete policies and actions that facilitate decolonial repair and the conditions of the possibility of full human thriving for African Americans.

Decolonial Love

Frantz Fanon ends his classic *Black Skin, White Masks* by asking, "Was my freedom not given to me then in order to build the world of the *You*? At the conclusion of this study I want the world to recognize, with me, the open door of every consciousness."[9] He turns his desire for recognition and an open consciousness into a prayer: "Oh my body, make of me always a man who questions!"[10] Fanon's prayer conveys his sensing bodily the existential

---

[8]Cecelia Cissell Lucas, "Decolonizing the White Colonizer?," PhD dissertation, University of California–Berkeley, 2013, 2, https://digitalassets.lib.berkeley.edu/etd/ucb/text/Lucas_berkeley_0028E_13606.pdf, 35 and 45. I draw upon Lucas's elucidation of a "philosophy and praxis of p/reparations" to articulate a decolonial, Christian mystical-political praxis.

[9]Frantz Fanon, *Black Skin, White Masks*, trans. Charles Lam Markmann (New York: Grove Press, 1967 [1952]), 232.

[10]Ibid.

geopolitical predicament of the *damnés de la terre*. Philosopher Lewis Gordon contextualizes Fanon's conclusion in terms of double consciousness. In the context of colonial oppression, "embodied consciousness is overly determined inward," creating anxiety and alienation, whereas Fanon's final prayer to always embody questioning is "double-consciousness born of dialectical critique."[11] Gordon explicates the way Fanon shifts his question ("Was not my freedom given . . .") away from himself to the general reader—"in order to build the world of the *You*?" Fanon uses the personal, informal "you" here (*toi* in French) instead of the formal (*vous*). He notes that the personal you, in terms of the existential thought of philosopher Martin Buber, concerns the "*I* and *You*" that will "leave no room for 'it' formulations."[12] In Buber's formulation, the personal "you" respects "you in your humanity. It is, as we say, *personal and intimate*."[13] By recognizing the humanity of you, such respect faces the "'open consciousness of all consciousness' (*'la dimension ouverte de toute conscience'*), another human being devoid of overdetermined presumptions."[14]

Unlike modern European epistemology that asserts universal claims from an unacknowledged provincial perspective, Fanon's bodily prayer is a way of thinking geopolitically whereby "the biographical sensing of the Black body in the Third World" anchors "a politics of knowledge that is both ingrained in the body and in local histories."[15] In the context of French colonized Algeria, Fanon enacts bodily epistemic disobedience, whereby his sensing "created the conditions to link border epistemology with immigrant consciousness and, consequently, delink from territorial and imperial epistemology grounded on theological (Renaissance) and egological (Enlightenment) politics of knowledge."[16]

In contrast to Fanon's bodily sensing of the geo- and political-historical predicament of *les damnes de la terre*, modernity's theo- and ego-politics of knowledge are grounded in a suppression of bodily sensing,[17] in which European modernity claims universality of knowledge and "hides coloniality and prevents pluriversal, dialogic, and epistemically democratic systems of

---

[11]Lewis R. Gordon, *What Fanon Said: A Philosophical Introduction to His Life and Thought* (New York: Fordham University Press, 2015), 140.

[12]Ibid. Gordon cites Martin Buber, *I and Thou*, trans. Ronal Gregor Smith (New York: Scribner's and Sons, Collier Book, 1958).

[13]Gordon, *What Fanon Said*, 140, citing Buber (Gordon's emphasis).

[14]Ibid.

[15]Walter Mignolo, "Geopolitics of Sensing and Knowing: On (De)coloniality, Border Thinking, and Epistemic Disobedience," *Confero* 1, no. 1 (2013): 129–50, here 132.

[16]Ibid., 132–33.

[17]See also Margaret Farley's critique of Western dualism, embodiment, and coloniality in her *Just Love: A Framework for Christian Sexual Ethics* (New York: Continuum, 2006), 114–15 and 63–65.

thought from unfolding."[18] Fanon's prayer is a bodily way of practicing epistemic disobedience, which is the first step in unlearning modernity/coloniality.

It would be an understatement to say that this presents a problem for Christian spirituality and theology. Walter Mignolo describes a fundamental problem in which Christianity remains epistemologically rooted in the imperial designs of coloniality. Christian spirituality and theology—even when they might be critical of modernity—tend not to question the rules of the game set by modernity/coloniality. Mignolo includes theologies of liberation in his criticism because "as in the disputes between (neo)liberalism and (neo) Marxism, both sides of the coin belong to the same bank: the disputes are entrenched within the same rules of the game, where the contenders defend different positions but do not question the terms of the conversation."[19]

In contrast to epistemologies that do not question the rules of the game set by modernity, Mignolo (and other decolonial theorists)[20] seek to "work out genealogies of thought" that "are connected through the common experience of the colonial wound—of sensing in one way or another, one belongs to the world" of the *damnés*. Decoloniality shifts the "rules of the game" by unveiling the rhetoric and promises of modernity, showing its "darker side" and "advocating and building global futures that aspire to fullness of life rather than encouraging individual success at the expense of the many and the planet."[21]

To return to a question I asked in the previous chapter, how do white colonial settlers in North America even begin to sense our geopolitical and historical ties to coloniality? This is an enduring problem of white settler colonialism because white American settlers and their churches actively suppress the violence upon which the nation was built. For example, Catholic parishes in predominantly White neighborhoods display the US flag, while few, if any, even begin to acknowledge the fact that we are white settlers living on land that First Peoples lived on for millennia. How many White Americans know anything about the US history of colonization, dispossession of Native American lands, and genocide? I did not begin to learn about colonization, dispossession of Indigenous lands, and genocide from Native American perspectives

---

[18]Walter Mignolo, *The Darker Side of Western Modernity: Global Futures, Decolonial Options* (Durham, NC: Duke University Press, 2011), 82.

[19]Ibid., 92.

[20]See, for example, Gloria Anzaldua, *Borderland / La Frontera: The New Mestiza* (San Francisco: Aunt Lute, 1987); Nelson Maldonado-Torres, *Against War: Views from the Underside of Modernity* (Durham, NC: Duke University Press, 2008); Linda Tuhiwai Smith, *Decolonizing Methodologies: Research and Indigenous Peoples* (Dunedin: University of Otago Press / Zed, 1999); and Sylvia Wynter, "Unsettling the Coloniality of Being/Power/Truth/Freedom: Towards the Human, After Man, Its Overrepresentation: An Argument," *New Centennial Review* 3, no. 3 (2003): 257–337.

[21]Mignolo, *Darker Side*, 122.

until I was in graduate school. I am writing this chapter on ancestral lands of Mohican people, which means "people of the waters that are never still." A common white settler assumption in this region, the Berkshire Mountains of western Massachusetts, is that the colonial period is past. In other words, we don't perceive the ways in which coloniality is our contemporary reality. Where, when, and how do white settlers recall that "under the crust of that portion of the Earth called the United States of America . . . are interred the bones, villages, fields, and sacred objects of American Indians?"[22] Historian of Native American studies Roxanne Dunbar-Ortiz begins her courses with a simple exercise. She invites students to draw a rough outline of the United States at the time it gained independence from Britain. She finds that most students draw a picture of the United States that reflects the twenty-first-century shape of the country from the Atlantic to the Pacific. She assures them that they are not alone in this assumption that "reflects the seeming inevitability of U.S. extent and power, its destiny, with an implication that the continent had been *terra nullius*, a land without people."[23]

Perhaps there is nothing that prevents a White body from recognizing how coloniality works in other non–Western European bodies, but as Mignolo observes, "That would be rational and intellectual but not experiential."[24] He continues, "For a white European body to think decolonially means to give; to give in a parallel way that a body of color formed in colonial histories has to give if that body wants to inhabit postmodern and poststructuralist theories."[25]

I asked in the previous chapter what it would mean for a white colonial settler body "to give" in a way that inhabits—dwells within—a disobedient, decolonial way of being in the world. Intellectual questioning does not necessarily involve bodily sensing, as in Frantz Fanon questioning with his entire body or W. E. B. Du Bois sensing double consciousness bodily, socially, intellectually, morally, and spiritually.[26] Decolonial dwelling, Mignolo argues, demands an *aesthesis*,[27] which involves one's entire way of being in the world, including sensing and feeling with and for other human beings. Nelson Maldonado-Torres describes decolonial aesthesis as embodied subjects "who can not only reflect about but also mold, shape, and reshape subjec-

---

[22]Roxanne Dunbar-Ortiz, *An Indigenous Peoples' History of the United States* (Boston: Beacon Press, 2014), 1.

[23]Ibid., 2.

[24]Mignolo, "Geopolitics of Sensing," 145.

[25]Ibid.

[26]W. E. B. Du Bois, *The Souls of Black Folk* (New York: Barnes and Nobles Classic, 2003 [1903]); see especially chapter 1, "Of Our Spiritual Strivings."

[27]Walter Mignolo and Rolando Vazquez, "Decolonial AestheSis: Colonial Wounds/Decolonial Healings," *Social Text*, July 15, 2013, https://socialtextjournal.org.

tivity, space, and time."[28] Mignolo describes the aesthesis of decoloniality as "disobedient conservatism," that is, the "energy that engenders dignified anger and decolonial healing."[29]

As noted in the previous chapter, the main goals of decolonial aesthesis as disobedient conservatism include: 1) de-linking from modernity in order for people to re-exist on their own terms; and 2) re-linking with the "legacies one wants to preserve in order to engage in modes of existence with which one wants to engage."[30] Calling modernity/coloniality into question, however, is not a call to anarchy. Maldonado-Torres develops decolonial love as an "attitude" and "unfinished project," whereby the dynamic action of giving oneself over to diverse struggles of the *damnés* builds an open "world of the you."[31] In other words, Maldonado-Torres grounds his articulation of decoloniality in a "preferential option for the condemned of the earth," whereby love "acquires the dimension of passionate and intimate body-to-body encounter, which is a critical part of forming communities of 'loving and understanding'—in this sense the decolonial philosopher is by necessity an erotic being and erotics is part of decoloniality as first philosophy."[32] Decolonial "erotics" is not the reductionist sexual desire that tends to dominate American misogynist culture. It is not a self-interested eros in contradistinction to the "other-oriented" love of agape. Rather, decolonial love encompasses a more complex integration of eros and agape in which "the affective entrance into the lived experience and cosmology of communities that suffer on the underside of modernity is already a method of resistance, as is the relationality that exists within these communities."[33]

In summary, decolonial love is a geopolitical embodiment in three critically interrelated ways. First, it begins in bodily sensing and critique that unmoors dominating Western and American epistemologies, including the idolatry of anti-black white supremacy. Second, it is a particular, local communal praxis that creates space for a consciousness open to alternative ways of being in the world that retrieve genealogies of decolonial praxis. And third, decolonial love is a "catalyzing and authenticating historical movement" that creatively quickens the end of colonial oppressions.[34]

---

[28]Nelson Maldonado-Torres, "Outline of Ten Theses on Coloniality and Decoloniality," Frantz Fanon Foundation, http://fondation-frantzfanon.com.

[29]Walter Mignolo, "Coloniality Is Far from Over, and So Must Be Decoloniality," *Afterall: A Journal of Art, Context and Enquiry*, no. 43 (Spring/Summer 2017): 38–45.

[30]Ibid.

[31]Maldonado-Torres, "Outline of Ten Theses," 27, especially thesis 8: "Decoloniality involves an aesthetic, erotic, and spiritual decolonial turn whereby the *damné* emerges as creator."

[32]Ibid., 28.

[33]Joseph Drexler-Dreis, "James Baldwin's Decolonial Love as Religious Orientation," *Journal of Africana Religions* 3, no. 3 (2015): 251–78, here 255.

[34]Joseph Drexler-Dreis, *Decolonial Love: Salvation in Colonial Modernity* (New York: Ford-

Christian Decoloniality as Mystical-Political Praxis

Black, Indigenous, and Latinx theologians and communities have drawn upon and generated genealogies of thought and being that are connected through the common experience of colonial wounds—of dwelling in the world of the *damnés*.[35] M. Shawn Copeland's nonromanticized, critical elaboration of the "dark wisdom of slaves" invites a decolonial counterimagination and love. Drawing deeply upon slave narratives, histories of slave resistance to chattel slavery, and spirituals, Copeland elucidates how Africans drew upon "root paradigms—cognitive and moral orientations, fragments of rite and ritual, cultural memory—emerged from the interstices of loss and pushed upward in recovery and revision, in change and transformation, in improvisation."[36] In the midst of the violence of chattel slavery, "enslaved people opposed the violation of their liberty, although not always, not always successfully, and never completely. Eruptions of their defiance should never be romanticized or uncritically appropriated."[37]

Slaves resisted through diverse means, including backtalk or "sass," strategic organizing to disrupt a plantation's system of work, running away, or "feigned madness."[38] Anyone who judges slaves' responses as "deficient," Copeland retorts, ignores the asymmetrical power relations in which the master utilized the slave's body as a legal commodity with monetary value that objectified human life as a thing. In this context of "thingification," to recall Césaire's description of coloniality,[39] the lives of slaves became a "paradoxical tension of '*death in life.*' "[40]

Yet it is precisely in this context of objectification that enslaved people struggled for life and liberty by praying, learning to read and write, and creating rites and rituals in the hush of night—all of which defied the master's rule and death-dealing distortion of Christianity. Not only did the slaves demonstrate that "being human is a praxis,"[41] Copeland notes, their praxis is highly

---

ham University Press, 2019), 11.

[35]Ibid., 50. Drexler-Dreis cites a growing number of scholars who are developing a decolonial theological and spiritual project, including Vine Deloria Jr., Marcella Athaus-Reid, Ivan Petrella, Delores S. Williams, Ivone Gebara, James A. Noel, Jawanza Eric Clark, Noel Leo Erskine, Ada María Isasi-Díaz, Mayra Rivera, An Yountae, and Josiah Ulysses Young III.

[36]M. Shawn Copeland, *Knowing Christ Crucified: The Witness of African American Religious Experience* (Maryknoll, NY: Orbis Books, 2018), 8.

[37]Ibid.

[38]Ibid.

[39]Aimé Césaire, *Discourse on Colonialism*, trans. Joan Pinkham (New York: Monthly Review Press, 2000), 42.

[40]Copeland, *Knowing Christ Crucified*, 13–14.

[41]Ibid., 36.

suggestive of ways to delink from coloniality. "The vocabulary, characters, places, and events sung in the spirituals," she asserts, "reflect how enslaved people transformed 'the Book of Religion of the dominant peoples' into the prophetic, apocalyptic, emancipatory religion of the enslaved. And, what is most astonishing, perhaps cannot be argued: *the conversion of the God of slave masters to the cause of the emancipation of the enslaved.*"[42]

Most importantly, in the context of chattel slavery that objectified Black women's bodies for economic production, reproduction, and sexual violence, enslaved people "risked abuse, assault, even martyrdom to withdraw to secret spaces in woods and gullies to commune with the Author and Source of freedom."[43] Slave communities created "counter-discourses and practices," where they "knew themselves as 'new creatures in Jesus, the workmanship of his hand saved from the foundation of the world.'"[44]

Although it may be anachronistic to name Jesus's praxis as decolonial, he knew in his body "refugee status, occupation and colonization, social regulation and control" under Roman imperial rule in Palestine.[45] Jesus, Copeland rightly claims, "inserted" his body into the tension between resisting the oppression of Roman imperial rule and God's desire to realize fully the *basileia tou theou*.[46] His praxis of compassion that we find in the stories that he told, his practice of healing through touching ostracized bodies, and his critique of unjust wealth and power meant that Jesus identified his entire life and being with people treated as less than human. The prophetic praxis of Jesus is "on behalf of the reign of God" and renews Israel as it denounces "oppressive Roman rule."[47] Embracing lepers and people who were blind, paralyzed, and deaf, among others, Jesus invites an entirely new practice of table fellowship. As the parable of the Great Banquet (Lk 14:12-14 and Mt 22:9-10) testifies, Jesus overturns societal conventions regarding commensality. The host fills the banquet table with people who are poor, ostracized, and physically disabled so that people will be "'reclining next to anyone else, female next to male, free next to slave, socially high next to socially low, ritually pure next to ritually impure.'"[48] Jesus's practice of welcome signified a *basileia tou theou*

[42]M. Shawn Copeland, "Foundations for Catholic Theology in African American Context," in *Black and Catholic—The Challenge and Gift of Black Folk: Contributions of African American Experience and Thought to Catholic Theology*, ed. Jamie T. Phelps, OP (Milwaukee: Marquette University Press, 1998), 126 (italics in original).

[43]M. Shawn Copeland, *Enfleshing Freedom: Body, Race, and Being* (Minneapolis: Fortress Press, 2010), 38.

[44]Copeland, *Knowing Christ Crucified*, 33. Copeland is citing voices of ex-slaves in Clifton H. Johnson, ed., *God Struck Me Dead: Voices of Ex-Slaves* (Cleveland: Pilgrim Press, 1969), 111.

[45]Copeland, *Enfleshing Freedom*, 58.

[46]Ibid., 59.

[47]Ibid.

[48]Ibid., 60. Copeland cites John Dominic Crossan, *Jesus: A Revolutionary Biography* (New

that embodied egalitarianism, disrupted the perverse "'pleasures of hierarchy' and domination, and abolished the etiquette of empire."[49]

Jesus embodies a reverent, passionate, and compassionate way of being that "honors and prompts our deepest yearnings for truth and life; and validates our refusal of docility and submission in the face of oppression."[50] Jesus exemplifies "an eros for others, he gave his body, his very self, to and for others, to and for the Other" in a way that "resists every temptation to use or assimilate the other and the Other for our own self-gratification, purpose, or plan."[51]

Jesus's praxis of solidarity interrupts dominative relationships. Jesus clearly did not practice elite forms of piety and respectability. On the contrary, his unmistakable desire to be with and for oppressed people threatened the economic, political, and religious elites and reveals God's love and justice. Indeed, his preferential compassion for people who have been damned by society in any shape or form led to his crucifixion. The social doctrine of the church recognizes this reality today when it states that those who "stand up against [racial] oppression by certain powers" will "face scorn and imprisonment."[52]

The acid test of a decolonial, mystical-political solidarity, to draw upon the measure described by moral theologian Bryan Massingale, "is how it is lived in the midst of reality, that is, in the midst of social conflict."[53] The Black radical tradition forms a geopolitical genealogy of thought and practice, whether in the perspective of the "dark wisdom of the slaves," or the life and teaching of W. E. B. Du Bois, Richard Wright, Malcolm X, or Sylvia Wynter that dislocate Eurocentric epistemology and generate other ways of being in the world. In other words, Massingale's appropriation of Malcolm X demands "'unmasking the contradictions in logic and practice of the established order.'"[54] Malcolm X's critique of White Christianity means constantly questioning the assumptions of the established American order, including Catholic Christianity's "truth of how it has served as a rationalization of vested interests."[55]

York: Harper & Row, 1994), 68.

[49]Copeland, *Enfleshing Freedom*, 62. She attributes the "pleasures of hierarchy" to Paul Anthony Farley, "The Black Body as Fetish Object," *Oregon Law Review* 76 (1997): 459 and 464.

[50]Copeland, *Enfleshing Freedom*, 64.

[51]Ibid., 65.

[52]The Vatican, Pontifical Commission on Justice and Peace, "The Church and Racism: Toward a More Fraternal Society," 1988, no. 26.

[53]Bryan N. Massingale, "*Vox Victamarum, Vox Dei*: Malcolm X as a Neglected 'Classic' for Catholic Theological Reflection" *Proceedings of the Catholic Theological Society of America* 65 (2010): 63–88, here 63.

[54]Massingale, "*Vox Victamarum, Vox Dei*," 78. Massingale quotes Africanist scholar and activist Maulana Karenga, "The Oppositional Logic of Malcolm X: Differentiation, Engagement, and Resistance," *Western Journal of Black Studies* 17, no. 1 (Spring 1993): 7.

[55]Massingale, "*Vox Victamarum, Vox Dei*," 78.

Practicing solidarity in the midst of social conflict means fully embracing the moral claims of Black Lives Matter in mind, body, and spirit. That means, I believe, putting our White bodies on the line to protect Black Americans in the midst of public protest, giving the substance of our lives socially, economically, and politically so that Black Americans may thrive. Giving our lives with and for Black people demands that we "work to convert whites who think and act in racist ways."[56]

A concrete example, drawn from my own experience, is the anti-racist Community Organizer's Roundtable (COR) in New Orleans. Led by African American and Latinx community organizers, lawyers, and other nonprofit leaders, COR is oriented to establishing just and equitable institutions. As a White activist and scholar, I, along with other White people, followed the lead of Black and Latinx leaders, and we White folks worked primarily to address anti-black white supremacy in predominantly White communities. I have found through over twenty years of anti-racist work that White people's resistance to confronting our own privilege confirms Massingale's fundamental point, paraphrasing Frederick Douglass, that "power concedes nothing without a demand" and a struggle.[57] Until we White folks join bodily in a geopolitical struggle for justice and equality led by Black Lives Matter and confront racism in our own White communities, the colonial system of domination will endure.

P/reparations

I now outline one way of thinking about p/reparations theologically, morally, spiritually, and practically that integrates ecclesial, institutional, local, personal, and national dimensions of reparations work. I begin by discussing p/reparations as: truthful remembering, racial equity practices through covenant and caucusing, the African American ritual of Maafa, and embodying a "blues hope." The chapter concludes with a discussion of equitable redistribution of resources at both the national and local levels.

Truthful Remembering

Truthful remembering is a condition of the possibility of authentic repentance and reconciliation in Catholic social teaching.[58] Truthful remembering,

---

[56]Ibid., 83.

[57]Ibid., 82. Massingale quotes Frederick Douglass, "West Indian Emancipation Speech," on August 4, 1857 in Lerone Bennett Jr., *Before the Mayflower: A History of Black America*, 5th ed. (New York: Penguin Books, 1982), 160–61.

[58]Pontifical Council for Justice and Peace, "Contribution to World Conference against Racism,

theologian Jeremy Bergen explains, is more than a mode of knowledge. Truthful remembering must become a practice, a way of life.[59] Truthful remembering means that the Church's witness "cannot be done apart from the testimony of those who experience the distortion of that witness and its life-denying effects."[60] As such, the Church cannot be in control of a listening process in terms of setting deadlines or determining outcomes. Authentic listening demands a fundamental openness to hearing the pain, suffering, anger, and cries for justice of people who experience anti-black supremacy.

Eucharistic solidarity begins in anamnesis, "the intentional remembering of the dead, exploited, despised victims of history."[61] As a practice, however, remembering cannot be "pietistic or romantic memorial," because the histories of suffering are "fraught with ambiguity and paradox. The victims of history are lost, but we are alive."[62] The depth of who we are in the Mystical Body of Christ intimately intersects with histories of unjust suffering. As M. Shawn Copeland writes, "We owe all that we have to our exploitation and enslavement, removal and extermination of despised others."[63] And as Cheryllyn Branche and other descendants of slaves sold by Georgetown University urge, "We need the truth to be shared. Our Catholic faith demands truth."[64]

An "embodied account of the truth" measures the authenticity of an ecclesial process of listening.[65] That is to say, if the church confesses sin in its past, it must engage dialogically with the groups most impacted and hurt by those sins. The account of those most hurt—in this case, African Americans—must be living African Americans, both inside and outside the church, who alone can provide an embodied, truthful, and comprehensive picture of what really happened and is happening in the church's complicity in slavery and racism. Only an open-ended, transparent process of public dialogue offers the possibility of truthful remembering. If the church attempts to retrieve the past on its own without dialogue with people most impacted by its sin, it must recognize that such a retrieval would likely "obscure the account that may be given of that sin."[66] In other words, truthful remembering and apology ought not to be "a soliloquy."[67] An embodied dialogical process in the pres-

---

Racial Discrimination, Xenophobia and Related Intolerance," Vatican, 2001, nos. 6–12.

[59]Jeremy M. Bergen, *Ecclesial Repentance: The Churches Confront Their Sinful Pasts* (New York: T&T Clark International, 2011), 190–91.

[60]Ibid., 254.

[61]Copeland, *Enfleshing Freedom*, 100.

[62]Ibid.

[63]Ibid.

[64]Cheryllyn Branche, "My Family's Story in Georgetown's Slave Past," *New York Times*, September 2, 2016.

[65]Bergen, *Ecclesial Repentance*, 125.

[66]Ibid.

[67]Ibid., 280.

ent is the only way to "jointly own a new account of the past"—and "the mutuality and respect presupposed by it will already contribute to a healing of those relationships."[68]

In their recent pastoral letter *Open Wide Our Hearts*, the US Catholic bishops issued an apology for the Church's complicity in racism. The document proclaims,

> Acts of racism have been committed by leaders and members of the Catholic Church—by bishops, clergy, religious, and laity—and her institutions. We express deep sorrow and regret for them. We also acknowledge those instances when we have not done enough or stood by silently when grave acts of injustice were committed. We ask forgiveness from all who have been harmed by these sins committed in the past or the present.[69]

Although this statement rightly admits complicity, the problem is that it wholly lacks any process of open-ended, ongoing dialogical engagement with Black, Latinx, or Indigenous Catholics. The request for forgiveness is generic and lacks any direct conversation with persons and groups who have suffered harms due to the church. The voices of Black, Latinx, and Indigenous Catholics are not being heard. *Open Wide Our Hearts* was written and approved by the hierarchy without any transparent dialogical process.

While no process can adequately redress past wrongs of the Atlantic slave trade, *Open Wide Our Hearts* did not even afford Black Catholics the dignity and worth of speaking for themselves to establish a public record to which the Church could be held accountable. It appears that the document was written and issued as a soliloquy. A monological pastoral letter has consequences that tend to serve the status quo by maintaining the silence of marginalized voices within the Church and society. Furthermore, Catholic institutions, including parishes that tend to be predominantly White and affluent, are preemptively acquitted of any concrete examination of conscience that would foster accountability. Most importantly, a monological proclamation fails to engage White Catholics in a living dialogical process oriented to the specific voices of individuals and communities most impacted by anti-black white supremacy.

Finally, truthful remembering as a process of dialogue is a concrete way to counter American mythologies of innocence and incessant progress. Rather than obscuring the past, truthful remembering holds the people of God to

---

[68]Ibid., 125.

[69]United States Conference of Catholic Bishops, *Open Wide Our Hearts: The Enduring Call to Love, A Pastoral Letter against Racism* (Washington, DC: United States Conference of Catholic Bishops, 2018), 22, https://www.usccb.org.

account by focusing us on decolonial healing that happens in and through the Mystical Body of Christ. It refuses to induce *ressentiment* or numbing guilt. Truthful remembering centers the prayer and work of the church on the Mystical Body of Christ, who "retunes" our entire being in concert with our shared intimate relationship with one another in God, who alone guides our journey "on that absolute future that only God can give."[70]

Racial Equity Practice

In contrast to monological ecclesial statements, racial equity practice recognizes that the process of dialogue itself must contend with the reality of inequality. Racial equity practice is not naïve or idealistic about the prospects of cross-racial dialogue—creating authentic dialogue means contending with the dynamics of power and conflict that tear apart the Body of Christ. As a former member of the Pax Christi USA Anti-Racism Team (PCART), I have learned that racial equity practice includes the kind of social and historical analyses that I develop in Part I of this book. Now I focus on a practical process of building moral accountability through dialogue.

Racial equity practice begins with prayer and creating, or re-creating, a living covenant. Like covenants in Holy Scripture, a covenant is how we bind ourselves to one another and God. The work of establishing the covenant involves listening and attending to the diverse ways that respect is practiced. The covenant establishes a safe space where we can speak our truth, be with discomfort and work through conflict together in a safe and confidential space, commit to nonclosure or keeping the conversation going, embrace paradox and humor, and seek always to learn from one another, rather than trying to be perfect or in control.

After an anti-racism team or collective creates the covenant, racial identity caucusing (RIC)[71] is an indispensable process for developing the moral accountability of White people through dialogue. RIC structures three dimensions of dialogue: 1) White people addressing internalized superiority and racism within a white caucus, 2) people of color (POC) addressing internalized inferiority within a POC caucus, and 3) dialogue between both caucuses. Caucusing creates intentional space both for White people and people of color to focus on their respective work to dismantle racism and build racial equity.

The work of each caucus is interrelated but different. Caucusing respects the choice and need of people who have been marginalized to support one

---

[70]Copeland, *Enfleshing Freedom*, 103. See also Bergen, *Ecclesial Repentance*, 254.

[71]Crossroads Anti-Racism, "Racial Identity Caucusing: A Strategy for Building Anti-Racist Collectives," (Matteson, IL: Crossroads Antiracism Organizing and Training, undated), https://www.seattlechildrens.org/globalassets/documents/clinics/diversity/racial-identity-caucusing.pdf.

another and addresses the dynamics of internalized oppression. For POC, caucusing is a place where White people are not at the center of attention and where POC need not accommodate or assimilate to the ways White people tend to resist the emotional and conflictual nature of racial equity work. POC caucusing facilitates full expression of people's experience of macro- and micro-racial harms and trauma and ways of healing.

White caucusing embraces responsibility for exposing how white superiority operates. Making white culture visible is a critical first step in making intentional changes within the dominant culture. When the caucusing process makes white culture visible, it enables questioning and deliberate examination of white privilege and power and associated processes that reproduce white settler coloniality. White people together need to work through whiteness, its privileges, its conscious and unconscious dynamics, and the fears, anger, discomfort, and guilt that arise from the process of undoing internalized superiority.

Racial equity practice for White people means learning how to relinquish control. It means fostering the humility to orient ourselves to the voices and experience of Black and Indigenous people, and other people of color. Relinquishing control of the process is an integral way that White people practice authentic listening—by bending one's ear and being open to the experience of people of color. Too often, however, conversations on race place undue burdens on people of color to be teachers, thereby obfuscating the responsibility of White people to do our own work. White culture tends to leave its superiority uninterrogated and White people unresponsible. I have observed this dynamic within institutions of higher education when multicultural offices fail to develop concrete processes for dominant groups to become accountable.

In contrast to unstructured conversations and "one-off" events, racial equity caucusing nurtures awareness and empathy through personal encounter and responsible intellectual preparation, prepares people for healing and creative action for change in society, invites people to take sides with Black people and shoulder the burden of suffering, and facilitates a process of moral accountability in grassroots organizing and institutional transformation that "create[s] new cultural conditions that make more likely the voluntary assumption of responsibility for structured harm by the perpetrators and guilty beneficiaries to whom such responsibility is assigned."[72] Creating the conditions of the possibility for White people to take responsibility for repairing harm "must be practiced in the context of an anti-racism collective struc-

---

[72]Michael P. Jaycox, "Payback, Forgiveness, Accountability: Exercising Responsible Agency in the Midst of Structured Racial Harm," *Religions* 10, no. 528 (2019): 1–16, here 13.

tured by appropriate interracial accountability to persons of color."[73] Racial
identity caucusing is one integral piece of moral accountability that ought to
be integrated with rituals of remembrance and repair, to which I now turn.

Maafa

One ritual that African Americans practice in New Orleans and to which
the Catholic Church is invited to participate is Maafa.[74] *Maafa*, a Kiswahili
word for "great tragedy," is a ritual of music, dance, prayer, and intentional
remembering of the victims of the Atlantic slave trade that is practiced
throughout the United States. The Ashé Cultural Arts Center, which organizes
the annual Maafa commemoration in New Orleans, describes it as "an opportunity for the entire community to pause and reflect on a horrific transgression
against humanity, and how to personally, as a community, agree to distance
ourselves institutionally in word and deed from that transgression, its legacy,
and the evolved practice of racism in our civic, social, spiritual, and personal
lives."[75] Maafa is inclusive and invites all participants to remember their own
ancestors, whether enslaved or not, and to recall how the whole of creation
is united spiritually with the cosmos and the earth. Since I left New Orleans,
I miss the opportunity to participate in this ritual because my colleagues
from the Institute for Black Catholic Studies there and fellow members of
Black Catholic parishes cofacilitated the process. Maafa inspired within me
a newfound spiritual openness to seeing the world from the descendants of
the enslaved. More than a dozen different faith traditions, including Christian, Muslim, and Jewish faith leaders, offer prayer in the annual ritual in
Congo Square.

The commemoration of Maafa remembers and reenacts the practices of
Africans during the slave trade in New Orleans. As historian Freddi Williams
Evans describes the gatherings in Congo Square, "African descendants spoke
and sang in their native languages, practiced their religious beliefs, danced
according to their traditions, and played African-derived rhythmic patterns
on instruments patterned after African prototypes."[76] M. Shawn Copeland
describes how the ritual walk of Maafa "honors the Many Thousand Gone,
the enslaved ancestors of the Middle Passage and its brutal fulfillment, and
the Black Catholic dead."[77] Copeland elucidates how Bakongo and Roman

---

[73]Ibid.

[74]*Maafa* is a Kiswahili term for disaster, calamity, or great tragedy. Maafa commemorations
of the transatlantic slave trade, held in cities throughout the United States and beyond, honor
African ancestors and pray for a different future.

[75]See the Ashé Cultural Center's Maafa website, https://www.ashenola.org/maafa.

[76]Freddi Williams Evans, *Congo Square: African Roots in New Orleans* (Lafayette: University
of Louisiana Press, 2011), 1.

[77]M. Shawn Copeland, "Tradition and Traditions of African American Catholicism," *Theo-*

Catholic traditions "compenetrate one another" in the ritual to honor the dead, who are "believed capable of intervening in daily affairs[. B]estowing blessing or meting out punishment, the ancestors must be venerated properly and faithfully according to ritual and custom."[78] MAAFA invites both bodily questioning of coloniality and embodying a "blues hope," an integrally related dimension of decolonial repair.

Embodying a "Blues Hope"

One of the marks of retuning and decolonial repair is in laying our lives down for our friends (Jn 15:13). Decolonial repair means loving our neighbor as ourselves by giving our lives for others. If there is a way where there is no way, it is lamenting with and for people afflicted by anti-black violence and following the lead of Black Catholics that we may yet glimpse the possibilities of new birth in God's Beloved Community. Laying our lives down for others means embodying freedom *with and for*, that is, *being on the side of* Black people. Paradoxically, perhaps, one of the critical conditions of the possibility of decolonial repair means embodying a "blues hope," to draw upon Copeland's felicitous phrase of a mystical and prophetic womanist theology. Copeland is not alone in calling America to live the blues. Cornel West, the iconoclastic philosopher, reflected on being Black post-9/11 in a conversation with Toni Morrison:

> Since 9/11, all Americans feel unsafe, unprotected, subject to random violence and hatred, and that's been the situation of Black folks for 400 years. In that fundamental sense, to be a nigger is to be unsafe, unprotected, subject to random violence and hatred. And now the whole nation is niggerized, and everybody's got to deal with it. And I think that we are at a moment now when a blues nation has to learn from a blues people.[79]

In her "Meditation on the Blues," Copeland invites readers to contemplate multiple meanings of a spiritual journey to "the crossroads." She begins by explaining that in African spirituality the cross is two intersecting roads "where earthly and the spirit worlds meet" to "nourish each other."[80] She evokes im-

logical Studies 61, no. 4 (December 2000): 632–55, here 649.

[78]Ibid.

[79]Toni Morrison and Cornel West, "We Had Better Do Something: Toni Morrison and Cornel West in Conversation," *The Nation*, May 6, 2004, www.thenation.com.

[80]M. Shawn Copeland, "Theology at the Crossroads: A Meditation on the Blues," in *Uncommon Faithfulness: The Black Catholic Experience*, ed. M. Shawn Copeland, LaReine-Marie Mosely, SND, and Albert J. Raboteau (Maryknoll, NY: Orbis Books, 2009), 97–107, here 97.

ages both of a crossroads where Jesus was crucified and of the blues musician Tommy Johnson, who invites musicians to go to the crossroads at midnight to retune their instruments. "Figuratively," she writes, the "crossroads not only evoke potentiality, openings, and creativity but also improbability, caution, even chaos."[81] She explains that in "African American expressive aesthetics,"

> the multiple meanings of the cross and crossroads condense in the blues, in the creativity, style or "cool" (meaning appropriate conduct), power or *áshe* of the blues player. Keenly attuned to the indistinguishable yearnings of Saturday night and Sunday morning, the blues are jagged, raw, liminal, bursting with *eros*, shocking, yet true. The blues reverberate the depth of sorrow and hurt experienced by men and women who live hidden and in uncommon faithfulness in the shadows at the crossroads.[82]

The blues did "not just happen," rather, they are the "musings and moanings of African people in response to their 'peculiar experience' in the new world."[83] While the blues are not a set of propositions "nor a reductive interpretation of the Black lifeworld,"[84] Copeland celebrates theologian James Cone's description of the blues as "the essential ingredients that define the essence of the Black experience . . . the blues as a state [of] mind in relation to the Truth of the Black experience."[85]

Copeland invites all of us to bring our body, heart, mind, and soul to the crossroads where "heaven and earth" meet before the cross of Jesus, where we may experience graced retuning both individually and collectively. Walking to that crossroads of the dangerous memory of the life, ministry, death, and resurrection of Jesus Christ will be no easy task for people of privilege and power. At a time when Black Americans are crying out to breathe with George Floyd and yearning to live free of police, state, and vigilante violence, privileged white Americans find themselves in a different bind at the crossroads of this historical moment. Too many White people of faith are segregated from the pain, sorrow, and cries of brothers and sisters who struggle to live at the crossroads between the death-dealing scourge of a pandemic that disproportionately devastates communities of color and the scourge of anti-black police and vigilante violence.

---

[81] Ibid., 97–98.

[82] Ibid., 98.

[83] Ibid., 99.

[84] Ibid.

[85] Ibid. Copeland cites James Cone, *The Spirituals and the Blues: An Interpretation* (Maryknoll, NY: Orbis Books, 1972), 114.

Loss of lament, the biblical scholar Walter Brueggemann warns, means losing a relationship to God oriented to a covenantal praxis of economic and social justice.[86] However, when laments are submitted to God, a growth of mature faith develops that moves toward ritually, liturgically, rhetorically, and emotionally relinquishing power, privilege, and economic advantage in favor of restoring justice and covenantal relations devoted to caring for the most vulnerable first. That relinquishment is expressed in thanksgiving and praise to God. Lament makes a difference in Israel's life because it "shifts the calculus" of the status quo of power and ignites a transformation in the distribution of power. The crucial question that Brueggemann asks is, "What happens when the appreciation of lament is lost in our time?"[87] Where lament is lost, he answers, "docility and submissiveness are engendered," and the consequence of "social practice is to reinforce and consolidate the political-economic monopoly of the status quo."[88] However, where covenantal people lament suffering and injustice,

> it shifts the calculus and *redresses the distribution of power* between the two parties, so that the petitionary party is taken seriously and that the God who is addressed is newly engaged in a way that puts God at risk. As the lesser petitionary party (the psalm speaker) is legitimated, so the unmitigated supremacy of the greater party (God) is questioned, and made available to the petitioner.[89]

In a spirit of becoming a blues people who embody lament, it is time that we as the people of God acknowledge and seek to repair the maldistribution of resources and power.

P/reparations as Equitable Redistribution of Resources

Decolonial repair, I argue, means embracing a process that redresses the maldistribution of resources and power initiated by the Atlantic slave trade and reinscribed by Jim Crow and enduring discrimination against, and criminalization of, Black people. Material reparations restores survivors to their condition before the injustice occurred or to a condition that they would have attained if the injustice had not been inflicted. Drawing upon the 2001 state-

---

[86]Walter Brueggemann, "The Costly Loss of Lament," in *The Psalms: The Life of Faith*, ed. Patrick D. Miller (Minneapolis: Fortress Press, 1995), 98–111.

[87]Ibid., 102.

[88]Ibid.

[89]Ibid., 101 (italics in original).

ment of the International Law Commission of the United Nations, Catholic social teaching affirms,

> As far as possible, reparation should erase all the consequences of the illicit action and restore things to the way they would most probably be if that action had not occurred. When such restoration is not possible, reparation should be made through equivalent reparation.[90]

This document asserts that the "responsible State is under an obligation to make full reparation for the injury caused by the wrongful act."[91] This includes providing restitution by reestablishing the situation in place before the wrongful act was committed, if this is reasonably possible.[92] It is not possible, obviously, to "restore those who were enslaved to a condition preceding their enslavement, not only because those who were enslaved are now deceased but also because many thousands were born into slavery."[93] However, we can respect the memory of the enslaved by moving "their descendants toward a more equitable position commensurate with the status they would have attained in the absence of the injustice(s)."[94] Ultimately, effective reparations as restitution would "eliminate racial disparities in wealth, income, education, health, sentencing and incarceration, political participation, and subsequent opportunities to engage in American political and social life."[95]

Decolonial repair will, undoubtedly, unsettle those who are beneficiaries of the matrix of domination. Decolonial repair brings an end to the structures and ethic of coloniality. Decolonization "is not a metaphor"; it begins in incommensurability.[96] Incommensurability means that my white wealth and well-being are *"constituted in Afro" (as well as in Indigenous people and other people of color) "American impoverishment."*[97] That is to say, "their loss is my gain. The relationship is utterly asymmetrical and the asymmetry is utterly

---

[90]Pontifical Council for Justice and Peace, *Contribution to World Conference against Racism, Racial Discrimination, Xenophobia and Related Intolerance*, Vatican, August 29, 2001, no. 12, https://www.vatican.va/roman_curia/pontifical_councils/justpeace/documents/rc_pc_just-peace_doc_20010829_comunicato-razzismo_en.html.

[91]International Law Commission, "Responsibility of States for Internationally Wrongful Acts," United Nations, 2001, Article 31. Text reproduced as it appears in the annex to General Assembly resolution 56/83 of December 12, 2001, and corrected by A/56/49 (Vol.I)/Corr.4.

[92]Ibid., Article 35.

[93]William A. Darity and A. Kirsten Mullen, *From Here to Equality: Reparations for Black Americans in the Twenty-First Century* (Chapel Hill: University of North Carolina, 2020), 3.

[94]Ibid.

[95]Ibid.

[96]Eve Tuck and K. Wayne Yang, "Decolonization Is Not a Metaphor," *Decolonization: Indigeneity, Education, & Society* 1, no. 1 (2012): 1–40.

[97]James Perkinson, *White Theology: Outing Supremacy in Modernity* (New York: Palgrave Macmillan, 2004), 15 (italics in original).

relational."[98] In other words, the consequences of anti-black white supremacy are so disproportionate that extreme inequality defines racial relationships. Redressing the extreme inequality instituted over the past five hundred years, therefore, requires white economic divestment and dispossession.

Unsurprisingly, some people object to reparations for African Americans. For instance, economist William A. Darity and folklorist A. Kirsten Mullen refute thirteen arguments against reparations for descendants of slaves.[99] I focus on two primary objections to reparations. The editors at the *National Review* succinctly state their objection: "Paying for reparations is a terrible idea because there is no one to pay reparations and no one to pay them to."[100] Echoing this claim, *Boston Globe* columnist Jeff Jacoby argues that reparations to African Americans is "unworkable and unjust."[101] Contending that slavery was abolished in the Northeast within fifteen years of the American Revolution and that 75 percent of Whites never owned slaves during the height of southern slavocracy, Jacoby asserts that the time for reparations is when slaves were alive.

First, against the erroneous assumption of northern innocence, the North in fact "promoted, prolonged, and profited from slavery."[102] Second, slavery was not so long ago; many African Americans are only separated two or three generations from enslaved ancestors.[103] Third, contrary to the illusory assumption that slavery "is past, so get over it," economic historians illustrate how it is impossible to understand America's "spectacular economic development without situating slavery front and center."[104] African Americans continue to bear the brunt of racism in "labor market discrimination, grossly attenuated wealth, confinement to neighborhoods with lower levels of amenities and safety, disproportionate exposure to inferior schooling, significantly greater dangers in encounters with police and the criminal justice system writ large, and a general social disdain for the value of Black people's lives."[105] Reparations provide the most comprehensive way to redress the enduring legacy of slavery, Jim Crow, and structural racial inequalities.

---

[98]Ibid.

[99]Darity and Mullen, *From Here to Equality*, chapter 12, "Criticisms and Responses."

[100]The Editors, "The Reparations Primary," *National Review,* February 26, 2019, www.nationalreview.com.

[101]Jeff Jacoby, "Reparations Are Unworkable and Unjust," *Boston Globe,* March 29, 2019, www.bostonglobe.com.

[102]Anne Farrow, Joel Lang, and Jennifer Frank, *Complicity: How the North Promoted, Prolonged, and Profited from Slavery* (New York: Ballantine Books, 2006).

[103]Darity and Mullen, *From Here to Equality*, 242–43. The authors retrieve hereditary lines to slavery for over a dozen families.

[104]Sven Beckert and Seth Rockman, *Slavery's Capitalism: A New History of American Economic Development* (Philadelphia: University of Pennsylvania Press, 2016), 27.

[105]Darity and Mullen, *From Here to Equality*, 6.

Grounded in the gospel call that the first be last and the last first (Mt 20:16),[106] decolonial repair is not about any kind of "reconciliation" that would rescue white settler normalcy for individuals or institutions.[107] God's preferential love for the despised constitutes an incommensurable ethic that prioritizes Black and Indigenous sovereignty; it is not primarily concerned with the comfort of those in dominant positions. Partisanship favoring the oppressed is not only justified by the preferential option for the poor in Catholic social teaching, it is demanded by the disproportionate inequality of coloniality.[108] Indeed, Catholic social teaching demands a "firm and persevering commitment" to the common good and preferential love for the poor that means losing oneself "for the sake of the other rather than exploiting" others, and to serve people who are oppressed instead of oppressing others "for one's own advantage."[109]

But too often, Catholic calls for solidarity lack an engagement of struggle that includes white economic dispossession.[110] Decolonial repair necessarily redresses the historical and economic processes of white wealth "accumulation by dispossession."[111] Accumulation by dispossession interconnects multiple processes of coloniality and racial capitalism that shift "resources, land, wealth, power, sovereignty, free time, etc.," from colonized peoples to the elite few at the top of the racial hierarchy.[112] Appeals to solidarity tend to omit the historical context of colonial dispossession and therefore fail to recommend adequate forms of redress. For example, although public policies aimed at improving financial literacy, elevating educational achievement, increasing savings, and encouraging entrepreneurship would help African Americans, these policies ultimately fail to redress a wealth gap that is rooted in slavery.

Although racial economic dispossession is a constitutive feature of American life, "most Americans are in an almost pathological denial about the depth of Black financial struggle."[113] A recent interdisciplinary study at Yale University by five scholars from diverse fields, including management, psychology,

---

[106]See also Mt 19:30; Mk 10:31; Lk 13:30; and Frantz Fanon, *The Wretched of the Earth* (New York: Grove Press, 1968), 37.

[107]Tuck and Yang, "Decolonization Is Not a Metaphor," 3 and 35.

[108]Patricia McAuliffe, *Fundamental Ethics: A Liberationist Approach* (Washington, DC: Georgetown University Press, 1993), 61–63 and 124–25.

[109]Pope John Paul II, *Sollicitudo Rei Socialis* [On Social Concern of the Church], Vatican, 1987, no. 38, www.vatican.va.

[110]Massingale, "*Vox Victamarum*," 81–82.

[111]Cissell-Lucas, "Decolonizing the Colonizer?," 49. The term "accumulation by dispossession" was coined by David Harvey. Cissell-Lucas cites David Harvey, *The New Imperialism* (Oxford: Oxford University Press, 2003), and David Harvey, *The Enigma of Capital and the Crises of Capitalism* (London: Profile Books, 2011).

[112]Cissell-Lucas, "Decolonizing the Colonizer?," 49.

[113]Nikole Hannah-Jones, "What Is Owed?," *New York Times Magazine*, June 28, 2020, 51.

and social and policy studies, examining the misperception of racial economic inequality, found that White Americans vastly underestimate the racial wealth gap.[114] Nearly 97 percent of survey respondents overestimated Black-White wealth equality, and over 94 percent believe that Black households hold $90 in wealth for every $100 in wealth held by White households.[115] In fact, Black households actually hold $10 in wealth for every $100 in white wealth.[116]

Contrary to the widely held American belief that strong effort, tenacious motivation, and high academic achievement are sufficient to achieve racial economic well-being, Darity and Mullen demonstrate that given the existing distribution of "financial and real resources, *Blacks cannot close the racial wealth gap by independent or autonomous action.*"[117] Citing data from the 2016 Survey of Consumer Finances, they show that for every dollar the median white household possesses in wealth, including assets like homes, cash savings, and retirement funds, the median Black household retains a mere ten cents.[118] Even when Black youth attain more years of education and credentials than White youth for comparable levels of family socioeconomic status, Black households with one or more members holding a college or university degree possess ten thousand dollars less than white households that never completed high school.[119]

The central problem contributing to persistent racial wealth inequality is that the "primary sources of the capacity for sustained wealth building for most people are inheritances, in vivo transfers, and the economic security borne of parental and grandparental wealth."[120] Studies of the longitudinal Panel Study of Income Dynamics demonstrate a close linkage between older generations' net worth and the wealth outcome for the third generation. Given that Blacks held nearly no wealth at Emancipation, the dynamics of intergenerational wealth transfers "work sharply to their disadvantage."[121] Wealth inequality was further exacerbated by the Homestead Acts (1860s to 1930s) that disproportionately transferred public assets to whites, including 246 million acres of land, an area that approximates that of Florida, Alabama, Georgia, South Carolina, and North Carolina, and Virginia combined.[122] Recall too that white vigilante violence often destroyed Black property and

---

[114]Michael W. Kraus, Ivuoma N. Onyeador, Natalie M. Daumeyer, Julian M. Rucker, and Jennifer A. Richeson, "The Misperception of Racial Economic Inequality," *Perspectives on Psychological Science* (2019): 1–23, https://spcl.yale.edu/sites/default/files/files/Kraus_etal2019PoPS.pdf.

[115]Ibid., 4–6.

[116]Ibid., 6.

[117]Darity and Mullen, *From Here to Equality*, 31.

[118]Ibid.

[119]Ibid., 33.

[120]Ibid., 34.

[121]Ibid., 36.

[122]Ibid., 37.

financial assets, including, for example, destruction of 191 businesses that comprised Black Wall Street and burning over twelve hundred homes in Tulsa, Oklahoma, during a two-day siege in 1921.[123] Over the last fifty years banks and the real estate industry, in tandem with local, state, and national policies, have undermined Black homeownership and the value of homes in predominantly Black communities.[124]

Darity and Mullen evaluate every existing method to calculate the monetary cost of a reparations bill. Most scholars propose some form of reparations for slavery based upon "present value calculation" either for unpaid wages, the purchase price of human property, or land promised to the enslaved.[125] The "present value calculation" is generated by increasing values at the time of slavery at compound interest until today.[126] Most of these calculations range from trillions to tens of trillions in US dollars. Don't forget: "When millions of people have been cheated for centuries," Martin Luther King Jr. declared, "restitution is a costly process."[127]

In contradistinction to values derived from the time of slavery, Darity and Mullen argue that the present racial wealth gap is the most effective way to calculate the cumulative economic effects of white supremacy. Ultimately, the nation and all faith communities must redress the fact that severe differentials in wealth transfer capture *"the cumulative effects of racism on living Black descendants of American slavery."*[128] Grounded in this reality, Darity and Mullen propose a formulation for reparation:

> *The magnitude of ongoing shortfalls in wealth for Blacks vis-à-vis whites provides the most sensible foundation for the complete monetary portion of the bill for reparations.*[129]

Utilizing the 2016 Survey of Consumer Finances, the gap in mean household wealth by race is $795,000.[130] Darity and Mullen multiply $795,000 by the US Census Bureau's estimate of nearly ten million Black households,

---

[123]Ibid., 18. Darity and Mullen discuss other specific communities due reparations because of White vigilante massacres in Wilmington, North Carolina (1898), and Rosewood, Florida (1923), among others.

[124]Keeanga-Yamahtta Taylor, *Race for Profit: How Banks and Real Estate Industry Undermined Black Homeownership* (Chapel Hill: University of North Carolina Press, 2019), 261–62.

[125]Ibid., 259.

[126]Ibid.

[127]Martin Luther King Jr., "Testament of Hope," in *A Testament of Hope: The Essential Writings of Martin Luther King Jr.*, ed. James M. Washington (San Francisco: Harper & Row, 1986), 314.

[128]Darity and Mullen, *From Here to Equality*, 264.

[129]Ibid (italics in original).

[130]Ibid., 263.

yielding a total reparations bill of $7.95 trillion. They utilize the gap in mean household wealth rather than the median because "it is the appropriate target measure for calculating the sum required *to eliminate the racial wealth gap.*"[131] The mean is the appropriate measure because it includes Whites in the upper two quintiles of wealth distribution, which "must be taken into account when gauging the magnitude of the debt owed."[132]

Another measure that could be utilized to close the racial wealth gap would give Black Americans a share of the nation's wealth that is proportionate to their share of the nation's population. Currently, African Americans constitute 13 percent of the US population. Thirteen percent of the nation's total household wealth of $107 trillion in 2018 amounts to $13.91 trillion.[133] African Americans currently hold 3 percent of the nation's wealth or $3.21 trillion. Eliminating the racial wealth gap would require a "reparations outlay of $10.7 trillion, or an average outlay of approximately $267,000 per person for 40 million eligible Black descendants of American slavery."[134]

Darity and Mullen recommend a portfolio of reparations that would include immediate direct payments that could be allocated over time, similar to the monthly direct payments Germany pays to victims of the Nazi Holocaust.[135] The portfolio could also include trust funds to which eligible Blacks could apply for asset-building projects, homeownership, additional education, or start-up funds for self-employment, as well as funds to endow historically Black colleges and universities.[136] Other scholars have called for a "reparations superfund" that would pool government funding with contributions from the corporate and educational institutions that benefitted from slavery, Jim Crow, and contemporary dispossession of Black Americans.

In addition to a national program of reparations, scholar Katherine Franke contends that a collective moral reckoning should also include local and state initiatives. Faith communities could advance such initiatives at the local level to deter white gentrification; remove housing from speculative, for-profit real estate markets; and put property back into the hands of Black communities in a contemporary form of General Sherman's land grants. Franke's recommendations include "innovative models such as reinvestment in Black communities through community land trusts, limited equity housing cooperatives, mutual housing associations, and deed-restricted housing—sometimes referred to as 'third sector housing'—all used to empower Black communi-

---

[131]Ibid.

[132]Ibid.

[133]Ibid., 264.

[134]Ibid.

[135]Ana Lucia Araujo, *Reparations for Slavery and the Slave Trade: A Transnational and Comparative History* (New York: Bloomsbury, 2017), 129.

[136]Darity and Mullen, *From Here to Equality*, 264–65.

ties by transferring resources and property back into those communities."[137]

It is time for decolonial repair. The institution of processes of p/reparations is long overdue. It is time for the church and the nation to pay its moral and economic debt. "It is time," Nikole Hannah-Jones concludes, "for reparations."[138] Or as it is written in Matthew 20:16, "So the last will be first, and the first will be last."

[137]Katherine Franke, "Making Good on the Broken Promise of Reparations," *New York Review of Books,* March 18, 2019, www.nybooks.com.
[138]Hannah-Jones, "What Is Owed?," 53.

6

Embracing Ecological Intimacy

The struggle for racial and ecological justice is one—undoing and unlearning anti-black supremacy is constitutive of practicing ecological intimacy. White supremacy intricately connects exploitation of people and the earth. W. E. B. Du Bois presciently recognized this reality when he described whiteness as "ownership of the earth forever and ever. Amen."[1] The critical point I take from Du Bois is that whiteness as ownership is a perversion of relationships between human and nonhuman kin such that social relations of reciprocity, mutuality, and common care are torn asunder.[2] This chapter elucidates some of the ways that modernity/coloniality has divided "nature" from society, and in turn, we human beings have lost a living sense of the radical intimacy, interconnection, and interpenetration of human and nonhuman ecologies within the whole web of life. The same colonial, dualistic ways of thinking and being that gave rise to the Atlantic slave trade and genocide of Indigenous Peoples throughout the Americas, as I discussed in Part I, are at the very source of the objectification and exploitation of all of creation.

If we, as the people of God, are going to live by the integral ecological praxis recommended by Pope Francis, we will need to shift away from seeing ourselves as separate from the web of life and retrieve a deeper, living sense of the radical intimacy of the whole of creation. Thomas Merton understood the interconnection between economics and ecology when he criticized White people for being "victim to the same servitudes which he has imposed on the Negro: passive subjection to the lotus-eating commercial society that he has tried to create for himself, and which is shot through with falsity and unfreedom from top to bottom."[3] If we are going to live in ways that sustain

---

[1] W. E. B. Du Bois, *Darkwater: Voices from within the Veil*, introduction by David Levering Lewis (New York: Washington Square Press, 2004 [1920]), 22.

[2] Du Bois was among the first sociologists to examine the relationship between racism and environmental degradation. See Sylvia Hood Washington, *Packing Them In: An Archaeology of Environmental Racism in Chicago, 1865–1954* (Lanham, MD: Lexington Books, 2005), 50.

[3] Thomas Merton, *Seeds of Destruction* (New York: Farrar, Strauss, and Giroux, 1964), 86.

the regenerative capacity of the lotus flower's ecology and the entire web of life, "we need an intellectual state shift to accompany" the new epoch that has already emerged.[4] The problem, however, is that we remain wed to a disease of capitalist growth "that eats your flesh—and then profits from selling your bones for fertilizer, and then invests that profit to reap the cane harvest, and then sells that harvest to tourists who pay to visit your headstone."[5] Tragically, it seems that our civilization is in "a sort of terminal spiral of thanaticism," that is, a gleeful will for death,[6] or, as Pope Francis laments, a "spiral of self-destruction."[7]

I begin by drawing upon Pope Francis's passionate embrace of Saint Francis to frame the ecological vision and praxis of this chapter. Second, I outline a brief history of how our economic assumptions have been killing the planet and human beings for five hundred years. The problem is not only capitalism but our idolatry of capitalist growth over and against living ecosystems that sustain the global common good. We tell ourselves a happy story of how capitalism naturally developed from feudalism and universally extended the human life span. This happy story is just that—a nice-sounding fairy tale with no basis in history. The real history of the shift from feudalism to capitalism is quite different and instructs humanity on the need for shifting from growthism, the belief that "growth is the costless, win-win solution to all problems,"[8] to a new paradigm that de-commodifies public human goods like health, education, housing, and transportation and prioritizes reciprocal relations with the local and global ecological commons.

Third, I engage the deeper cultural dialogue with Indigenous perspectives invited by Pope Francis. He promotes a way of cultural dialogue that is constitutive of practicing an authentic integral ecology. Fourth, drawing upon *Laudato Si'* and ecological scholarship, I outline how the "degrowth" paradigm, perhaps ironically, nurtures ecological conversion to the overflowing giftedness of God's creation. Finally, I offer an open-ended "in/conclusion" to invite readers to learn ways of living in harmony with nature from African American ecological traditions, and dwell in Jayne Cortez's ecological poem "I got the blues-ooze."

---

[4]Raj Patel and Jason W. Moore, *A History of the World in Seven Cheap Things* (Oakland: University of California Press, 2017), 2.

[5]Ibid., 18. Patel and Moore cite M. S. Graham Dann and A. V. Seaton, "Slavery, Contested Heritage, and Thanatourism," *International Journal of Hospitality and Tourism Administration* 2, nos. 3–4 (2001): 1–29.

[6]McKenzie Wark, "The Capitalocene," *Public Seminar*, October 15, 2015, www.publicseminar. org.

[7]Pope Francis, *Laudato Si': On Care for Our Common Home* (Washington, DC: United States Conference of Catholic Bishops, 2015), no. 163.

[8]Herman Daly, "Growthism: Its Ecological, Economic, and Ethical Limits," Local Futures: Economics of Happiness, March 21, 2019, https://www.localfutures.org.

A Franciscan Vision of Ecological Intimacy

Pope Francis provides a contemplative and critical way of framing this chapter in terms of three interrelated and fundamental crises of our time: ecological, socioeconomic, and spiritual-cultural. In the midst of a culture of climate-change denial and a fossil-fuel-based economy, it seems nearly impossible to even begin to adequately address the ecological crisis that threatens the very life of the planet. As the global, neoliberal economic way of life threatens Earth, it simultaneously spawns a socioeconomic crisis in which the wealth of society is directed to the richest, while the most vulnerable bear ever-increasing and death-dealing burdens. These ecological and economic crises are fundamentally intertwined with three spiritual-cultural divides: between persons and nature, between individuals and others, and between society and authentic ecological development—that is, the full thriving of human and planetary biodiversity. The profound disconnection between the imperative for infinite growth in current economic logic and the finite resources of the earth threaten all of life as we know it. Human and nonhuman kin who experience oppression seem only to cry out more.

In his encyclical *Laudato Si'* ("On Care for Our Common Home"), Pope Francis invites a shift in our entire way of living and being from an egocentric to an ecologically centered way of life. Pope Francis calls people of faith, personally and collectively, to an "integral ecology" that truly cares for and celebrates the radical intimacy of the whole of God's creation. The title of the encyclical *Laudato Si'* heralds Saint Francis's *Canticle of the Creatures*, "Praise be to you, my Lord," where "Francis of Assisi reminds us that our common home is like a sister with whom we share our life and a beautiful mother who opens her arms to embrace us."[9] Like Black and Brown sisters who cry out for racial justice, our Sister Mother Earth "cries out to us because of the harm we have inflicted upon her by our irresponsible use and abuse of the goods with which God has endowed us."[10] The source of this violence is

> present in our hearts, wounded by sin, [and] also reflected in the symptoms of sickness evident in the soil, in the water, in the air and in all forms of life. This is why the earth herself, burdened and laid waste, is among the most abandoned and maltreated of our poor; she "groans in travail" (Rom 8:22).[11]

---

[9]Francis, *Laudato Si'*, no. 1.
[10]Ibid., no. 2.
[11]Ibid.

We need to remember with Pope Francis that we are made of the dust of the earth (Gen 2:7), and that from this ground of humility we surrender to the mystery of God's creation because "our bodies are made up of [the earth's] elements," as "we breathe her air and we receive life and refreshment from her waters."[12]

Laudato Si' draws deeply upon Saint Francis of Assisi because he is "the example par excellence of care for the vulnerable and of an integral ecology lived out joyfully and authentically."[13] Saint Francis demonstrates with his joy, generosity, and openheartedness "just how inseparable the bond is between concern for nature, justice for the poor, commitment to society, and interior peace."[14] *Laudato Si'* highlights the witness of Francis of Assisi to help open us to the "awe and wonder" of gazing at the sun, the moon, or the smallest of creatures.[15] Pope Francis invites us to "the heart of what it is to be human" and to be united, like Saint Francis, by "bonds of affection" with all creatures in the intimacy of God's creation.[16] If we lose the language of mutuality and beauty in all our relationships with creation, the pope warns, "our attitude will be that of masters, consumers, ruthless exploiters, unable to set limits on [our] immediate needs."[17] However, "If we feel intimately united with all that exists, then sobriety and care will well up spontaneously."[18] The poverty and austerity of Saint Francis's spirituality, Pope Francis writes, is "something far more radical" than "a mere veneer of asceticism"; rather, Francis of Assisi refuses to turn God's creation "into an object simply to be used and controlled."[19] In the spirit of Saint Francis, the pope invites us to "see nature as a magnificent book in which God speaks to us and grants us a glimpse of his infinite beauty and goodness."[20] Pope Francis calls us to joyful, contemplative transformation with the whole of God's creation.

I believe his focus on Saint Francis is fitting for our time. Saint Francis emulates the kind of relationship with nature that ecologists invite today, that is, a humble way of listening to, attending to, and caring for our nonhuman kin. However, we who are overprivileged seem to have lost that intimate sensibility of interrelating to the whole of creation. I recall noticing this inattentiveness when I was nine years old and dressed up as Saint Francis for Halloween. While I looked silly in a fake beard and Franciscan tunic, I remember adults making fun of how Saint Francis interrelated with creatures and nature. Even

---

[12]Ibid.
[13]Ibid., no. 10.
[14]Ibid.
[15]Ibid., no. 11.
[16]Ibid.
[17]Ibid.
[18]Ibid.
[19]Ibid.
[20]Ibid., no. 12.

in my divinity school and doctoral theological education, teachers tended to view Saint Francis as a bit out of touch with reality.

In the context of ecological disaster, however, radical reorientation of our entire being with the earth, plants, animals, water, and air is a necessity for all of life. Saint Francis models the kind of reciprocal relationship with local and global ecosystems that we need to sustain life for all of our human and nonhuman kin. By drawing upon the witness of Saint Francis, perhaps our first Jesuit pope invites us to notice the "intimacy, porosity, and permeability" of all human and nonhuman kin within the multidimensional relationships in "which there are no basic units, only webs within webs of relations: 'worlds within worlds.' "[21] In their study of gut microbiota in diverse vertebrates, including zebrafish, mice, and humans, Ruth E. Ley and her colleagues reveal how human gut microbiota evolved within diverse forms of microbial life over 3.25 billion years ago, interconnecting habitats "all over the biosphere" that "likely required whole microbial communities to have exchanged innovations."[22]

Dynamic webs within webs of living relations hint at a deeper level of transformation through God's creation, to which Saint Francis witnesses. I cannot prove this, and proving is not the point of the mystery of God's creation. My point here is that Saint Francis was humbly open to being transformed by Brother Sun and Sister Moon and Mother Earth and all of God's creatures. Our Western anthropocentric perspective has socialized us to assume that we humans only act upon nature and that nature does not act upon us. Western dualism's splits between mind and body and society and nature have blinded us to the ways that the entire web of life is inside of us and that we are inside of nature, and to how the interaction between body, society, and nature transforms us. Saint Francis is not alone in the way that he witnesses to a profound intimacy with and between the entire web of life. This chapter listens to voices of peoples and cultures that herald humble respect and affinity for the entire creation. Pope Francis invites all of us into this deeper level of sociality when he writes that "a true ecological approach must also be a social approach," because we need to integrate questions of human and ecological justice and "hear *both the cry of the earth and the cry of the poor.*"[23]

Pope Francis emphasizes how the climate is a global common good "belonging to all and meant for all" because it is a "complex system linked to

---

[21]Jason W. Moore, *Capitalism in the Web of Life: Ecology and the Accumulation of Capital* (New York: Verso, 2015), 8. Moore quotes Ruth E. Ley, Catherine A. Lozupone, Micah Hamady, Rob Knight, and Jeffrey I. Gordon, "Worlds within Worlds: Evolution of the Vertebrate Gut Microbiota," *Nature Reviews Microbiology* 6, no. 10 (2008): 776–88.

[22]Ley et al., "Worlds within Worlds," 776.

[23]*Laudato Si'*, no. 49.

many of the essential conditions for human life."[24] He underscores how we are "witnessing a disturbing warming of the climatic system." The consequences of climate change are "a global problem with grave implications: environmental, social, economic, political, and for the distribution of goods."[25] The pope invites us to notice that when plants and animals cannot adapt to climate change, "this in turn" unleashes a whole series of consequences that impact the "livelihood of the poor, who are forced to leave their homes, with great uncertainty for their future and that of their children."[26]

The Problem of Growthism

Western societies take it as an article of faith that capitalism is the best economic system ever created. In the US political system, while there are wide-ranging views on the role of government and how best to distribute goods, it is difficult to find any political party or politician who questions whether we need economic growth. In a recent essay discussing the need to reimagine capitalism, the author asserted that "Entrepreneurial capitalism remains the best system ever invented to create and distribute prosperity and if you look at the billion-plus people in China, India and elsewhere who were lifted from poverty in the past two decades, it remains easy to sing its praises."[27] Two Catholic authors reiterate the basic claim that capitalist, market economies serve the common good.[28] Yet does the happy story of capitalism inexorably serving human progress and the common good stand up to scrutiny?

Our "origin story" of capitalism claims that human beings by nature are self-interested, profit-seeking, and maximizing agents known as *Homo economicus*, as all college students learn in Economics 101.[29] The story we tell ourselves contends that humanity's competitive, self-interested, profit-maximizing nature guided us to break free from the "constraints of feudalism and the chains of serfdom" and establish capitalism as the way of prosperity for all.[30] However, this deeply ingrained cultural belief—that capitalism naturally emerged to serve human freedom and the common good—is not true. Historians tell a different story.

---

[24]Ibid., no. 23.

[25]Ibid., no. 25.

[26]Ibid.

[27]Randall Lane, "Reimagining Capitalism: How the Greatest System Ever Conceived (and Its Billionaires) Need to Change," *Forbes*, March 31, 2019, www.forbes.com.

[28]See, for example, Arthur Brooks, "Confessions of a Convert to Catholicism," *America*, February 6, 2017, and Stephanie Slade, "A Libertarian Case for the Common Good," *America*, August 6, 2018.

[29]Jason Hickel, *Less Is More: How Degrowth Will Save the World* (London: Penguin Random House, 2020), 40.

[30]Ibid.

As is the case with much of Western culture that stresses the "humanistic river" of instrumental reason and *Homo economicus*,[31] we tend to forget that it was peasant-driven revolutions, not capitalism, that brought an end to feudalism. Organized peasant rebellions in the early 1300s, ecological anthropologist Jason Hickel explains, began the process of revolt against the feudal system all across Europe.[32] Social and political crises were accelerated by the bubonic plague that killed one-third of Europe's population in 1347. Unexpectedly, because the plague decimated the labor force while land remained abundant, commoners realized that they had gained bargaining power. They took advantage of their newfound collective power to demand lower rents and higher wages.

Revolts spread across Europe, including, for example, a peasant revolt in England in 1381, people taking over city government in Ciompi, Italy, in 1382, and Parisians establishing a "workers' democracy" in 1413.[33] Commoners across Europe wanted nothing less than revolution, with a complete overturning of the feudal system. Hickel quotes historian of European political economy Silvia Federici's summary of their goal: " 'The rebels did not content themselves with demanding some restrictions to feudal rule, nor did they bargain for better living conditions. Their aim was to put an end to the power of the lords.' "[34] Although many rebellions were crushed and rebels executed, feudalism was indeed overturned. In its place, "Free peasants began to build a clear alternative: an egalitarian, co-operative society rooted in principles of local self-sufficiency" and collective care for natural resources.[35] Notably, historians call this period from 1350 to 1500 the "golden age of the European proletariat."[36] Even more remarkably, Hickel adds, it was "a golden age for Europe's ecology, too."[37]

Feudalism devastated the ecological commons because lords pressured peasants to deforest and overgraze to the point of eroding soil fertility. Peasant rebellions after 1350, however, reversed the devastating ecological impacts of feudalism and "inaugurated a period of ecological regeneration."[38] Once they gained control of the land, peasants established a "more reciprocal relationship with nature: they managed commons and pastures collectively, through democratic assemblies, with careful rules that regulated tillage, grazing and

[31] Walter D. Mignolo, *The Darker Side of Western Modernity: Global Futures, Decolonial Options* (Durham, NC: Duke University Press, 2011), 1–2.
[32] Hickel, *Less Is More*, 41–42.
[33] Ibid., 42.
[34] Ibid., 43. Hickel quotes Silvia Federici, *Caliban the Witch: Women, the Body, and Primitive Accumulation* (Brooklyn, NY: Autonomedia, 2004), 46.
[35] Hickel, *Less Is More*, 42–43.
[36] Ibid., 44.
[37] Ibid.
[38] Ibid.

forest use."[39] The key lesson is that where the ecological commons is a fundamental value, soils and forests can regenerate.

While it is often assumed that capitalism evolved from feudalism, Hickel illuminates how such a transition was impossible. Capitalism depends upon "piling up excess wealth for large-scale investment."[40] We will never know how an egalitarian, cooperative peasant society might have evolved because it was systematically destroyed by nobles, the Church, and merchant bourgeoisie through land privatization.[41] Historians describe the period from 1350 to 1500 as the "golden age of the European proletariat" because a series of peasant rebellions throughout Europe (briefly described earlier) enabled serfs to become free farmers "with free access to commons: pasture for grazing, forests for game and timber, [and] waterways for fishing and irrigation."[42] While the feudal system had been an ecological disaster because lords extracted more from the land, forests, and soil than nature was able to regenerate, the reintroduction of a collective commons that carefully managed tillage, grazing, and forest use helped forests and soil to regenerate.[43] Since they were unable to re-enserf peasants, Europe's elites violently forced people off their lands through "a continent-wide campaign of evictions."[44] The public commons of collectively managed pastures, forests, and rivers "were fenced off and privatized for elite use. They became, in a word, *property.*"[45]

This process of placing physical boundaries between privately owned land, forests, and rivers is known as "enclosure." The enclosure movement destroyed "thousands of rural communities" by ripping up and burning crops and razing villages to the ground.[46] The Reformation only added "fuel to the bonfire of dispossession" by dismantling Catholic monasteries across Europe that were confiscated by nobles. Revolts by commoners failed in the 1500s, and over the next three centuries "huge swathes of land were enclosed," thereby removing millions of people from their lands, which in turn triggered "an internal European refugee crisis."[47] In England, "poverty," a word that had rarely been used in texts of that time, became useful for describing the mass of paupers and vagabonds created by enclosure and privatization. Enclosure worked like "magic" for capitalists because it inaugurated what Adam Smith called "previous accumulation," that is, appropriating vast amounts of land and natural resources that had previously been in the public domain of the

---

[39]Ibid.

[40]Ibid., 45.

[41]Ibid.

[42]Ibid., 43–45. The "golden age of the European proletariat" is attributed to Fernand Braudel, *Capitalism and Material Life: 1400–1800* (New York: Harper & Row, 1967), 128ff.

[43]Hickel, *Less Is More*, 43.

[44]Ibid., 45.

[45]Ibid.

[46]Ibid.

[47]Ibid.

commons.[48] As Smith and economic textbooks tell the story, this accumulation came about by innocent hard work and savings. Contrary to this idyllic tale, which historians call "naïve," a more accurate term for the process of enclosure is "plunder," or what Karl Marx called "primitive accumulation," a term that defines the violent ways capitalists appropriated labor and natural resources through

> *Restructuring of the relations of reproduction—human and extra-human alike—so as to allow the renewed and expanded flow of Cheap labor, food, energy, and raw materials into the commodity system.*[49]

As capitalism commodified everything, including land and raw materials, the consequences of enclosure were devastating for peasants. Enclosure also created something else capitalism has historically depended upon: plentiful, cheap labor.[50] Peasants were thrust into an intolerable choice: starve or subsist on rock-bottom wages. Neither slaves nor serfs, they were proletarians wholly dependent upon wages, facing a predicament "utterly new in world history."[51] Far from the economists' happy story of a peaceful and inevitable transition from feudalism to capitalism, "organized violence, mass impoverishment, and the systematic destruction of self-sufficient subsistence economies" actually inaugurated the new system.[52] The devastating consequences of primitive accumulation included driving wages down 70 percent, creating conditions of famine and starvation, which in turn dramatically lowered population as "average life expectancy at birth fell from 43 years in the 1500s to the low 30s in the 1700s."[53]

We often hear and tend to assume that from its inception capitalism increased life expectancy, but the opposite is the case. Industrial capitalism erupted with disastrous public health impacts. In Manchester and Liverpool, two of the giants of industrialization, life expectancy dropped precipitously in comparison to nonindustrialized parts of England. One of the world's leading experts on the history of public health, Simon Szreter, has demonstrated that life expectancy dropped in industrialized cities to levels "not seen since the Black Death in the fourteenth century."[54] The same pattern was found in other European cities, and for its first three centuries "capitalism generated misery to a degree unknown in the pre-capitalist era."[55] Major boosts to life

---

[48]Ibid.

[49]Moore, *Capitalism in the Web of Life*, 98 (italics and capitalization in original).

[50]Patel and Moore, *A History of the World in Seven Cheap Things*, 97.

[51]Hickel, *Less Is More*, 47.

[52]Ibid., 46.

[53]Ibid.

[54]Ibid., 49.

[55]Ibid. Hickel cites Simon Szreter, "The Population Health Approach in Historical Perspective," *American Journal of Public Health* 93, no. 3 (2003): 421–31, and Simon Szreter and

expectancy, Szreter explains, did not occur until public investments were made in public plumbing, that is, in separate water and sewerage systems in the late 1800s.[56] Capitalists opposed public investments in water and sewerage systems.

Primitive accumulation through colonization was even more devastating than Industrialization in Europe. The same elites who achieved enclosure in Europe were colonizing "new frontiers" in Africa, the Americas, and South Asia. For example, in the same year (1525) that German nobles massacred 100,000 peasants, the "Spanish king Carlos I awarded the kingdom's highest honor to Hernan Cortés, the conquistador who slayed 100,000 Indigenous people as his army marched through Mexico and destroyed the Aztec capital of Tenochtitlán."[57] In his multidisciplinary study of the Americas before the arrival of Columbus, Charles C. Mann observes that "from Bartolome de Las Casas on, Europeans have known that their arrival brought about a catastrophe for Native Americans."[58] Indeed, after Cortés, "the population of the entire region" of central Mexico collapsed from over 25 million people to 730,000 by 1625.[59]

Capitalism is not a fairy tale of human evolution. Rather, "It hinged on commodities that were produced by slaves, on lands stolen from colonized peoples, and processed in factories staffed by European peasants who had been forcibly dispossessed by enclosure."[60] Consider, for example, how European colonizers, from the 1500s to the 1800s, extracted more than 220 million pounds of silver from the Andes. Hickel invites us to a thought experiment about the scale of wealth stolen by siphoning silver: "If invested in 1800 at the historical average rate of interest, that quantity of silver would today be worth $165 trillion—more than double the world's GDP."[61] Reflect further that the calculation does not include the gold extracted from South America during the same period. That is not all. Colonization also provided raw materials like cotton, which was the most important commodity for Britain's economic rise,[62] and sugar, which was a "key source of cheap calories for Europe's industrial workers."[63]

Remember that at least 5 million Indigenous peoples were enslaved to

---

Graham Mooney, "Urbanization, Mortality, and the Standard of Living Debate: New Estimates of the Expectation of Life at Birth in Nineteenth-Century British Cities," *Economic History Review* 51, no. 1 (1998): 84–112.

[56]Ibid.

[57]Hickel, *Less Is More*, 50.

[58]Charles C. Mann, *1491: New Revelations of the Americas before Columbus*, 2nd ed. (New York: Vintage Books, 2011), 146.

[59]Ibid.

[60]Hickel, *Less Is More*, 51.

[61]Ibid.

[62]Moore, *Capitalism in the Web of Life*, 155–56.

[63]Hickel, *Less Is More*, 52.

power the mines and plantations in South America, and 15 million "souls were shipped across the Atlantic from Africa during three centuries of state-sponsored human trafficking."[64] Consider another thought experiment: "If enslaved Africans had been paid at least the US minimum wage, with modest interest, it would add up to $97 trillion today—four times the size of the US GDP."[65]

A "subtler form of appropriation" was at work in the way the British extracted $45 trillion in taxes from India between 1765 and 1938, a process that enabled Britain to buy "strategic materials like iron, tar and timber which were essential to the country's industrialization."[66] Britain also used these taxes to fund new white-settler colonies like Canada and Australia. Hickel notes that many contemporary politicians justify colonization on the grounds that Britain helped India to develop when, in fact, "The opposite is true: India developed Britain."[67] Far from a process of natural human evolution, capitalism was achieved through violent processes of enclosure, enslavement, extraction, and colonization.

The long history of capitalism, Hickel finds, far from a story about human evolution, is that capitalist growth has always depended upon commodification and enclosure. He describes the "Lauderdale Paradox," first articulated by James Maitland in 1804, the Eighth Earl of Lauderdale (the peerage of Scotland), "which holds that an increase in 'private riches' is achieved by choking off 'public wealth.'"[68] Maitland noticed that colonizers were "burning down orchards that produced fruits and nuts, so that people who once lived off the natural abundance of the land would be forced instead to work for wages and purchase food from Europeans."[69] Mahatma Gandhi's nonviolent protests against the British salt tax demonstrate perhaps the most iconic example of the Lauderdale Paradox. Salt was abundantly available to everyone along India's coasts—all people had to do was scoop it up. The British made something that was abundant scarce by enclosing the coasts and imposing a tax. Not only did the British acquire free value from the public commons, "they also created artificial scarcity" that produced revenue for the colonial government and sabotaged the commons "for growth."[70] The point is that capitalism, rather than protecting freedom, instead encloses, extracts, colonizes, and expropriates public wealth for the sake of growth and private enrichment.

---

[64]Ibid.

[65]Ibid.

[66]Ibid.

[67]Ibid.

[68]Jason Hickel, "Degrowth: A Theory of Radical Abundance," *Real-World Economics*, no. 87 (2019): 54.

[69]Hickel, *Less Is More*, 60.

[70]Ibid.

The happy story we tell ourselves about capitalism perpetuates another perversity: "The proponents of capitalism believed it was necessary to *impoverish* people in order to generate growth."[71] The intellectual history of capitalism includes philosopher David Hume's claim that "'Tis always observed, in years of scarcity, if it not be extreme, that the poor labor more, and really live better.' "[72] John Locke was more straightforward, admitting "that enclosure was theft from the commons, and from commoners, but he argued that this shift was morally justifiable because it enabled a shift to intensive commercial methods that increased agricultural output."[73] Locke argued that any increase in output was for the greater good of humanity, and he applied the same argument to defend colonization. Yet, as Hickel explains, Locke is making an "alibi" for capitalism to shift from meeting human needs and the common good to using production for profit and private wealth. "Today," the very same alibi is "routinely leveraged to justify new rounds of enclosure and colonization—of lands, forests, fisheries, and of the atmosphere itself."[74] Today, the alibi is called "growth."

Before I turn to the ways that the preoccupation with capitalist growth is killing humanity and the planet, it is important to understand that the Church's role in advancing what Walter Mignolo calls the "colonial matrix of power" was not only through colonization of land and peoples. The Church also played a role in suppressing ecologically healthy ways of human living, simultaneously facilitating the rise of capitalism. Commoners had taken responsibility for caring for the earth because they saw it as a nurturing, even divine, mother. The historian Carolyn Merchant describes how, in precapitalist times, "The image of the earth as a living organism and nurturing mother had served as a cultural constraint restricting the actions of human beings. . . . As long as the earth was considered to be alive and sensitive, it could be considered a breach of human ethical behavior to carry out destructive acts against it."[75]

Although Pope Francis rightly celebrates the Franciscan tradition that nurtures intimate connection and co-relationship with the whole of creation, there is also a long history in Catholic Christianity of the *contemptus mundi* tradition.[76] In brief, *contemptus mundi*, literally contempt for the world, is

---

[71]Ibid., 58.

[72]Ibid. Hickel's quote of Hume is derived from Michael Perelman, *The Invention of Capitalism: Classical Political Economy and the Secret History of Primitive Accumulation* (Durham, NC: Duke University Press, 2000).

[73]Hickel, *Less Is More*, 55.

[74]Ibid.

[75]Ibid., 66. Hickel quotes Carolyn Merchant, *The Death of Nature: Women, Ecology, and the Scientific Revolution* (San Francisco: Harper & Row, 1981), 3.

[76]See, for example, Lothario di Segni (Pope Innocent III), *The Misery of the Human Condition: De miseria humane conditionis*, ed. Donald R. Howard, trans. Margaret Mary Dietz (New

obsessed with the salvation of the soul beyond this world and disdains all things biological and physical, including the body. As theologian Elizabeth Johnson has shown, this contempt issued in a dualism that made women and the earth passive agents, at best.[77] *Contemptus mundi* is, perhaps, a precursor to the tradition of dualism that locates society and economics outside of nature, so that capitalism disrupts nature from the outside.

This dualistic worldview is fundamental to the violence of capitalism.[78] Pope Francis focuses his critique of dualism on the *"undifferentiated and one-dimensional"* technocratic paradigm that "exalts the concept of a subject who, using logical and rational procedures, progressively approaches and gains control over an external object."[79] Francis laments the way this technocratic paradigm is a "technique of possession, mastery and transformation."[80] That technique of possession, furthermore, "has made it easy to accept the idea of infinite or unlimited growth," which "is based on the lie that there is an infinite supply of the earth's goods and this leads to the planet being squeezed dry beyond every limit."[81] World-ecology scholars[82] express a critique similar to that of Pope Francis: Cartesian dualism is a root philosophical orientation and colonial practice that not only separates mind from body but also divides "thinking things" from "extended things."[83] Ecologists Patel and Moore explain that European ruling classes viewed most human beings, including "women, peoples of color, Indigenous peoples—as extended, not thinking beings."[84] It is upon this division of mind and body, nature and society, that Descartes argued that "we" Europeans must become "'the masters and possessors of nature.'"[85] Dualism "was recruited in order to justify not only the land of colonies, but the bodies of the colonized themselves."[86]

York: Bobbs-Merrill, 1969).

[77]Elizabeth Johnson, *She Who Is: The Mystery of God in Feminist Theological Discourse* (New York: Crossroad, 1997), 51–54.

[78]Moore, *Capitalism in the Web of Life*, 5 and 30.

[79]Pope Francis, *Laudato Si'*, no. 106.

[80]Ibid.

[81]Ibid.

[82]Giorgis Kallis, Vasilis Kostakis, Steffan Lange, Barbara Muraca, Susan Paulson, and Mattias Schmelzer, "Research on Degrowth," *Annual Review of Environment and Resources* 43 (May 2018): 291–316, here 294. The authors state, "The economic sphere was construed as a relatively autonomous, self-equilibrating sphere governed by different laws than nature, and distinct from the state." They cite Michel Foucault, *The Order of Things: An Archaeology of Human Sciences* (New York: Vintage, 1994), and Margaret Schabas, *The Natural Origin of Economics* (Chicago: University of Chicago Press, 2009), for this argument.

[83]Patel and Moore, *History of the World*, 52.

[84]Ibid.

[85]Ibid. Patel and Moore cite René Descartes, *Philosophical Writings: Volume I*, trans. John Cottingham, Robert Stroothoff, and Dugald Murdoch (Cambridge: Cambridge University Press, 1985), 142–43.

[86]Hickel, *Less Is More*, 76.

Integral Ecology and Cultural Dialogue
on Othering the Earth

Pope Francis prioritizes listening to Indigenous communities as a primary way of shifting from the technological paradigm to an integral ecological ethic. In this section I highlight how listening to Indigenous and Black communities facilitates deeper understanding of the interconnectedness of time and space within the web of life. *Laudato Si'* underscores the need for integrating diverse forms of knowledge into a "broader vision of reality" in the opening of chapter 4, "Integral Ecology."[87] In his openness to a broader vision of the interconnectedness of reality, Francis pays heightened attention to "cultural ecology" because he understands that "together with the patrimony of nature, there is also an historic, artistic, and cultural patrimony which is likewise under threat."[88] Indigenous communities and their cultural traditions deserve "special care" and "should be the principal dialogue partners" because the land "is not a commodity but rather a gift from God and from their ancestors who rest there, a sacred space with which they need to interact if they are to maintain their identity and values."[89]

In contrast to the multitude of ways that capitalism seeks to control and extract value from the web of ecological relations that make up all life, many cultures deemed "primitive" by modernity/coloniality celebrate radical intimacy, interdependence, and reciprocity within the web of life. For instance, the Anishinaabeg, whose original lands were in northeastern America (now Canada), have the word *"minbimaatisiiwin,"* which means "'a continuous rebirth' of reciprocal and cyclical relations between human and other life."[90] In southern African regions, "Bantu languages have *ubuntu*, human fulfillment through togetherness," and the Shona have *"ukama*, 'relatedness to the entire cosmos,' including the biophysical world."[91] The Chinese *shi-shi wu-ai* and the Maori term *mauri* express interrelatedness through the entire life force of the cosmos.[92]

Professor Lisa Brooks recovers the way her Abenaki ancestors mapped native space in the northeast, the region white settlers call New England.[93] Mapping, for the Abenaki, is itself a language of communication within the entire interdependent and interconnected landscape. A central metaphor Abenaki use to describe their mapping of the Northeast is the "Common

---

[87]Pope Francis, *Laudato Si'*, no. 138.
[88]Ibid., no. 143.
[89]Ibid., no. 146.
[90]Patel and Moore, *History of the World*, 19.
[91]Ibid.
[92]Ibid.
[93]Lisa Brooks, *The Common Pot: Recovery of Native Space in the Northeast* (Minneapolis: University of Minnesota Press, 2008).

Pot" or *Wlôgan*, which "is that which feeds and nourishes. It is the wigwam that feeds the family, the village that feeds the community, the networks that sustain the village."[94] The "pot" is made from birch trees, the clay of the earth, and is the *Wlôgan* or "dish" of interconnected social and ecological interrelationships. Women play a central role in facilitating cocreative relationships in the Common Pot. "All our relations" are evoked in the Common Pot, and the closely related Abenaki word *wlidôgawôgan* proclaims "thanks to all our relations."[95] The Common Pot interrelates the whole of existence, including the divine, as the pot is "our mother" who is "Sky Woman's body, the network of relations that must nourish and reproduce" life itself.[96]

Rather than just nice words or rhetoric, these diverse ways of describing the radical interdependence of the whole web of life reflect ways of living that actually protect the world's biodiversity. Although traditional Indigenous lands have been reduced to 22 percent of the earth's land area, scientists have found that "80 percent of the world's biodiversity is found on territories stewarded by Indigenous peoples."[97] As capitalist processes appropriate land and "'modernize' indigenous ways of life," and "accelerate consumerism and urbanization," these and other factors "are driving a cultural die-off."[98] Scientists have linked linguistic diversity with the plentitude of biodiversity. As the world loses one language every two weeks, eroding the diversity of seven thousand languages, we also lose local species.[99] Cultural diversity and linguistic diversity are integral to full thriving for all human and nonhuman kin.

A central concern to Indigenous peoples is the question of how to mark time, including geological time and the current epoch. Consider, for example, how a group of scientists recently voted to designate a new epoch "the Anthropocene."[100] The Anthropocene coincides with measurable impacts of the "great acceleration" of human activities over the past century.[101] This new human-dominated geologic epoch generates unprecedented global impacts that geologists measure in layers of the earth. Geologists find no analogue for the period we now navigate.

However, if we dig a little deeper into how we mark geologic time, we find startling revelations about coloniality. Geologists Simon L. Lewis and Mark A. Maslin advance two hypotheses that date the Anthropocene to

---

[94]Ibid., 4.

[95]Ibid.

[96]Ibid., 4 and 253–54.

[97]Hickel, *Less Is More*, 264. Hickel cites Hannah Rundle, "Indigenous Knowledge Can Help Solve the Biodiversity Crisis," *Scientific American*, October 12, 2019.

[98]Jessica Stites, "There's a Vanishing Resource We're Not Talking About," *In These Times*, January 31, 2019, www.inthesetimes.com.

[99]Ibid.

[100]Meera Subramanian, "Anthropocene Now: Influential Panel Votes to Recognize Earth's New Epoch," *Nature*, May 21, 2019, www.nature.com.

[101]International Geosphere-Biosphere Program, "Great Acceleration," January 2015, www.igbp.net.

1610.[102] Their first hypothesis concerns how the ecosystems of Europe and the Americas were reshaped through the exchange of plants and animals. The evidence for this change is found in the kinds of biomass accumulated in European and American continents. Lewis and Maslin's second hypothesis, far more terrifying, examines geological strata that reveal how carbon dioxide levels dropped when genocide eviscerated Indigenous peoples throughout the Americas. While 54 million to 60 million people lived in the Americas in 1492, by 1650 there were only 6 million. Lewis and Maslin call this the "Orbis spike" of 1610, because the onset of globalization (*Orbis* is Latin for "world") in the form of European colonization coincides with dramatic geological changes in landmass and carbon dioxide levels. They conclude that the "Orbis spike implies that colonialism, global trade and coal brought about the Anthropocene."[103]

Indigenous scholars, however, invite decolonization of the Anthropocene. Decolonization begins with exposing how the concept of the Anthropocene makes Eurocentric assumptions about the relationship between time and space invisible, neutral, and global. Simultaneously, it erases Indigenous knowledges. In the wake of slavery, the Anthropocene extends colonialist logics that sever relations between humans and soil, plants and animals, and even "between minerals and our bones."[104] Consider Métis scholar Zoe Todd's reflection on the entanglements across time between other-than-human and human kin that heralds Black and Indigenous ways of attending to mutually complex interrelationships between rocks, fish, and human kin.[105] Todd invites contemplation of Christina Sharpe's reflection *In the Wake: On Blackness and Being*. Sharpe invites readers to imagine the historical, hydrological wake of an Atlantic slave ship in order to recall enslaved peoples who were deliberately drowned in the Middle Passage.

People who drowned during the slave trade still endure through "residence time," the amount of time it takes for a substance to enter the ocean and then leave it. Sharpe learns what "residence time" is from a colleague who is a marine geographer. The colleague explains that human blood is salty, and that sodium has a residence time of 260 million years.[106] Sharpe then asks, "And what happens to the energy produced in the waters? It continues cycling like atoms in residence time. We, Black people, exist in the residence time of the wake, a time in which 'everything is now. It is all now.' "[107]

[102]Simon L. Lewis and Mark A. Maslin, "Defining the Anthropocene," *Nature*, March 12, 2015, 171–80, www.nature.com.
[103]Ibid., 177.
[104]Zoe Todd, "On Time," November 7, 2018, www.zoestodd.com.
[105]Ibid.
[106]Christina Sharpe, *In the Wake: On Blackness and Being* (Durham, NC: Duke University Press, 2016), 41.
[107]Ibid. Sharpe quotes Toni Morrison, *Beloved* (New York: Plume, 1987), 198.

Sharpe reflects on multiple levels of the meaning of living in the wake left by slave ships, including the historical, literal, and enduring consequences of enslavement of Africans. She invites meditation on the meanings of "wake" as the track left on the water's surface by a ship, and as all the disturbances left by a wake, including mourning the dead and living in a state of wakefulness and consciousness.

She writes that "living in/the wake of slavery is living 'the afterlife of property' and living the afterlife of *partus sequitur ventrem* (that which is brought forth follows the womb) in which the Black child inherits the non-status, the non/being of the mother."[108] The historical inheritance of non/being and non/status as human, Sharpe writes, "is everywhere apparent in the ongoing criminalization of Black women and children."[109] This inheritance also includes "the gratuitous violence of stop-and-frisk and Operation Clean Halls," mind-boggling rates of incarceration, and "the immanence of death as 'a predictable and constitutive aspect of *this* democracy.'"[110]

I wonder whether and how residence time, in the wake of Atlantic slavery, even register in white settler being? Zoe Todd and Heather Davis pragmatically deploy the Orbis spike of 1610 to thread interwoven ties between the Anthropocene and colonization.[111] Todd and Davis explain, however, that their interest goes deeper than a scientific marker—"We are interested in how rock and climate are bound to flesh."[112] Sharpe's residence time registers that relationship. If we attend to residence time, it offers the possibility of learning from Black and Indigenous ancestors whose bodies endure in landmasses and oceans as "oxygen, hydrogen, and atoms."[113] Returning to the residence time of the Middle Passage, which she must honor as an Indigenous woman in order to survive, Todd asks, "What if the rocks are working in concert with those residence times of those who were violated by the nightmares that white supremacy has summoned?"[114] Her question haunts, and nurtures wonder. Will we white settlers turn toward a new way of being? Will we cultivate a tender way of co-sensing our mutual relationality, interconnectedness, and obligations with and for Indigenous and Black kin as well as other-than-human kin?

The reality of the Orbis spike and the interconnections between human and nonhuman kin that Sharpe, Todd, and Davis help us to perceive expose how Western time is not natural, no matter how much we Westerners may think that today's date on the Gregorian calendar is so. My point is not to

---

[108]Sharpe, *In the Wake*, 15.
[109]Ibid.
[110]Ibid.
[111]Zoe Todd and Heather Davis, "On the Importance of a Date, or Decolonizing the Anthropocene," *ACME: An International Journal for Critical Geographers* 16, no. 4 (2017): 761–80.
[112]Ibid., 769.
[113]Todd, "On Time."
[114]Ibid.

dismiss the practical dimension of marking time on a daily calendar; rather, we need to notice how the Western conception of time divides us from the larger reality of beings rooted in a global ecosystem that is the source of all life as we know it. Western time orients humanity to control and domination over the earth to accelerate production and consumption without limits or regard for Sister Earth.

Consider, for example, the summary report released May 6, 2019, from the Intergovernmental Science-Platform on Biodiversity and Ecosystem Services (IPBES), an independent body comprising more than 130 member governments and often called the "IPCC for biodiversity." The report finds that "nature is declining globally at rates unprecedented in human history—and the rate of species extinction is accelerating, with grave impacts on people around the world now likely."[115] Planetary biodiversity is "humanity's most important life-supporting safety-net," a net that "is being stretched almost to breaking point," said Professor Sandra Diaz of Argentina, who cochaired the global species assessment.[116]

The report states, "The health of ecosystems on which we and all other species depend is deteriorating more rapidly than ever."[117] Finding that more than one million plant and animal species are threatened with extinction, and at a greater pace than ever in human history, the report warns, "We are eroding the very foundations of our economies, livelihoods, food security, health and quality of life worldwide."[118]

Degrowth: A Way of Radical Abundance

It should be clear by now that we can't pursue capitalist growth and simultaneously reverse environmental racism and breakdown of the ecological commons. We need new ways of thinking and being in relationship with Mother Earth. An alternative economic way of being, oriented toward hope and radical abundance, began to emerge at least fifty years ago with the Club of Rome's[119] study of the devastating ecological implications of unabated economic growth.[120] While the Club of Rome found that the current myopic

---

[115]Intergovernmental Science-Platform on Biodiversity and Ecosystem Services, "Nature's Dangerous Decline 'Unprecedented'" (Bonn, Germany: ISPBES, May 2019), www.ipbes.net.

[116]Ibid.

[117]Ibid.

[118]Ibid.

[119]The Club of Rome describes itself as a "network of thought leaders from a rich diversity of expertise" whose "goal is to actively advocate for paradigm and systems shifts which will enable society to emerge from our current crises, by promoting a new way of being human, with a more resilient biosphere." See "About the Club of Rome," https://www.clubofrome.org/about-us/.

[120]Donella H. Meadows, Dennis L. Meadows, Jørgen Randers, and William W. Behrens III,

focus on economic growth is unsustainable, they were joined by other thinkers who articulated paradoxical ways of living in radical abundance and harmony with the planet without economic growth.[121] These alternative perspectives have recently congealed into a multi- and interdisciplinary ecological field of "degrowth," a movement that emerged in the early 2000s and a term that was first used in a collection of essays titled *Demain la Décroissance: Entropie—écologie—économie (Tomorrow's Degrowth: Entropy—Ecology—Economy)*.[122] Degrowth may sound impractical and disruptive to American ears that can easily miss its ecological meaning. The French word *"décroissance"* and the Italian *"la decresita"* evoke an ecological imagination to French and Italian ears because these words mean "a river returning to its regular flow after a flood."[123] Degrowth, paradoxically, is not about living in Scrooge-like misery—it is about living in the radical abundance of God's creation. Jason Hickel delineates the outlines of a vision of degrowth:

> Degrowth stands for de-colonization, of both lands and peoples and even our minds. It stands for de-enclosure of the commons, the de-commodification of public goods, and the de-intensification of work and life. It stands for the de-thingification of humans and nature, the de-escalation of ecological crisis. Degrowth begins as a process of taking less. But in the end it opens up new vistas of possibility. It moves us from scarcity to abundance, from extraction to regeneration, from dominion to reciprocity, and from loneliness and separation to connection with a world that's fizzing with life.[124]

In *Laudato Si'*, Pope Francis implicitly promotes degrowth in his recognition of the limits of capitalism. He writes that the environment "cannot be adequately safeguarded or promoted by market forces."[125] He urges that we "reject a magical conception of the market" that prioritizes private and corporate gain over the fundamental value of biodiversity.[126] We need an entirely new approach that prioritizes care for the living organism Earth and

---

The Limits to Growth: A Report for the Club of Rome's Project on the Predicament of Mankind (New York: Universe Books, 1972).

[121]See, for example, Ivan Illich, *Tools for Conviviality* (New York: Harper & Row, 1973), and E .F. Schumacher, *Small Is Beautiful* (New York: Harper & Row, 1973).

[122]Nicholas Georgescu-Roegen, *Demain la Decroissance: Entropie—Écology—Économie*, preface and translation by Jacques Grinevald and Ivo Rens (Lausanne: Pierre Marcel Favre, 1979). Cited in Ksenija Hanacek, Brototi Roy, Sofia Avila, and Giorgos Kallis, "Ecological Economics and Degrowth: Proposing a Future Research Agenda from the Margins," *Ecological Economics* 169 (2020): 1–13, here 12.

[123]See "What Is degrowth?" at https://www.degrowth.info/en/what-is-degrowth/.

[124]Hickel, *Less Is More*, 287.

[125]Pope Francis, *Laudato Si'*, no. 190.

[126]Ibid.

people who are most vulnerable to environmental destruction. It ought to be evident that growth for its own sake produces "more illth than wealth" when the ongoing pursuit of growth in high-income nations produces more inequality and instability, stress, and depression from overwork, along with "ill health from pollution, diabetes and obesity, and so on."[127] This contradiction "cannot be considered progress," writes Pope Francis, because too often "people's quality of life actually diminishes—by the deterioration of the environment, the low quality of food or the depletion of resources—in the midst of economic growth."[128] We need to find a way other than growthism. Pope Francis recommends,

> We know how unsustainable is the behavior of those who constantly consume and destroy, while others are not yet able to live in a way worthy of their human dignity. That is why the time has come to accept decreased growth in some parts of the world, in order to provide resources for other places to experience healthy growth.[129]

We tend not to perceive how economic growth delivers diminishing returns. There are, for example, dozens of countries that attain higher life expectancy with significantly less per capita income than the United States, including Japan, South Korea, Portugal, and even the European Union (which has 36 percent less income than the United States).[130] A similar pattern emerges in terms of education. Finland, Estonia, and Poland attain the best educational systems in the world despite per capita income levels that are respectively 25 percent, 66 percent, and 77 percent less than the United States.[131] The critical point is that it is possible to achieve high levels of human development and protect the environment with much lower levels of Gross Domestic Product (GDP).

In fact, United Nations data show that nations can succeed in a wide variety of social indicators, including health, education, employment, nutrition, social support, democracy, and life satisfaction, "with as little as $10,000 per capita while staying within planetary boundaries."[132] If we use a metric that accounts for inequality and the social and environmental costs of economic activity, which GDP does not measure, it becomes clear that "past a certain point" growth "begins to have a *negative impact*."[133] While the Genuine Prog-

---

[127]Hickel, *Less Is More*, 175.
[128]Pope Francis, *Laudato Si'*, no. 194.
[129]Ibid., no. 193.
[130]Hickel, *Less Is More*, 174.
[131]Ibid.
[132]Ibid. Hickel cites Daniel O'Neill et al., "A Good Life for All within Planetary Boundaries," *Nature Sustainability* (2018): 88–95.
[133]Hickel, *Less Is More*, 176.

ress Indicator (GPI) begins with personal consumption expenditure just like GDP, it also accounts for both benefits and costs to provide a more holistic perspective on the economy. Global GPI grew with GDP until the mid-1970s, but has declined since because the "social and environmental costs of growth have become significant enough to cancel out consumption-related gains."[134]

At the same time, although income levels have quadrupled in the United States and tripled in the United Kingdom since the 1950s, levels of happiness have declined. As economist Joseph Stiglitz demonstrates, inequality exacerbates economic inefficiencies, erodes trust and social cohesion, undermines democratic institutions and civic participation, and creates a sense of unfairness and disillusionment.[135] It ought not be surprising, then, that countries with higher levels of inequality tend to be less happy while countries with "robust welfare systems have the highest levels of human happiness, when controlling for other factors."[136] There are many countries with significantly less GDP per capita than the United States that experience higher levels of well-being.[137] Interestingly, the economically poor Nicoya region of Costa Rica has one of the highest life expectancy rates in the world. Researchers found the reason for higher life expectancy in Nicoya was not genes or diet but community—even in old age people felt valued through connections with family, friends, and neighbors.[138] Drawing upon comprehensive studies of happiness, Hickel finds that "when people live in a fair, caring society, where everyone has access to social goods, they don't have to spend their time worrying about how to cover their basic needs day to day—they can enjoy the art of living."[139] In fact, the more generous the welfare system, the "happier everyone becomes."[140]

[134]Ibid., 177.

[135]Joseph Stiglitz, *The Price of Inequality: How Today's Divided Society Endangers Our Future* (New York: W. W. Norton & Company, 2012); see especially chapter 4, "Why It Matters," and chapter 5, "Democracy in Peril."

[136]Hickel, *Less Is More*, 177.

[137]Ibid., 178. Hickel's list of countries include Germany, Austria, Sweden, the Netherlands, Australia, Finland, Canada, and Denmark.

[138]Ibid., 180n20. "Sixty-year-old Nicoyan men have a median lifetime of 84.3 years (a three-year advantage over Japanese men), while women have a median lifetime of 85.1." Hickel cites Luis Rosero-Bixby et al., "The Nicoya Region of Costa Rica: A High-Longevity Island for Elderly Males," *Vienna Yearbook of Population Research* 11 (2013); Jo Marchant, "Poorest Costa Ricans Live Longest," *Nature*, September 3, 2013, 10.1038/nature.2013.13663; Luis Rosbero-Bixby and William H. Dow, "Predicting Mortality with Biomarkers: A Population-Based Prospective Cohort Study for Elderly Costa Ricans," *Population Health Metrics* 10, no. 1 (2012): 11, doi: 10.1186/1478-7954-10-11.

[139]Hickel, *Less Is More*, 178.

[140]Ibid., 180. Hickel cites Adam Okulicz-Kozaryn, I. V. Holmes, and Derek R. Avery, "The Subjective Well-Being Political Paradox: Happy Welfare States and Unhappy Liberals," *Journal of Applied Psychology* 99, no. 6 (2014): 1300–1308; and Benjamin Radcliff, *The Political Economy of Human Happiness: How Voters' Choices Determine the Quality of Life* (Cambridge: Cambridge University Press, 2013).

Degrowth, argues Jason Hickel, is an "antidote" to capitalist growth by "calling for a fairer distribution of existing resources and the expansion of public goods," and "releasing both humans and ecosystems from its grip."[141] Growth in material consumption, even so-called green growth, is undesirable because it does not keep humanity within ecological boundaries. When people live in a fair and equal society with universal health care, unemployment insurance, pensions, paid holiday and sick leave, affordable housing, daycare, and strong minimum wages, and are not stressed about covering basic needs, they "can enjoy the art of living" and "build bonds of social solidarity."[142]

We need a social, moral, and ecological compass that will guide us in living in ways that enable every human being and community to live in dignity and well-being while also protecting global ecological systems. Kate Raworth created such a compass when she was working at Oxfam in 2012. She calls her compass the "doughnut" because it "combines two concentric radar charts to depict the two boundaries—social and ecological—that together encompass human wellbeing."[143] The inner boundary, she explains, is a social foundation that establishes a floor below which are shortfalls in well-being, including water, food, health, housing, education, work, peace and justice, political voice, social equity, gender equality, networks, and energy. The minimum standards for these indicators are based upon internationally agreed-upon minimum standards established by the 2015 Sustainable Development Goals adopted by all UN member-states.[144] The outer boundary of the doughnut delineates an ecological ceiling, above which is represented "overshoot of pressure on Earth's life supporting systems," including climate change, ozone layer depletion, air pollution, biodiversity loss, land conversion, freshwater withdrawals, nitrogen and phosphorus loading, chemical pollution, and ocean acidification.[145] We are now living above and beyond the ecological ceilings for climate change, biodiversity loss, land conversion, and nitrogen and phosphorus loading, according to the planetary boundaries framework.[146]

---

[141] Jason Hickel, "Degrowth: A Theory of Radical Abundance," *Real-World Economics Review*, no. 87 (2019): 54.

[142] Hickel, *Less Is More*, 180.

[143] Kate Raworth, "A Doughnut for the Anthropocene: Humanity's Compass in the 21st Century," *The Lancet: Planetary Health* 1, no. 2 (May 1, 2017), www.thelancet.com.

[144] United Nations, Department of Economic and Social Affairs, Sustainable Development Goals, https://sdgs.un.org/goals.

[145] Raworth, "A Doughnut for the Anthropocene."

[146] Ibid. Raworth cites W. Steffen, K. Richardson, and J. Rockstrom et al., "Planetary Boundaries: Guiding Human Development on a Changing Planet," *Science* 347, no. 6223 (February 2015): 1–10.

In/conclusion:
Toward Racial and Ecological Intimacy

In his 2009 book *Farewell to Growth*, French economist Serge Latouche explains how a postgrowth, post-GDP world has no room for racism: "We resist, and must resist all forms of racism and discrimination (skin color, sex, religion, ethnicity). Unfortunately, they are all too common in the West today."[147] Environmental racism in the United States, sadly, compounds the injustices of anti-black racism because those who are viewed as "being threats to the larger social body are usually the ones who end up being" subjected to the most degraded geographical spaces and the many illnesses that result from living in those spaces.[148] The way ecological issues in the United States tend to be perceived as the "exclusive dominion of European-Americans," Black Americans might be legitimately skeptical about proposals for degrowth.[149] The tendency of the larger ecological movement to be led by affluent White people is exacerbated when "'environmental justice' (the movement and the issue) is populated by Black Americans, native Americans, working class European Americans and Latinos."[150] Not only are people who are poor and/ or Black or Indigenous or other people of color constructed as the "environmental lepers,"[151] the larger society misses how Africans in diaspora and Indigenous peoples fostered intimate relationships with nonhuman kin.[152]

Drawing upon the ecological traditions of her African ancestors, Kimberly Ruffin demonstrates how Africans' adaptiveness and capacity to cultivate their own love of nature, biophilia, enabled their survival through enslavement.[153] Retrieving African ecological traditions is a critical piece of becoming an "ecosocial" citizen who cultivates "civic participation informed by the interconnectedness of ecological and social worlds."[154] Ruffin believes, rightly so, that we need a broader concept of citizenship and democracy that nurtures biophilic fitness for these times. By "biophilic fitness" she means

---

[147]Serge Latouche, *Farewell to Growth* (New York: Polity Press, 2010), 99.

[148]Washington, *Packing Them In*, 21.

[149]Brian Gilmore, "The World Is Yours: 'Degrowth,' Racial Inequality and Sustainability," *Sustainability* 5 (2013): 1282–303, here 1287.

[150]Ibid. Gilmore quotes Kimberly N. Ruffin, "Writing African-American Ecological Ancestors," in *Proceedings of Land and Power: Sustainable Agriculture and African Americans, 2007 Environmental Thought Conference*, Jeffrey L. Jordan, Edward Pennick, Walter A. Hill, and Robert Zabawa, eds. (Washington, DC: US Department of Agriculture, Sustainable Agriculture Research and Education Program [SARE], 2007), www.sare.org.

[151]Washington, *Packing Them In*, 30.

[152]Kimberly Ruffin, "Biophilia on Purpose: A Declaration to Become an Ecosocial Citizen," *Intervalla* 3 (2015): 44–48, here 46.

[153]Ibid., 45.

[154]Ibid.

that human beings have an innate affinity for the natural world "that must be cultivated and supported."[155] "Going forward," both for global elites and African Americans, she writes,

> human beings need both social and ecological vitality, what I will call the presence of "ecosocial security," if planet Earth is going to continue to be the stage for their biophilia. Contemporary African Americans cannot fully enjoy self-certified biophilia if their status in the social sphere remains compromised. And while their geographic and social mobility is enviable, [elite] citizens cannot shield themselves from ecological collapse through their purchased entry into human systems that confer "alternative" citizenship. Simply put, our future in our current life support system is predicated on our ability to strengthen interconnected ecosocial security.[156]

Ruffin's point is clear in our current predicament of impasse: "neither ecological nor social affiliation can be enjoyed exclusive of the other. Human beings are an intimate part of nature whose notions of rights, responsibilities, obligations, and freedoms have both a social and ecological context."[157] She demonstrates how a focus on slavery's commodity crops may miss insight into the richness of African American ecological agency. African traditions of botanical knowledges enabled them "'to ward off hunger, diversify their diet, reinstate customary food preferences, and to treat illness.'"[158] Developing an interconnected sense of racial and ecological intimacy, I believe, means recognizing and retrieving the ways "African Americans have a triumphant record of self-certified biophilia that enriched their connections to nonhuman nature and emboldened them to change human systems built to exclude them."[159]

In her book *Black on Earth: African-American Ecoliterary Traditions*, Ruffin draws upon diverse African American artists, poets, musicians, and slave narratives as ways of thinking and working through ecological crises. She celebrates the ecological blues poetry of Jayne Cortez (1934–2012) for the way Cortez viscerally articulates our physical entanglements with landscapes we have rendered surreal. For example, in her "I got the blue-ooze," Cortez laments,

[155] Ibid.
[156] Ibid., 47.
[157] Ibid., 48.
[158] Ibid., 46. Ruffin quotes Judith Carney, "Seeds of Memory: Botanical Legacies of the African Diaspora," in *African Ethnobotany in the Americas*, ed. Robert Voeks and Johan Rashford (New York: Springer, 2013), 30.
[159] Ruffin, *Biophilia on Purpose*, 46.

I got the fishing in raw sewerage blue-ooze
I got the toxic-waste dump in my backyard blue-ooze
I got the contaminated water blue-ooze
I got the man-made famine blue-ooze
I got the dead house dead earth blue-ooze.[160]

Ruffin urges readers/listeners to sit with Cortez's images and sounds as a way of embracing the ecological emergencies of our day. She reflects on Cortez's ecological poetry:

> Disruptive, memorable and unexpected images in angry tones push the reader/listener to expand their ecological consciousness and think with an epistemological orientation that is not stunted by the alienation of modern daily living. Those who are in ecological crisis may find in Cortez's poetry artful acknowledgment and advocacy. Those sheltered from ecological crisis may find their buffer eroding from her acidic vision.[161]

My hope is that people malformed by anti-black supremacy will be disrupted enough in this moment of ecological disaster to delink from modernity/coloniality and relink with Black and Indigenous cultural traditions that draw us into ways of living an authentic integral ecology.[162] When we begin living in loving concert with our human and nonhuman kin, then we may yet nurture the shared labor of liberation and intimate belonging to which Sophia-Wisdom draws us in creating the *basileia tou theou*.

---

[160]Kimberly Ruffin, *Black on Earth: African American Eco-Literary Traditions* (Athens: University of Georgia Press, 2010), 145. Ruffin cites Jayne Cortez, "I got the blue—ooze," in *Jazz Fan Looks Back* (Brooklyn, NY: Hanging Loose Press, 2002), 60.

[161]Ruffin, *Black on Earth*, 150.

[162]Pope Francis, *Laudato Si'*, no. 138 and following.

Index

wealth inequality history, 22-23
  New Deal legislation exacerbating, 24
West, Cornel, on 9/11 and the blues, 97-98,
  123
Western time, Gregorian calendar, unnatural,
  149-50
whiteness
  definition, normative, 48
  cash value, 35
  Christian imagery of good and evil, xxxix
  culture of unity, unions, 36
  ignorance, cultivating, 49
  innocence, assume, xxxix, 48, 50
  lie, 4, 48-49
  politics of racial resentment killing every-
    one, xxxvii
  possessiveness, 35
white nationalism, rage, backlash during
    Emancipation, xxxviii
white people
  "All Lives Matter" enforcing supremacy,
    30
  belief, deserving privilege, 9, 48
  bias, intellectual and moral horizons, 48
  Black people, unheard, 38, fear of, 48
  Catholic, silence, 96
  Christian innocence, fantasy, xxxix
  commodified society, subjection to, 5
  domination, absolving, 6
  false identity, 4
  fragility, 86
  gun suicides, xxxvii
  household net worth, 24
  individualism, 30
  identity, unmarked and invisible, 5, invis-
    ibility/visibility dynamic, 47, normal,
    48
  idolatry of white superiority, xxxviii
  moderate, obstacle to freedom, "Letter
    from Birmingham Jail," 29
  "past is over, get over it," rhetoric, 22
  reparation discourse, 108
  social alexithymia, lack cross-racial empa-
    thy, 40, 49
  "Souls of White Folk," and violence, 50
  terrorism, 23

theological, moral, and spiritual, problem,
  4
white settler coloniality, 12
white supremacy
  "All Lives Matter," 30
  chosen, 38
  cultivating, 49
  defined, xxxix, 21
  empathy, lack, social alexithymia, 40, 49
  habitus, xxxix, 21, 31, structured struc-
    ture, 32. *See also* white habitus.
  historical white class formation, xxxix, 21
  highway system, 45-46
  illusion of superiority and forgetfulness,
    xxiv
  mind-set, 28-29
  myth of de facto, 37
  poison, 39
  political economy, 44
  positional alchemy, xxxix, 21, 48
  primary socialization, xxxix, 21
  self-deception, 48
  social sin, 4, 51-52
  symbolic hierarchical order, xxxix, 21, 48
  segregation, 21
  white habitus, defined, 30-31, 46-47, 48,
    86. *See also* ecosystem and Eduardo
    Bonilla-Silva.
White, T. Kirk, history of racial wealth gap,
  22-23
Wilkerson, Isabel, 39
Williams, Freddi, 122
Wink, Walter, 10-11
World War II. *See* GI Bill
Wynter, Sylvia, 57, 76

X, Malcolm, 6, 103-04. *See also* Benjamin
  Karim; Bryan N. Massingale; unlearning

Yancy, George, 6, 46, 48, 51

zero-point epistemology, Santiago Castro-
  Gómez, 15
zoning, anti-black and expulsive, 40-41
Zurara. *See* Azurara, Gomes Eannes

CPSIA information can be obtained
at www.ICGtesting.com
Printed in the USA
LVHW070059080623
749170LV00005B/664